Greening Food and Beverage Service: Operations & Management

Greening Food and Beverage Service: Operations & Management

Viniti Sharma

AMIGA PRESS INC.

DELHI (INDIA)

AMIGA PRESS INC.
H.O.: 28-A, Indra Park, Chander Nagar
Delhi-110051 (India)
Tel.: 011-22504028, +91-98736-57000
E-mail: amigapub@gmail.com
Website : www.amigapress.co.in

This edition is published by Amiga Press Inc.

ISBN: 978-93- 87295-03-2

First Published 2019

Printed and bound by Amiga Press Inc. New Delhi-India

Preface

Hotel industry offers several services. Food and beverage is one of the basic services, provided by the hotel industry. Quality of diet, nutritional quantity, vitamin contents and proper cooking are vital elements, the management has to keep in mind, while providing food services. In this age of globalization, competition in providing food services is on increase. Even MNCs have entered the arena and they are delivering better food and beverage services.

In fact, it is a big challenge for Indian hotel industry, to cope with the situation. In India, food services are not up to the mark as per global standards. In this consumer age, takers are well aware of all aspects and very cautious about what they are getting. 'Better services' is the present day mantra. Food and Beverage Services are of vital significance in modern times. Preparing different foods with appropriate nutrition value is a scientific exercise while serving it is an art.

Modern hotels and restaurants pay much attention towards their food and beverage services. Since catering industry has flourishing prospects, this book is designed as an introductory text on the topic, highlighting all salient features." It is a matter of contentment for us to make this book available to readers, researchers, and academics. Suggestions from serious readers are highly welcome.

– Author

Contents

1

Introduction

The provision of food and beverages away from home forms a substantial part of the activities of the hospitality industry and, indeed, of the economy as a whole. Like the industry of which it is a major part, food and beverage operations are characterized by their diversity. Outlets include private and public sector establishments and range from small independently owned and operated units to large multinational corporations managing global brands and from prison catering to catering in the most luxurious hotels in the world. It is however very difficult to get hold of consistent statistics about the hospitality industry and about food and beverage operations as there is no one single definition of what the boundaries of the various industry sectors and sub sectors are and therefore what should and should not be included.

SIZE AND SCOPE OF FOOD AND BEVERAGE OPERATIONS

If the hospitality industry is considered to cover all undertakings concerned with the provision of food, drink and accommodation away from home, this will naturally include all food and beverage outlets. In other words, food and beverage provision is simply one element of a broader hospitality industry. In conceptual terms, this raises few problems except possibly with take-away food establishments where in some cases the food may be taken home for consumption even though it is prepared and provided away from home.

In practice, however, there are a number of difficulties in considering the hospitality industry as embracing all food and beverage establishments and outlets. This arises because, following a number of official and commercial attempts at definition, the hospitality industry is often considered to have a much narrower scope. The official definitions have excluded many food and beverage outlets. For example, the Standard Industrial Classification gives hospitality a reasonably broad coverage as shown in the Table but even here parts of employee and welfare catering are either omitted or included in other sectors. This book adopts the broadest possible approach, aiming to consider all types of food and beverage operation wherever they may appear.

Table. Size and Scope of the Hospitality Industry

Number of businesses	**SIC 92 Code**	**2001**	**2002**	**2003**	**2004**
Hotels and motels	55.11 and 55.12	10,890	10,800	10,535	10,416
Camping sites, etc.	55.21 and 55.23	3,928	4,175	4,370	4,702
Restaurants, cafes, takeaway food shops	55.30	52,633	54,340	55,475	57,667
Pubs, bars and licensed clubs	55.40	46,320	47,914	47,475	48,146
Canteen operator, catering contractor	55.51 and 55.52	5,217	5,485	5,636	5,765
Total	**55.00**	**118,988**	**122,714**	**123,491**	**126,696**
Turnover (£ million)	**SIC 92 Code**	**2001**	**2002**	**2003**	**2004**
Hotels and motels	55.11 and 55.12	12,047	11,824	12,172	13,009
Camping sites etc.	55.21 and 55.23	2,220	2,631	3,032	3,616
Restaurants, cafes, takeaway food shops	55.30	18,323	18,843	20,145	21,726
Pubs, bars and licensed clubs	55.40	19,163	20,681	21,392	24,481
Canteen operator, catering contractor	55.51 and 55.52	5,985	6,624	6,670	7,382
Total	**55.00**	**57,738**	**60,603**	**63,412**	**70,216**
Employment (Thousands)	**SIC 92 Code**	**2001**	**2002**	**2003**	**2004**
Hotels, motels and camping sites, etc.	55.1/55.2	370	365	369	379
Restaurants, cafes, takeaway food shops	55.30	509	547	575	594
Pubs, bars and licensed clubs	55.40	525	531	540	558
Canteen operator, catering contractor	55.50	256	265	267	267
Total	**55**	**1,660**	**1,708**	**1,751**	**1,798**

Table provides the latest figures on the size and scope of the India hospitality industry available from India government sources. The figures are based on a definition based on the SIC 1992. The data show a pattern of fairly consistent growth across the industry for the first few years of the 21st century. In terms of numbers of businesses, with the exception of the hotel and motel sector, all other sectors have grown substantially, with the restaurant, cafés and take-away sector in particular growing by around 10 per cent over these 4 years. The hospitality industry as described here has a total of nearly 127,000 separate businesses.

Looking at turnover provides a slightly different picture of the make up of the total of over `70,000 million. For example, hotels and motels show an increase in turnover from 2002 onwards even though the number of businesses has declined. This suggests either a consolidation of the sector with a smaller number of larger businesses or that each business is showing much better performance. The reality is probably somewhere between the two.

The restaurant and pubs, bars and clubs sectors have shown very strong growth in turnover and can be seen to be the dominant sectors of food and beverage operations as a large part of hotel turn over is dependent on room sales. The canteen and contract catering or contract food service sectors have also shown strong growth. In employment terms, restaurants are easily the largest sector, closely followed by pubs, bars and clubs, with the hotel sector growing more slowly, and the contract food service sector holding steady.

Standard Industrial Classification

For analytical purposes, economically similar activities may be grouped together into 'industries', for example, into agriculture, motor vehicle manufacture, retail distribution, catering and national government service. A system used to group activities in this way is described as an 'industrial classification'. Such a classification usually starts with a small number of broad groups of activities that are then subdivided into progressively narrower groups so that the classification can be used with varying amounts of detail for different purposes.

The first comprehensive SIC for the United Kingdom was issued in 1948. The classification has been revised on many occasions and in order to comply with EU data standards, the SIC was redrawn in 2007 and the new classification scheme will come into effect at the beginning of 2008. While the old SIC had only four main groups: hotels and other accommodation; restaurants, cafes and takeaways; pubs, bars and clubs; and canteens and contract catering, the new scheme is much more comprehensive. There is a lot of information here but it is worth looking in some detail at the various headings to understand the differences between the different classifications. In reading through the new classification, there are a number of interesting issues for note.

- First the very detailed nature of the descriptions and the very precise nature of the language used, including specifying types of activity that are included and also types of activity that are excluded. The activities excluded will appear in the national statistics under a different heading.
- Second, the definition of food and beverage operations as activities providing complete meals or drinks fit for immediate consumption. The emphasis here is on ready to eat food and drink and not on the manufacture or retail of food that needs reheating or reconstitution. This may cause some problems for supermarkets, who sell large amounts of sandwiches–for immediate consumption–for dinner. Where would a rotisserie chicken fit into this description?
- Third, the inclusion for the first time of mobile food stands, specifically mentioned in the classification.
- Fourth, the introduction of the category of event catering, which has seen substantial growth over the last few years, but perhaps strangely the inclusion of industrial or contract food service as part of this category. This 'other food services' category now also includes travel catering, catering at sports grounds, as well as factories, offices, hospitals or schools but only on a contract or concession basis and so still excludes the majority of public sector catering.
- Fifth, what is a beer parlour?

Classifying Food and Beverage Operations

There are many different ways of classifying food and beverage operations for different purposes. The SIC scheme is to allow the systematic collection and analysis of national economic statistics, which will now allow comparison across the whole of the EU.

Organizations such as Keynote, a well-respected market intelligence company, who prepare very detailed reports on a wide range of industries including hospitality and food and beverage operations, concentrate only on commercial operations in restaurants, fast food, contract food service, hotels, public houses and other. People 1st, the Sector Skills Council for the Hospitality, Leisure, Travel and Tourism industries, whose emphasis is on employees and the development of their skills to match industry needs, split the industry into 14, namely Contract food service providers, Events, Gambling, Holiday parks, Hospitality services, Hostels, Hotels, Membership clubs, Pubs, Bars and nightclubs, Restaurants, Self catering accommodation, Tourist services, Travel services and Visitor attractions.

This is a much broader description of the industry and by including in 'hospitality services' people who are employed 'in house', rather than by a contract caterer, to provide hospitality in travel, retail, education, health care, offshore locations, corporate hospitality, government and local authority provision such as care homes and prisons, as well as leisure venues and events, they capture many more people than the 'commercial' only definitions.

While these different definitions and classifications are interesting and useful, they do not provide any significant managerial insight. From this perspective, it is possible to make a number of distinctions between the many different types of food and beverage outlets. First, there is a distinction between those outlets that operate on a strictly commercial basis and those that are subsidized. A second distinction concerns the type of market served. In some cases, the market is confined to restricted groups, as for example, in a hospital or a prison or on a cruise ship, while in other cases the outlet is open to the public at large. A third distinction is between outlets where catering is the main activity of the undertaking, as for example, in a privately owned commercial restaurant, and those where it is a secondary activity, as is the case with travel catering or school meal catering. A final distinction appears between outlets that are in public ownership and those in private ownership. To a certain extent there is a rough compatibility between the distinctions. On the one hand, captive markets tend to be in public ownership and to be a subsidiary activity of the undertaking.

On the other hand, the commercial outlets tend to be in the private sector, to serve the general public and to be the main activity of the undertaking. In brief, the subsidized sector is not normally available to the public at large and normally provides catering only as an activity that is both secondary to the main business and available only to restricted groups. These broad divisions, however, do not hold true in all cases. Indeed, the exceptions are numerous and beyond the broad categories, they tend to devalue any generalizations. Using some of the distinctions, it is possible to classify food and beverage outlets into a number of broad sectors.

The purely commercial operations may be in public or private ownership and include outlets where catering is the main activity as well as those where it is a secondary activity, as for example, catering in the shops. In the case of the commercial sector, a secondary division is shown between outlets that have a restricted market and those which are open to the general public.

The subsidized operations similarly may be in public or private ownership. A distinction is drawn between catering in institutions where public ownership dominates and catering for employees where private ownership is also of importance. Almost by definition subsidized catering tends to be available only to restricted markets.

As with any classification, there are of course areas of overlap. There are two of particular importance here. The first overlap concerns catering in various private schools, colleges and hospitals, and in some offices and works canteens where the catering is not in any way subsidized but run on strictly on commercial lines.

These outlets appear under the heading of the commercial sector as commercial catering for a restricted market. The second issue concerns the many subsidized or welfare catering outlets that are operated by catering contractors who are themselves strictly organized on commercial lines.

These have not been separated out because although the operators themselves may be commercial companies, this does not affect the fact that the end product is normally subsidized for the market. There are two reasons for using this classification here. First, it provides a very broad coverage of food and beverage outlets–broader, for example, than many of the official definitions and classifications of the hospitality industry. The second reason for using this classification is that it is based on distinctions that have a significant bearing upon most aspects of the operation of the catering activity.

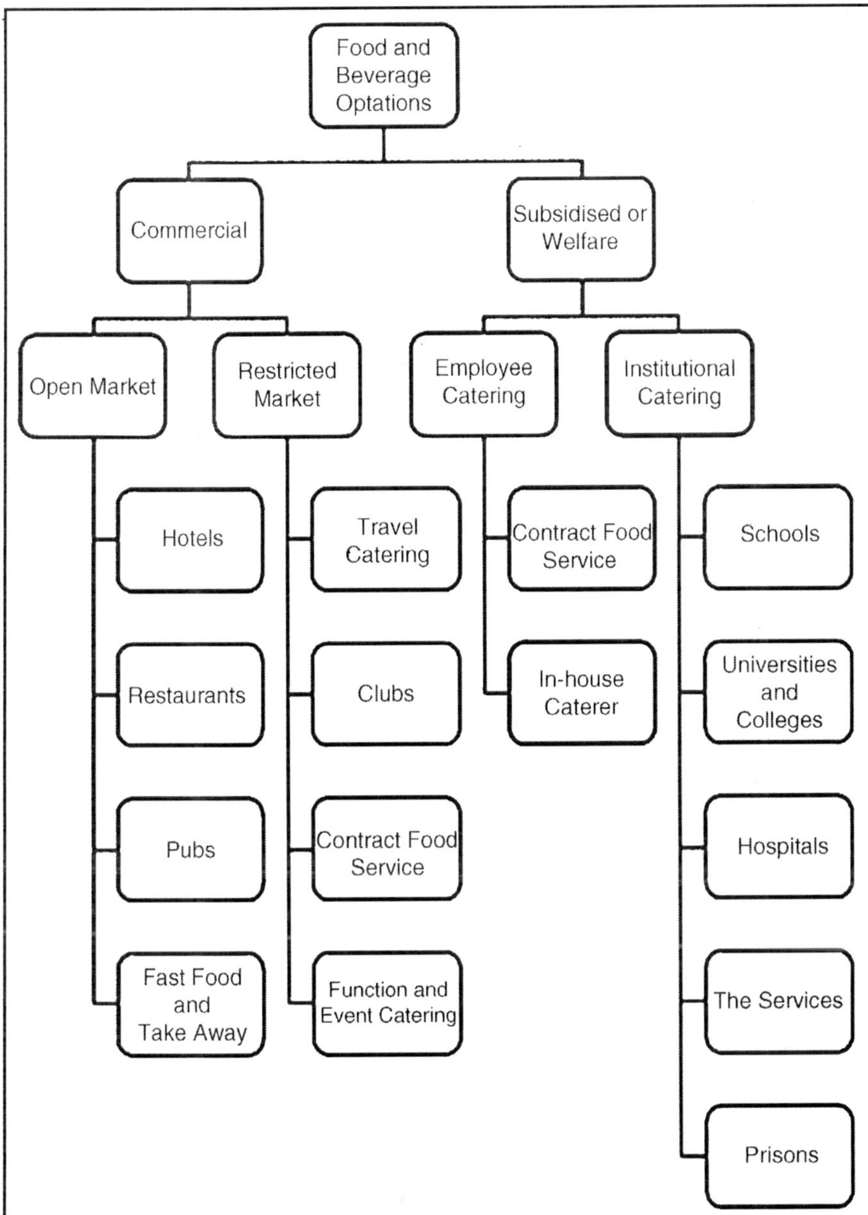

Fig: A Classification of Food and Beverage Operations

For example, the difference between subsidized catering and commercial catering not only embraces differences of objectives but also covers differences in the markets served, differences in the organizations involved and differences in their marketing and business strategy.

Cost and Market Orientation

It is then convenient at this point to discuss the broad distinction between cost and market orientation within the hospitality industry, as these two terms are closely associated with the particular sectors of the industry that have been identified. Examples of cost orientation are identified particularly in the welfare sector such as catering in prisons, for patients in hospitals and often for 'in-house' employee restaurants, while market orientation examples are found in the hotels, restaurants, popular and fast-food sectors. It is arguable that in fact all sectors of the industry need to employ a market oriented approach.

A market oriented business displays the following characteristics:

- A high percentage of fixed costs, for example rent, rates, management salaries, depreciation of buildings and equipment. This high percentage of fixed costs remains fixed regardless of any changes in the volume of sales. A hotel restaurant is an example of an operation with high fixed costs that have to be covered before profit can be made.
- A greater reliance on increases in revenue rather than decreases in costs to contribute to the profit levels of the establishment. The implication here is that in seeking to increase the business's profitability, more emphasis must be given to increasing sales rather than by reducing costs. For this reason the close monitoring of all sales in a market oriented business becomes of prime importance.
- An unstable market demand for the product, thereby requiring a greater emphasis on all forms of selling and merchandising of the product to eliminate shortfalls in sales and the need to manage the capacity of the business more closely.
- More likely to have a more flexible pricing policy in order to attract customers at off-peak times.

A cost oriented business displays the following characteristics:

- A lower percentage of fixed costs, but a higher percentage of variable costs such as food and beverage costs. The percentage of variable costs in cost oriented establishments varies with changes in the volume of the business's sales. Employee restaurants are often found with a lower percentage of fixed costs. This places less emphasis on achieving high sales volumes.

- A greater reliance on decreases in costs rather than increases in sales to contribute to the budgeted profit levels of the establishment. Thus in seeking to increase the performance level of a cost oriented business more emphasis would be given to reducing the overall costs of the operation in such areas as purchasing, portion sizes and labour levels.
- A relatively stable market demand for the product. In comparison to market oriented businesses, cost oriented operations enjoy a reasonably stable demand for their products. This makes planning and operating more predictable and controllable.
- More likely to have a more traditional fixed-pricing policy.

There are those areas of the hospitality industry that cannot be precisely defined as either cost or market oriented in that they display characteristics of both orientations at different times during their business. In the main, however, most hospitality establishments fall into one of these two categories and this has important implications for the catering and financial policies of the business, which are described later.

FOOD AND BEVERAGE MANAGEMENT

What do Managers Do?

There has been substantial interest in the nature and definition of the work of the manager over many years. Figure presents a model, which has been developed to synthesize much of this work for the hospitality industry.

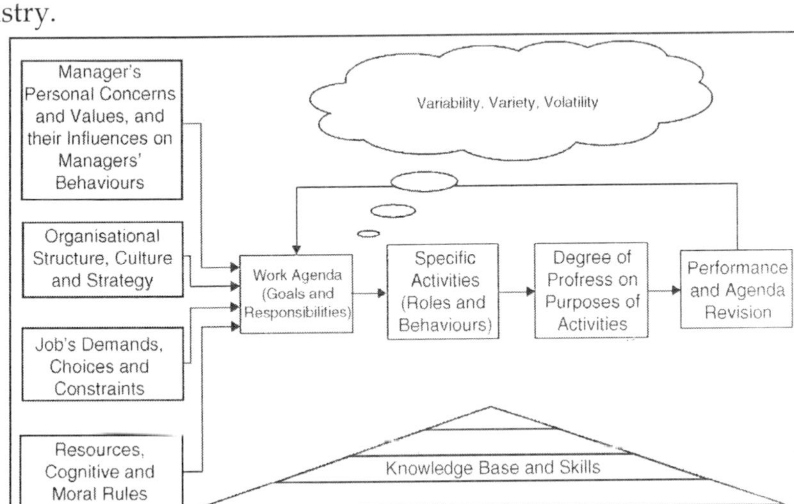

Fig: Exploring the Manager's Work in the Hospitality Industry

Hospitality managers have explicit and implicit goals, or responsibilities, which are concerned with ensuring the organization's continued success and survival, as well as their own personal interests, such as career progression. For hospitality firms, there are three main types of objectives that management must be concerned with, which are to ensure that the guest feels welcome, that facilities work for the guest, and that the operation will continue to provide service while also making a profit.

The goals that are set are shaped by factors, which include the organizational structure and culture, the economic situation, national culture, available resources, cognitive and moral rules, and their own personal attributes. Managers in the hospitality industry face a more uncertain and complex work environment than in many other industries due to its unique service characteristics.

This complexity is then coupled with the cultural differences of different business climates and environments and the managers' personal values. To reach the goals that have been set, managers in hospitality firms carry out various tasks and activities, covering the standard managerial roles such as planning, organizing, commanding, coordinating and controlling, sometimes extensive restaurant, conference and banqueting facilities, or the to the unexpected resulting from the changing environment. While managers undertake a diversity of managerial activities, what they do and/or what they choose to do are, to some extent, unpredictable and changeable.

The way that managers choose to perform the tasks is not always consistent either. Hence, the hospitality manager's work can be characterized by variability, variety and volatility, which represents the informal element of the hospitality manager's work. However, each managerial activity is often associated with a certain management function. In other words, the purpose of a managerial behaviour can be linked to one of the key functions of management.

For example, a restaurant manager may choose to speak to the customers to find out how they view the service offered. S/he will then be able to report on customer satisfaction. The manager may also recognize some weaknesses in service and, consequently, introduce appropriate training activities for staff. Since managers, including those in the hospitality industry, are responsible for the success of their organizations or organizational units, they also need to carry out these functional duties. This constitutes the formal nature of the hospitality manager's work. While the performance of managers is reflected by the degree of progress in achieving their goals, the effectiveness of the manager's performance is underpinned by their competencies including personal attributes, knowledge and skills. In the case of a food and beverage business, managers must have sufficient knowledge in order to manage daily operations and direct the business strategically. They must be competent in relating to employees and guests, accomplishing operational goals within financial constraints, and responding to customers' requirements immediately so that the quality of real-time service can be delivered. Within an international work environment, hospitality managers must be also competent in appreciating cultural differences and dealing with various situations appropriately. While this model sets the background to what managers should be doing, research conducted on behalf of the HCIMA by the University of Surrey was designed to identify the types of management activities that could be seen to be typical of different sectors of the hospitality industry across Europe.

Using a critical incident methodology, the research collected situations in which managers felt that their contributions or actions had made a significant difference to the outcome of a situation; somewhere the manager's skills and knowledge were used well, and somewhere the respondents felt their skills and knowledge were lacking. These incidents were then categorized into the four key areas of managing operations, managing the business, managing people and personal skills.

Each of these areas was then divided into categories. These 15 categories represent the key areas of skills and knowledge that any manager in the hospitality industry needs in order to be effective. The areas and subcategories are illustrated in Figure.

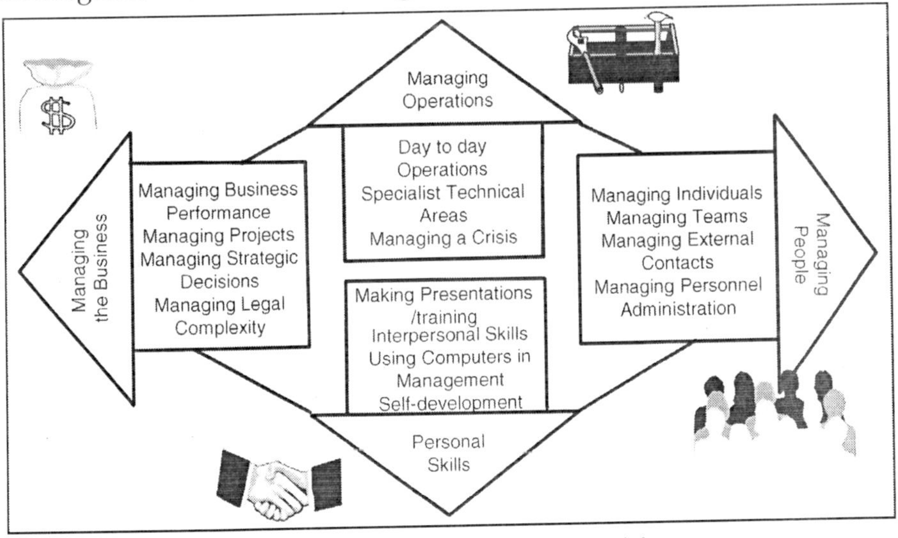

Fig: Main Areas of Management Activity

Analysing the incidents against the main category areas by level of management provides the data shown in Table.

Table: Cross Tabulation of Main Category Areas by Management Level.

Column%	Junior	Unit	General	Area	Director	Owner	Total%
Managing operations	40.3	30.2	20.9	13.4	17.8	29.3	29.0
Managing the business	11.8	23.0	32.6	41.2	41.1	32.0	25.2
Managing people	10.7	16.4	15.9	19.6	12.3	9.5	14.4
Personal skills	37.2	30.4	30.6	25.8	28.8	29.3	31.5
Total%	**23.2**	**36.5**	**19.6**	**6.3**	**4.8**	**9.6**	**100.0**

To allow for the differences in the titles and roles between industry sectors, the following management levels were used:

- **Department head/Junior management:** Managing a part within an operating unit. This would equate to the coffee shop manager in a hotel operation or the assistant manager of a fast-food operation.
- **Unit manager/Section manager:** Managing a complete unit or a section within a larger unit. This would equate to a unit catering manager working for a contract catering company, an executive chef, or the food and beverage manager of a small hotel.
- **General manager:** Overall control of one large unit composed of a number of sections or a collection of smaller units. This would equate to the food and beverage manager of a large hotel with manager of a small number of catering contracts.
- **Area manager:** Overall responsibility for a number of separate large units or geographic areas.
- **Director:** responsibility for the operation and management of a complete organization.
- Owner/proprietor/partner.

Managing operations recorded the second highest number of incidents across the three subcategories of managing day-to-day operations, specialist/ technical areas and managing crises. The analysis by managerial level, shown in Table shows a heavy emphasis in this area for the junior managers. This was strongest in day-to-day operations and specialist knowledge but when it came to a crisis the junior managers were more likely to call in their unit or general manager. Owners also get heavily involved in sorting out the crises that may occur within their businesses.

Sector comparisons show that hotels and restaurants reported the heaviest emphasis on managing operations while employee catering had the lowest. The area of managing the business included aspects of managing business performance, managing projects, managing strategic decisions and managing legal complexity. Across the whole sample, this area was in third place behind personal skills and managing operations. Although general managers, regional managers and directors show significantly more incidents in this area, junior managers and unit managers show a low emphasis.

This suggests that managers as a whole may be becoming more business oriented but only when they have reached a position of some seniority with an organization. Comparisons across the sectors of the industry reflect this emphasis, with hotels, restaurants and popular catering, sectors with large numbers of junior managers, showing a low emphasis on this area but other sectors, especially contract catering and local authority services, featuring positively.

The managing people area covered managing individuals, managing teams, managing external contacts and managing personnel administration. It was therefore surprising that, given the labour intensity of many sectors of the industry and the natural importance given to this area, there were relatively few reported incidents in this area. One explanation for this anomaly is that the interpersonal skills involved in managing people are not included in this part but are categorized as more generic personal skills.

Analysis across managerial level shows unit managers having the highest score in this area with junior managers and owners having low scores. The area of personal skills includes a range of generic or transferable skills that cover making verbal or written presentations, training, interpersonal skills, using computers in management and self-development. There were more incidents reported in this area than any other and most of these were in the interpersonal skills area, followed by making presentations and training.

Using computers in business showed comparatively few incidents and incidents to do with self-development were sadly, for an industry that seemingly values training highly, very sparse. All levels of manager reported large numbers of incidents in the area of interpersonal skills, especially the junior managers who would be new to having to handle these situations. Again there was an even spread across all sectors of the industry but a heavier than expected emphasis in popular catering or fast food. This is perhaps a reflection of the time managers spend dealing with interpersonal issues when the technological issues have been removed from consideration through systematized service delivery systems.

Responsibilities of Food and Beverage Management

The research described highlights the areas of activity that all managers are involved in but does not look at the specific responsibilities of the food and beverage manager. The significant contribution food and beverage sales can make towards total sales is evident but food and beverage costs can make equally significant inroads into sales. This necessitates the development of an effective system of control for all areas concerned with the food and beverage function. The development of such a total control system begins with the basic policy decisions–the determination of the financial, marketing and catering policies.

Working within these three broad policies of the establishment, the food and beverage department is then able to detail its objectives. Definitions of management are numerous with writers using different words and phrases to describe the same activity, but if allowance is made for this there is some broad agreement about managers' functions. First, they are involved in the planning process–setting objectives, making decisions about which direction the organization should take, that is, formulating policies. Second, managers decide how these objectives should be achieved and by whom.

This involves analysing tasks and assigning them to individuals or groups. Third, managers are involved in staff motivation in such a way as to move the organization through them in the direction formulated at the planning stage, to achieve the stated objectives. Fourth, managers have a controlling function including the comparison of actual performance to that forecast at the initial planning stage and taking any necessary steps to correct any deviation from agreed objectives.

The controlling may be done by observation, by analysis of accounting records and reports or by analysis of recorded statistical data. These four management functions–planning, organizing, motivating and controlling–can be translated into the functions of the food and beverage manager.

In a food and beverage department, the planning process involes the setting of several basic policies: a financial policy dealing with envisaged profitability or cost constraints of the establishment; a marketing policy defining the market to be catered for; and a catering policy defining the main objectives of operating the food and beverage facilities and the methods by which such objectives are to be achieved. Such policies would be decided at a senior level of management. The tasks needed to achieve these objectives would then be assigned to individuals who should receive job descriptions detailing the purpose of their tasks, the responsibilities of the individuals, who they are responsible to, etc. Here food and beverage managers work in conjunction with the personnel department in producing job descriptions and appointing on the job trainers to help train new staff.

The motivation of the staff of the food and beverage department is an important function of food and beverage managers. This may be undertaken in several ways–for example, by helping individuals who are undertaking common tasks to form into groups so that a 'team spirit' may develop, by encouraging staff–management committee meetings, or at a more basic level to see that full training is given so that job anxieties are reduced for employees from the beginning. Finally, there is the element of control in the food and beverage department. This involves the checking of actual performance against expectations or forecasts, and in the case of any wide deviations, to locate the problem area and rectify it, and to take whatever steps are possible to prevent the problem occurring again.

The functions of food and beverage managers in coordinating the food and beverage department are therefore numerous, and it is important that they should use all the tools of management available to them. An organization chart should be produced showing the position of the food and beverage department within the context of the total establishment. An organization chart presents graphically the basic groupings and relationships of positions, and a general picture of the formal organization structure.

In larger units, departmentalization becomes more apparent. Figure shows the organization of a food and beverage department in a large prestigious hotel. In this example, the food and beverage manager has six subordinate managers acting as departmental heads and then further levels of assistant managers and the operational teams themselves.

The food and beverage department can be seen to represent a major part of the hotel's total organization structure but clearly supported by other departments. Some units are, of course, too small to adopt anything like this type of organization structure. Indeed, in a small privately owned restaurant, it is often the owner who is 'manager' of all departments. In this instance, the proprietor would also operate as the control department, monitoring all incoming and outgoing revenues and costs, but overall the same main activities still have to be covered. It is also important to supplement the organization chart with a job description.

A job description is an organized list of duties and responsibilities assigned to a specific position. It may be thought of as an extension of the formal organization chart in that it shows activities and job relationships for the positions identified on the formal organization chart. An example of a food and beverage manager's job description may be seen in Table.

Some organizations also produce work schedules; these are outlines of work to be performed by employees with stated procedures and time requirements for their duties. Tasks are broken down into a careful sequence of operations and timed.

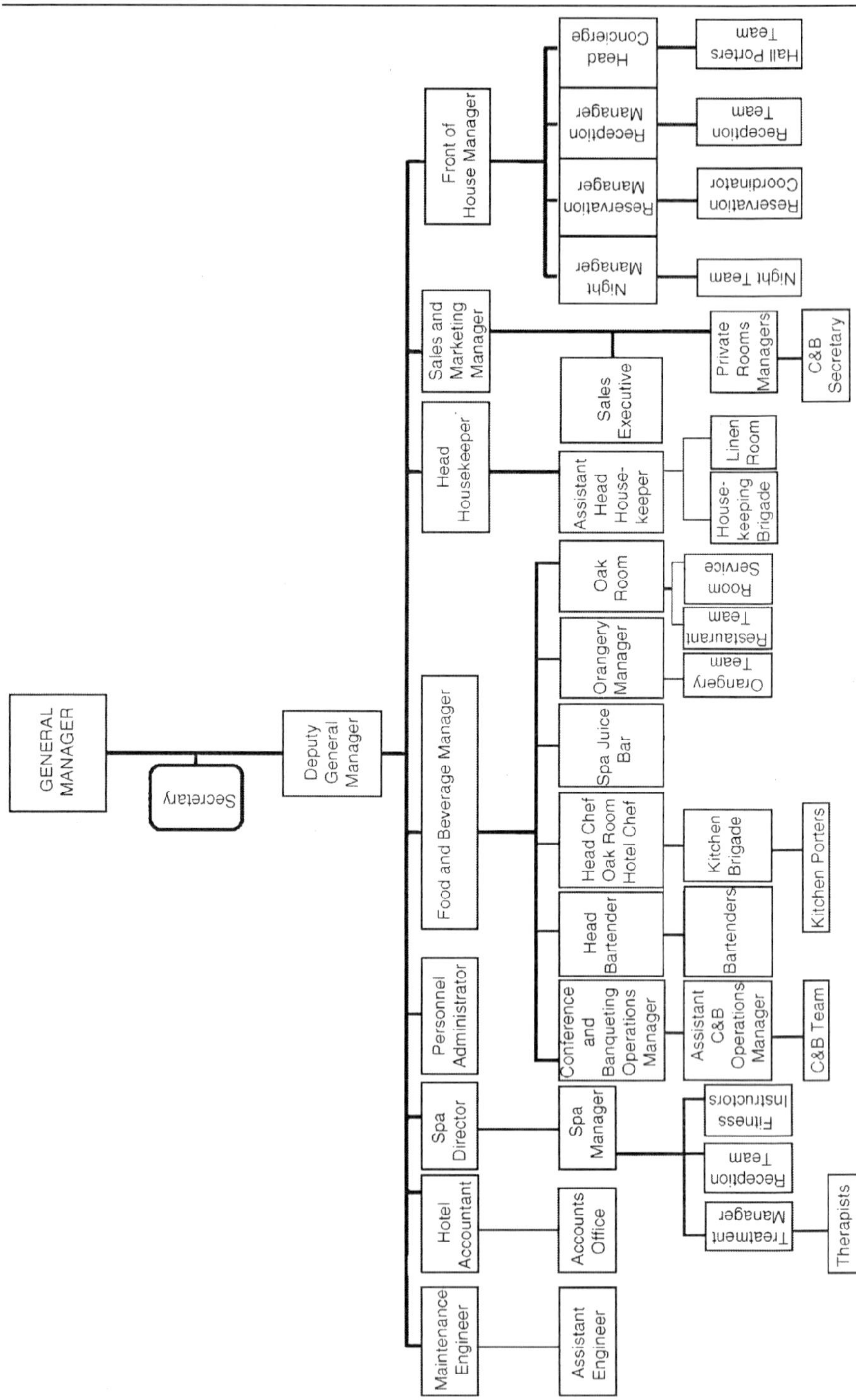

Fig: Danesfield House Hotel and Spa Organization Chart.

They are particularly useful in training new employees and for lower- grade jobs, but have a limited application at the supervisory and management level.

In general, the main responsibilities and objectives of the food and beverage department may be summarized as follows:

- The provision of food and beverage products and services catering for clearly defined markets to satisfy or exceed these customers' expectations.
- The purchasing, receiving, storing, issuing and preparation of food and beverages within the establishment for final provision and service to the customer.
- The formulation of an efficient control system within the food and beverage department with the purpose of:
  - Monitoring food and beverage prices and achieving competitive rates while still ensuring quality standards.
  - Pricing restaurant and special function menus to achieve desired profit margins.
  - Compiling on a daily, weekly and monthly basis, all relevant food and beverage information on costs and sales that may be used by management for forecasting, planning, budgeting, etc.
  - Reconciling actual and forecast costs and sales, and initiating corrective action if discrepancies occur, and finding out and eliminating the causes, for example bad portion control, incorrect pricing, etc.
  - Training, directing, motivating and monitoring of all food and beverage department staff.
  - Cooperating with other departments to become a significant contributor to the organization's short- and long-term profitability.
  - Obtaining in a regular, structured and systematic way, feedback from customers, so that their comments, complaints and compliments may be taken into account to improve the overall standard of service.

These are the major responsibilities and objectives of a food and beverage department. Other minor objectives do become important during the day- to-day running of the department, but these often tend to deal with sudden crises or short-term problems and would be too numerous to mention. However, achieving all these objectives is a far from easy task when managers are faced with the inherent complexity and variability of a food and beverage operation.

Constraints on Food and Beverage Management

The management of food and beverage departments has been described as the most technical and complex in the hospitality industry.

The specific factors that make food and beverage management relatively more complex are due to particular external and internal pressures.

External factors:

- The external factors are often seen as the 'major' problems of the food and beverage function. They originate outside the organization and for this reason internal action can rarely solve the problem adequately, although pro-active management may help to reduce their impact.

Government/political:

- Government legislation, for example, fire regulations, smoking regulations, health and safety legislation, EU regulations.
- Changes in the fiscal structure of the country, for example, regulations affecting business expense allowances.
- Specific government taxes, for example, VAT.
- Government policy on training and employment, economic development, regional development, etc.

Economic:

- Rising costs: Foods and beverages, labour, fuel, rates and insurance.
- Sales instability: Peaks and troughs of activity occur on a daily, weekly and seasonal basis.
- Changes in expenditure patterns and people's disposable incomes.
- Expansion and retraction of credit facilities.
- Interest rates on borrowed capital.

Social:

- Changes in population distribution, for example, population drifting away from certain areas or demographics such as age structure.
- Changes in the socio-economic groupings of an area.
- Change in eating patterns leading to a demand for more varied foods.
- Changes in food fashion, for example, current popularity of take-away foods, home delivery of fast foods, trends in healthy eating.

Technical:

- Mechanization, for example, of food production and food service equipment.
- Information technology, for example, data processing in hospitality establishments.
- Product development, for example, organic vegetables, increased shelf life of foods through irradiation, meat and dairy produce alternatives.lg1

Internal factors:

- Along with external factors, the food and beverage function also has many other day-to-day internal pressures. Internal problems are those originating within the organization and for this reason such problems can usually be solved adequately within the establishment if they can be identified and the root cause removed. The internal problems may be classified as follows.

Food and beverage:

- Perish ability of food and the need for adequate stock turnover.
- Wastage and portion control.
- Pilferage from kitchens, restaurants, bars and stores, sometimes referred to as 'shrinkage'.

Staff:

- General staff shortages or skill shortages within the industry.
- Achieving staffing levels to match peaks and troughs of sales activity.
- Absenteeism, illness, etc.
- Use of part-time or casual staff in some food and beverage departments.
- Poor supervision and training of new staff.
- High staff turnover, particularly in some areas.

Control:

- Cash and credit control and collection.
- Maintenance of all costs in line with budget guidelines and current volumes of business, for example, food, beverages, payroll, etc.
- Maintenance of a tight and efficient control of all food and beverage stocks.
- Maintenance of up-to-date costing and pricing of all menu items.
- Maintenance of an efficient food and beverage control system giving analysed statistical data of all business done.

Figure shows diagrammatically the potential sources of issues and problems that food and beverage managers need to be aware of if they are to maintain and improve the effectiveness of their operations.

Being a food and beverage manager is a challenging and demanding job but with the clear understanding and systematic approach that the following stages provide, it can also be a rewarding and satisfying one.

One key factor for all food and beverage managers is to understand their customers, the trends in the eating our market and the nature of the meal experience they need to provide.

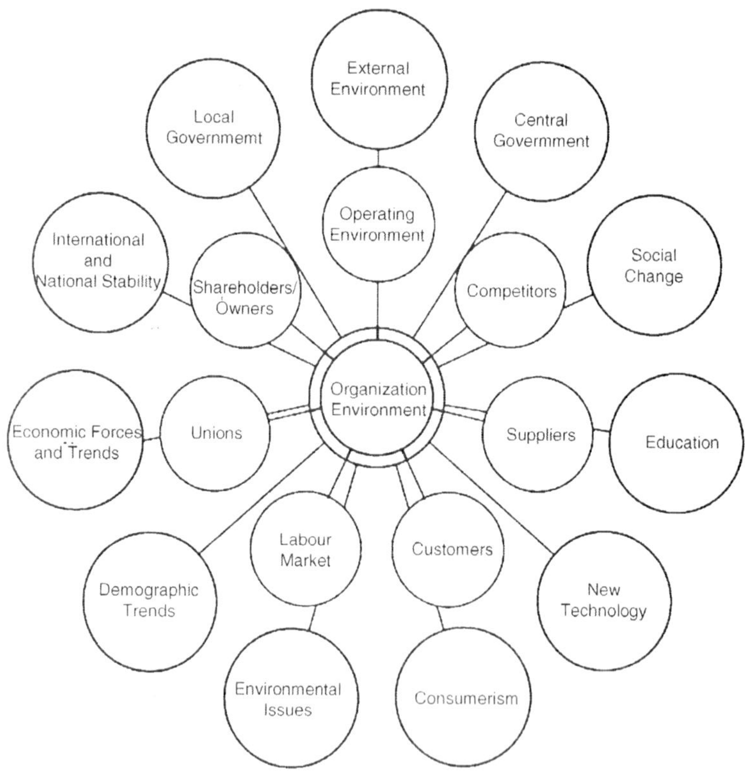

Fig: A Representation of Issues in the Business Environment

MANAGING THE MEAL EXPERIENCE

Service industries, such as food and beverage operations, differ from manufacturing in several ways. The customer is present at the time of both production and service. In manufacturing the customer is not present during the production process.

In food and beverage operations, the customer is involved in the creation of the service that is consumed at the point of production with little or no time delay between production and service.

The customer is not involved in the creation of manufactured products and there may be a considerable time lag between production and service. Services cannot be examined in advance, they are highly perishable and cannot be stored, all adding to difficulties in the quality control of service products; in manufacturing goods can be made in advance of demand and stored allowing more time for control procedures.

Finally, services have a larger intangible element in many of their products than manufactured goods do and for this reason have traditionally been more difficult to quantify and evaluate. For all these reasons, the time that the customer spends in the operation and what happens to them during that time is of particular importance. The 'meal experience' may be defined as a series of events–both tangible and intangible–that a customer experiences when eating out. It is difficult to define exactly where a meal experience actually starts, and indeed ends, although it is usually assumed that the main part of the experience begins when customers enter a restaurant and ends when they leave.

However, any feelings customers may have when they arrive at the restaurant, and when they leave, should also be taken into account and included as part of the total meal experience.

The series of events and experiences customers undergo when eating out may be divided into those tangible aspects of the product, that is, the food and drink, and those intangible aspects such as service, atmosphere, mood, etc.

These two components of the meal experience have also been labelled primary and secondary products or core and peripheral elements but although differing in descriptive terms, the underlying concept is the same.

It is the appreciation of the different components by the caterer that is important; the tangible and the intangible aspects must be integrated together to present a total product to the customer. If one or two components of the meal experience are out of harmony with the others, the whole product/service mix will be seen by the customer as a number of disjointed parts rather than as a totality.

This experience was first called the 'meal experience' in 1989 but is now a widely used term throughout the industry and has now been developed even further into the idea of the experience economy.

The Experience Economy

Food and beverage operations such as TGIFridays, the Hard Rock Café or Planet Hollywood have long understood that there is much more to the total customer experience than the food or the way that it is served.

They recognized in putting their concepts together that they needed to provide an additional 'theatrical' element to their operations that would make them memorable and provide added value to their customers. The Disney Corporation take this theatricality to an extreme by calling their hotel, restaurant and theme park employees 'cast members' and the uniforms they wear 'costumes'. Pine and Gilmore argue that in order to differentiate your operation in an era of high competition and the increasing commoditization of service there is a need to provide the customer with a memory of an experience that they can take away with them rather than just a good product or service. They argue that in order to do this the business needs to consider the complete staging of the experience from start to finish and to think of it as an almost theatrical performance expecting employees to act out their roles within a carefully crafted environment.

It could be argued that many restaurants have been in this business for a long time, but some operations are taking it even further.

Before customers set out to any operation for a meal, they may already have decided on the type of meal they want or feel would be most suitable for that particular occasion. This pre-meal experience decision may have been taken after the consideration of a number of variables and customers will choose the operation they consider satisfies all or most of their requirements.

The general factors affecting a customer's choice of meal experience include the following:

- **Social:** A social occasion is one of the most common reasons for eating out. Such family events as birthdays and anniversaries, special dates, a special event are all reasons for celebration and eating out. Equally, people decide to go to a restaurant for no other reason than to dine with friends. For those people who eat out infrequently, may be two or three times a year, the celebration of a special occasion is the most important reason. As the number of meal occasions per year rises, to over four times a year, there is a corresponding increase in the variety of reasons given, for example, to socialize with friends and relatives, as a treat for self or spouse, as a change from eating at home, etc.
- **Business:** Meals may also be taken away from home for business reasons. Generally speaking, the level of restaurant chosen will depend on the level of business being conducted, so that the more important and valued the business, the more expensive and up- market will be the restaurant. Business lunches and dinners are still the most common, although working breakfasts and afternoon teas are also common.

- **Convenience and time:** A food service facility may be convenient because of its location or because of its speed of service. A working couple arriving home may decide to eat out rather than prepare something at home; they do not wish to travel far, nor do they want an elaborate meal, so they choose a local pub, pizzeria or Thai restaurant. A family out shopping at the weekend decide to have lunch in a fast-food operation in the high street. A long-distance commuter has a meal onboard a train knowing that he will arrive home late that evening. Office workers or hospital staff with little time available decide to have lunch in the staff canteen. Housewives out shopping decide to stop for a snack in a shopping centre food court. All of these are typical examples of convenience eating away from home. They are convenient sometimes in terms of location, has for a meal, and very often a combination of the two. Most of the facilities used are associated with the mass-market end of the catering industry: fast-food operations; coffee shops; catering facilities in shopping centres; pizzerias; steak houses; cafés in leisure complexes; vending machines in schools; hospitals; offices and other work situations.
- **Atmosphere and service:** The atmosphere and environment of certain types of catering facilities and the social skills of the service staff can be particularly attractive to certain groups of customers. For example, wine and cocktail bars, and champagne and oyster bars in city centres appeal, in particular, to employees who have spent the day working together in offices and wish to meet together after work. The widespread use of 'Happy Hours' in such operations has further encouraged this trend for workers to go straight from their place of work to a catering outlet to socialize. These facilities are also often attractive because of their convenient locations.
- **Price:** The price level of an operation will significantly affect the restaurant choice of customers, particularly 'impulse' buying decisions. For the majority of customers, except perhaps for those few who can afford regularly to patronize high-quality restaurants, there exists a 'trade-off' point between the task and cost of preparing a meal at home, or paying for a meal out. Generally speaking, the higher the disposable income, the higher the trade-off level. For example, a couple may consider it quite acceptable spending up to ₹40 for an impulse meal

experience once a week; another couple may consider this price too high and would only be willing to pay up to that amount once a month. If they thought the meal was likely to cost more then they would trade-off the meal experience at a restaurant for a meal at home, or perhaps a cheaper take-away meal.

- **The menu:** Finally, a restaurant's menu may appear particularly interesting or adventurous, or have been recommended, enabling customers to enjoy a different type of meal from that cooked at home.

All of these factors will at some stage affect the buying decision of customers and hence their choice of meal experience, although it is unlikely that any of these variables will operate in isolation–usually two or three factors together will influence customers' choice of operation.

Once customers have decided on the type of meal they want, they will start to accumulate different expectations and anticipations. Just as the customers' buying decisions are influenced by a number of variables, so too is the meal experience itself.

Understanding Eating Out

Understanding the factors affecting customers' buying decisions an analysing who eats out and the frequency that they do is valuable data for all food and beverage managers. The analysis of who the customers actually are is also necessary information, not only for caterers in general, operational management in particular, but also for marketing management.

A review of this data shows that fast food as a sector has grown 23 per cent between 2002 and 2007, with more growth in chicken, perhaps fuelled buy health concerns and the introduction of new operations such as Nando's, and less growth in ethnic takeaways and fish and chips. In the restaurant sector, pubs have seen a growth rate of 35 per cent and restaurants including many of the branded chains growing 36 per cent. Much less growth has been seen in ethnic restaurants and in dining in hotels. The biggest growth, however, has been in the 'other' sector which includes cafes, coffee shops and other retail outlets. It would have been difficult over these last 5 years not to have noticed the number of new Costa, Caffè Nero, Starbucks and Pret A Manger operations appearing in towns and cities across the India. The analysis of those who eat out can be done in many ways. For example, it can be done by age, by gender, by socio-economic class and by the frequency of eating out–whether once, twice, or three or more times a week. Other examples of the types of analysis that may be done are by marital status, by the number of people in a household, by the number and age of children in the household, and by region within a country or of a specific area, etc.

Table. The UK Out Marketa, by Segment, 2002-2007

	2002	2003	2004	2005	2006 (est)	2007 (fore)	% change 2002-07
			Fast food				
Burgers	1.95	2.08	2.22	2.31	2.41	2.4	23
Ethnic takeaway	1.5	1.55	1.61	1.67	1.75	1.8	20
Pizza and Pasta	1.08	1.14	1.2	1.28	1.32	1.35	25
Fish and chips	0.87	0.91	0.95	0.99	1.02	1	15
Fried chicken	0.76	0.86	0.91	0.97	1.04	1	32
Other fast foodb	0.13	0.14	0.14	0.15	0.16	0.17	29
Total fast food	**6.28**	**6.67**	**7.03**	**7.36**	**7.7**	**7.72**	**23**
			Restaurants				
Pub catering	5.35	5.72	6.04	6.38	6.81	7.25	35
Hotel cateringc	3.94	3.99	4.02	4012	4.22	4.31	9
Restaurant meals	3.31	3.49	3.76	4.16	4.33	4.5	36
Ethnic restaurant	1.86	1.92	1.97	2.01	2.07	2	7
In-store	1.16	1.21	1.26	1.3	1.38	1.4	21
Roadside	0.47	0.48	0.49	0.51	0.53	0.53	11
Total restaurant	**16.09**	**16.81**	**17.53**	**18.48**	**19.34**	**19.98**	**24**
Otherd	1.7	1.77	1.95	2.28	2.56	2.75	62
Total	**24.07**	**25.25**	**26.51**	**28.12**	**29.59**	**30.45**	**27**

Note: Some historical data has been revised

[a]*xcl*: Institutional catering and other expenditure on food outside the home

[b]*incl*: Jacket potatoes, sausages, filled croissants etc.

[c]*incl*: Drinks revenue

[d]*incl*: Cafes, coffee shops and other retail outlets

The types of catering establishments that the public choose to eat out at, and the frequency that they do, is also valuable information.

Table. Frequency of Eating Out, by Venue Visited, March 2007.

	All %	Twice a week or more %	About once a week %	About once a fortnight %	At least once a months %	At least once every 3 months %	Less than once every 3 months %
Pub restaurant/ bar	51	67	64	69	52	50	27
Café/coffee shop	32	52	41	46	35	25	13
Chinese restaurant	27	45	39	37	28	17	10
Pizza/pasta restaurant	25	53	35	36	22	16	7
Fish and chip shop/restaurant	24	44	33	27	26	17	9
Indian restaurant	24	46	32	32	27	20	5
British restaurant	24	42	30	26	29	20	9
Burger/fried chicken bar	21	44	27	28	20	14	6
Hotel restaurant	18	36	28	25	17	10	8
In-store restaurant/ cafeteria	16	32	23	24	11	14	6
Other restaurant (e.g. Italian, vegetarian	16	33	23	19	16	11	4
Other ethnic restaurant (e.g. Thal, Mexican)	11	28	18	15	9	7	2

An example of an analysis of the types of establishment visited and frequency of visit based on a sample of 2,029 adults aged 15 and over is shown in Table.

- Major research of this nature is conducted by established market research organizations such as Mintel, Keynote and other consultancy companies, who undertake major studies for the industry in general. Specific and confidential studies to answer particular questions or for particular locations are also undertaken for individual companies. Research is also undertaken by the marketing departments of medium/large hospitality companies.

This does not preclude the smaller-size establishment from undertaking systematic research studies, although the sample size is likely to be smaller and the time available to do so is restricted. Ideally, basic information should provide:

- Sufficient data to aid decision-making;
- Accurate and up-to-date consumer profiles, so that an organization is more successfully able to meet the requirements of the consumer;
- Competitive analysis, so that an organization can in part measure its own performance.

Research of this nature to understand the needs of the customers should always be ongoing, and not just of an occasional nature.

Food and Drink

The type of food and drink that people choose to consume away from home depends on a number of factors which are of particular concern to food and beverage managers.

Table. Most Popular Eating Out Venues Visited, by Gender and Age, March 2007

	Any venue %	Pub restaurant %	Café/ coffee sho %	Chinese restau-rant %	Pizza/pasta restau-rant %	Fish and chip shop/ Restaurant %	British restau-rant %
All	86	51	32	27	25	24	24
Men	85	49	29	29	25	28	25
Women	87	52	35	25	25	20	23
16-19	91	52	30	35	45	40	18
20-24	90	50	26	33	44	28	21
25-34	93	53	34	38	40	30	24
35-44	90	56	41	32	29	28	29
45-54	85	48	36	26	20	18	26
55-64	84	53	31	22	15	20	25
65+	75	44	24	12	4	15	20

They include:

- The choice of food and drink available: Whether the menu is limited or extensive; whether the operation revolves around one particular product, for example, steak houses and pizzerias; or whether there is a varied choice, for example, coffee shops and wine bars.

- Able 1.7 shows an analysis of the most popular types of food and beverage outlets visited by age group and by gender in the last month, from a sample of 2,029 adults aged 15 and over. This shows that 86 per cent of the sample ate out at least once in the last month with pub restaurant and bars being the most popular choice, coffee shops growing strongly in popularity in second place and fish and chip shops and 'British' restaurants as the least popular.
- Looking at the gender differences, it would appear that women eat out more often than men and are more likely to visit pub restaurants and coffee shops. Men on the other hand are more likely to visit Chinese restaurants and fish and chip shops.
- Looking at the age differences, young people are more likely to eat out than older people, but everyone is happy to visit a pub restaurant. British restaurants appear to be more skewed towards an older clientele while pizza and pasta are skewed in the opposite direction.
- The quality of the product offered, for example, locally sourced fresh organics or convenience foods: château or estate bottled or cheaper wine varieties.
- The quantity of product offered, that is, the portion sizes. For example, does the restaurant offer children's meals or smaller portions for children or older people?
- The consistent standard of the product: customers returning to the restaurant for a second or subsequent occasion would expect the product to be of the same standard as they had eaten or drunk before.
- The range of tastes, textures, aromas and colours offered by a food dish, or the taste, colour and aroma offered by a drink.
- That the food and drink are served at the correct temperatures, for example, that the iced coffee is sufficiently chilled, or that hot food is hot when it reaches the customer.
- That the presentation of the food and drink enhances the product offered. This is important at all levels of catering, from cafeteria to fine dining service, where the visual presentation of the meal is very much part of the total experience.
- That the price and perceived value for money are both in line with customers' pre-meal experience anticipations.
- That the quality of the total meal experience matches or even enhances the expectations of the guests.

Variety in Menu Choice

The type of menu offered by an establishment and the variety of menu choice should also enhance the total meal experience. At the lower level of the market the choice of menu items in a restaurant is usually fairly limited for a number of reasons.

First, price. If a customer is paying ₹10–15 for a three-course meal the range of menu items that can be made available within the cost limits of such an operation is obviously more limited than in operations where the customer's average spending power is higher.

Second, the amount of time taken to consume meals at this level of the market may vary between half an hour and one hour, but will rarely exceed this. Proportionately, little of this time is spent studying the menu choice.

Third, it may be suggested that customers frequenting this lower level of the market may be uncomfortable if presented with a very large menu selection and may therefore prefer a more limited, but still varied menu choice. In fine dining restaurants where the average spending power may be well above ₹50 per head, the menu selection can be much greater. In these establishments which encourage a luxury meal experience, the minimum amount of time customers usually spend on a meal is one and a half hours, and may often be three hours, depending on the size of the group and the occasion.

The proportion of the time that may be devoted to reading the menu and selecting from the menu items is correspondingly greater. Customers frequenting these types of establishment would also expect to be offered not only a large menu selection, but also a number of chef' s and house specialities and wines. The menu choice offered by a restaurant is therefore dependent on a number of interrelated factors: the price the customer is willing to pay; the amount of time available for the meal experience; the level of the market in which the restaurant is situated and, consequently, the types of customer likely to frequent that type of operation. Further considerations affecting the choice of menu from the caterer' s point of view would be the production and service facilities available, the skills of the staff, the quality and availability of ingredients and the potential profitability of the menu.

Level of Service

Broadly speaking the higher the cost of the meal to the customer, the more service the customer expects to receive. In a food court where customers are spending around ₹5 for a meal, the degree of service received is comparatively little: customers collect and purchase their own food from particular food units, carry it to a table, and may be expected to clear their own dishes from the table at the end of their meal. As the cost of the meal to customers increases so will the amount of service they receive.

At the higher end of the eating out market, where customers may be paying over ₹40 per head for a meal, full service is most likely to be provided. However, the dominance of silver service at this level is increasingly challenged by chefs wishing to take direct control of the presentation of their dishes and so adopting a plated style of service. The actual service of the food and beverages to the customer may be described as the 'direct' service. Part of the restaurant' s total service, however, is also composed of 'indirect' or ancillary services. These might include the provision of cloakroom facilities; or access to the Internet.

It is necessary for a restaurant to identify the level of service it is going to offer in its offer and to extend this standard of service throughout all aspects of the operation. Thus, if a restaurant has a very formal type of food and beverage service, associated with some fine dining operations, the other aspects of the restaurant service should be equally formal–the speed, efficiency and dress of staff; the degree of personalization and courtesy the customers receives, and so on. It is important, therefore, for a restaurant operation to consider not only the service of the food and beverages for which the staff are usually adequately trained, but also to remember the indirect service aspect of the operation, which are all part of the customer' s meal experience.

Price and Value for Money

The concept of value for money will vary from one sector of the market to another and, indeed, from one customer to another. In the majority of cases, however, customers will frequent a restaurant not only because of its food and service, but also because they feel the price they are paying represents good value for money. At the popular end of the market, inclusive 'meal deals' are often offered.

For example, in the summer, a steak house operation might offer rump steak and strawberries at an inclusive and competitive price, so that a prospective client is aware in advance what the main cost of the meal will be, and this will help alleviate any concern the customer may have about the total cost. At the top end of the market, menu items are often charged for separately because at this level the total cost of the meal is not such an important factor to the customer as perhaps are the other aspects of the operation, such as the standard and range of food and beverages, the level of service offered and the degree of comfort, décor and atmosphere. However, there has been a growing emphasis recently on set price menus in quality and luxury restaurants, at both lunch and dinner.

Today, some establishments include a percentage service charge in the price of their meals, others will add it separately, while some operations do not include a service charge but leave it to the customer' s discretion. Prices charged within the India are inclusive of government taxes, while in some other countries the total amount of tax is shown separately. Some schools of thought consider that by not showing these 'added extras', such as a service charge in the price of the individual menu items, customers may be encouraged to spend more because the prices will appear very reasonable; others consider that customers prefer to know exactly what they are paying for and do not like to see these 'extras' added at the end of the bill.

Interior Design

The overall interior design of a restaurant is one of the first physical aspects of a catering operation that a customer will come into contact with. This first impression of the restaurant is very important. Potential customers passing by may like the look of the establishment and decide to come and eat there; customers who have actually planned to eat in the restaurant and like what they see when they enter, will feel pleased with their choice of restaurant.

The interior design of a restaurant is composed of many different aspects: the size and shape of the room; the furniture and fittings; the colour scheme; lighting; air conditioning; etc. As with the previously described aspects of a restaurant, there is a need for a sense of coherence in a restaurant' s interior design. The colour scheme of the restaurant should blend and balance and be enhanced by the lighting; tables and chairs should be ergonomically and aesthetically designed so that they not only satisfy their functional purpose, but also look attractive.

The interior design of a restaurant contributes greatly to the creation of its image. A self-service cafeteria in an industrial situation, for example, may consist of a very large dining area, tables and chairs of a standard design and shape, the colour scheme of the restaurant having few variations and lighting arrangements being purely functional. For this type of catering operation a consistently steady seat turnover is required, and this is encouraged by designing the interior of the restaurant so that it does not invite diners to linger over their meal; in addition a separate coffee lounge or area may be provided where customers may go afterwards and in this way vacate their seat for the next diner.

In a luxury restaurant, however, seat turnover is not so critical and, in fact, customers may be encouraged to stay in the restaurant to increase their average spend. In these types of establishment the interior design of the restaurant is made to be very comfortable: the lighting in the restaurant is quite subdued; the colour scheme has warmth and depth; there may be several particular points of interest in the restaurant, such as pictures, murals and large floral displays to hold the customer' s interest; tables are farther apart, and may be separated from one another in booths or by partitions; and the chairs are so designed that the customer may sit in them for several hours without feeling uncomfortable.

The interior design of a catering facility needs to be carefully considered at the initial planning stage and if necessary professional advice sought in order to avoid costly corrective measures later.

The life cycle of the operation also needs to be taken into account as this will significantly affect the financial investment in this aspect of the catering operation.

Atmosphere and Mood

The atmosphere or mood of a restaurant is a difficult aspect of an operation to define, but it is often described as an intangible 'feel' inside a restaurant. Not all restaurants have an obvious type of atmosphere, others try to deliberately create one. For example, some fine dining restaurants have a very formal atmosphere which is created by the dress and attitude of the staff, the decor of the restaurant, the service accompaniments, the type of clientele that frequent these restaurants, etc. Other restaurants, such as pub restaurants or pizza and pasta restaurants, try to create a relaxed informal atmosphere, and one that is very sociable to be a part of and seen in. The atmosphere of a restaurant is affected by many different aspects of the operation. They include the décor and interior design of the restaurant, the table and seating arrangements, the service accompaniments, the dress and attitude of the staff, the tempo of service, the age, dress and sex of the other customers, the sound levels in the restaurant, whether music is played, the temperature and the overall cleanliness of the environment and the professionalism of the staff.

Again, the harmony between the product itself, the service and the overall environment is important. If one of these aspects is out of unison with the others, disharmony may result in the customer gaining a confused image of the restaurant, and the customer will invariably leave feeling unsettled and remembering that one small aspect.

Expectation and Identification

A single customer or group of customers arriving at a restaurant for a meal bring with them a series of expectations regarding that restaurant– the type of service they will receive, the price they will pay, the expected atmosphere and mood of the restaurant, etc. The customer' s expectations may be varied and numerous, ranging from the restaurant which the customer frequents because they want to be seen there and participate in its social atmosphere, to the small quiet restaurant where the customer may go because of its intimate and personal nature.

Upon arrival at the restaurant, if the product presented to customers is in harmony with their expectations, it is very likely that they will be pleased with their choice and have a relaxed and enjoyable meal. Should customers sense disharmony, however, between their expectation of the restaurant and the actual product they find, they may not enter the restaurant but choose another. If disharmony is not realised until customers are seated at the table, it is unlikely that they will leave but will have a less than satisfactory meal. There is a need for customers to be able to identify and associate themselves with a particular restaurant for a particular meal occasion.

They may not always identify with the same restaurant, as their needs and expectations may vary from one meal experience to the next. For example, at a business lunch a customer may require an expensive restaurant with an atmosphere conducive to discussing business; such a restaurant, however, will not be suitable for the same customer to take their family for a special occasion.

A customer therefore has different needs and expectations on different meal occasions, and similarly at different times of the day, for example, lunch and dinner. These alternating needs of customers should be identified by a restaurant and catered for differently; for example, the restaurant offering formal business lunches may offer special function catering in the evening when the demand for business meals is minimal. There is a danger in these situations, however, that restaurants may be led into catering for mixed markets, and it is important for a restaurant offering different levels of service at different times of the day, to keep them completely separate, and not attempt to be 'all things to all people'.

Where different levels of markets are being catered for within the same establishment, it is sometimes possible for separate entrances to be used to service the different facilities, or functions timed so that the guests do not enter the operation all at the same time, and all require the use of the ancillary facilities simultaneously, such as cloakrooms, toilets, telephones, car parking spaces, etc.

In a hotel, for example, the speciality restaurant may be situated on the top floor featuring panoramic views, while the night club may be found on the lower ground floor; both facilities operating successfully within the same establishment, but both with separate entrances, ancillary amenities and catering to different types of clientele.

Location and Accessibility

The location of a food service facility has been said to be its most important feature. The location of a food and beverage operation must be made after careful identification of the market segments to which it is appealing. For example, a take-away fish and chip shop catering to a market segment identified as couples with children of CD1 socio-economic classification could not be situated further than two or three miles from this market; any distance greater than this and potential customers would consider choosing a fish and chip shop closer to their home.

The restaurant' s location in relation to its present markets should not only be considered but also its location to possible future markets. For example, a city restaurant may rely heavily on a number of large local companies for the majority of its lunchtime trade; should several of these companies leave the area the restaurant' s demand would be significantly affected. A roadside restaurant' s trade would also be affected by the expansion or relocation of a major nearby road and consequently an increase or decrease in the volume of traffic and hence customers.

The future expansion on a site with the possibility of catering to larger or more varied markets should also be considered and incorporated into the initial planning stage whenever possible. The accessibility to a catering operation is another important factor.

Customers arriving by car will expect adequate car parking facilities. If customers travel by public transport, the operation should be well served by buses, trains or taxis. If a high street take-away facility expects a large percentage of its business from passing trade there should be a heavy pedestrian flow past its doors.

Food and Beverage Service Employees

Staff employed by a restaurant operation should complement the meal experience of the customers, and they are able to do this in a variety of ways: their social skills; their age and sex; their uniform; the tempo of their service, and so on. The number of staff serving in a restaurant is closely related to the prices charged by the establishment and the level of service that it offers.

In self-service operations very few service staff is required; in some establishments the ratio of staff to customers being as low as one member of staff serving twenty to forty customers. However, in the fine dining restaurants offering full service, the ratio may be as high as one member of staff to eight or even less customers.

These latter types of operations are, however, charging the customers for this extra-attentive service and must therefore be seen to have an adequate number of staff. Not only does the number of staff in a restaurant contribute to the meal experience, but also their attitude to customers and the tempo of their service. In a large employee cafeteria where the ratio of service staff to customers may be low and speed of throughput important, the staff are required to work at a fast and efficient speed, and where possible leave the customers to serve themselves. In a luxury restaurant the tempo of the staff is considerably slower and more relaxed because of the higher ratio of service staff to customers.

It should be noted that the attitude of the staff is almost totally influenced by the management attitude and the employment climate in which they are working. The uniforms of the service staff should be appropriate for the level of the catering operation, and again this physical aspect of the restaurant must be seen to be a part of the establishment' s total image. At the end of the meal, staff can do a lot to reassure customers about their choice of meal experience. Because the intangible elements of a service are not visible, they are more difficult to evaluate.

Customers, therefore, particularly need reassurance about the product they have purchased. Food service staff may help in several ways: at a basic level by asking if the customers have enjoyed their meal– this verbal confirmation by customers reinforces that their decision was correct in having chosen a particular restaurant; by remembering to offer customers take-home tangible items provided by the restaurant, for example, matches, sample menus, the restaurant' s card; by pointing out a special promotion for a future date and enquiring whether the customer would like to make a reservation.

□

2

Packaging Food Preservation

One of the most common methods for preserving foods today is to enclose them in a sterile container. The term "canning" refers to this method although the specific container can be glass, plastic, or some other material as well as a metal can, from which the procedure originally obtained its name. The basic principle behind canning is that a food is sterilized, usually by heating, and then placed within an air-tight container. In the absence of air, no new pathogens can gain access to the sterilized food.

In most canning operations, the food to be packaged is first prepared in some way—cleaned, peeled, sliced, chopped, or treated in some other way—1and then placed directly into the container. The container is then placed in hot water or some other environment where its temperature is raised above the boiling point of water for some period of time. This heating process achieves two goals at once. First, it kills the vast majority of pathogens that may be present in the container. Second, it forces out most of the air above the food in the container.

After heating has been completed, the top of the container is sealed. In home canning procedures, one way of sealing the (usually glass) container is to place a layer of melted paraffin directly on top of the food. As the paraffin cools, it forms a tight solid seal on top of the food. Instead of or in addition to the paraffin seal, the container is also sealed with a metal screw top containing a rubber gasket. The first glass jar designed for this type of home canning operation, the Mason jar, was patented in 1858. The commercial packaging of foods frequently makes use of tin, aluminum, or other kinds of metallic cans. The technology for this kind of canning was first developed in the mid-1800s, when individual workers hand-sealed cans after foods had been cooked within them.

At this stage, a single worker could seldom produce more than 100 "canisters" (from which the word "can" later came) of food a day. With the development of far more efficient canning machines in the late nineteenth century, the mass production of canned foods became a reality.

As with home canning, the process of preserving foods in metal cans is very simple in concept. The foods are prepared and the empty cans sterilized. The prepared foods are then added to the sterile metal can, the filled can is heated to a sterilizing temperature, and the cans are then sealed by a machine. Modern machines are capable of moving a minimum of 1,000 cans per minute through the sealing operation.

DEVELOPMENT OF PACKAGING AND CANNING

In preindustrial society, packaging of food was far from being unknown. It was used for food storage at home and for transport from the production place, the farm, or workshop to the local or regional market. Examples are the transport of cereals or flour in bags, tea in wooden boxes or tinplate canisters, and oils in jars.

At the household level, people salted meat and pickled vegetables and preserved them in jars. In groceries at the end of the nineteenth century, most commodities were still unpacked and sold in bulk. Products such as tea, coffee, sugar, flour, or dried fruits were weighed out in front of the customer and wrapped in paper or put into a bag. In major cities in the 1880s, the milkman came around with a dipper and can to deliver milk, which was often dirty.

Origin of Modern Packaging and Canning

Early methods of sealing jars included waxed paper, leather, or skin, followed by cork stoppers and wax sealers. The beginning of modern food technology started with the experiments of the French confectioner Nicolas Appert. In 1795, the French Government offered a prize of 12,000 francs to anyone who could find a way to preserve food because Napoléon Bonaparte needed to provide the military with a safe food supply.

(The requirements of providing adequate food supplies for armies and navies have been of great significance in the history of modern packaging and food preservation.) After fourteen years of experimentation, Appert developed a method for preserving foods by heating. The food, meat, or vegetables, was first cooked in open kettles and placed in glass jars. After removing as much air as possible, the jars were carefully sealed with corks wired in place and then submersed in boiling water.

Appert chose glass for the container because he believed that it was air that caused the spoilage—glass is a material least penetrated by air. It is of importance to note that, in Appert's time, it was not known that microorganisms caused food to spoil. The processes involved in food spoilage were not understood until the second half of the nineteenth century as a result of the work of scientists such as Louis Pasteur on microorganisms. In 1810

Appert published his prize-winning essay on food preservation and the French emperor Napoléon awarded the 12,000-franc prize to him. Within a year, an English version appeared in London, and the new method of preserving food in glass spread quickly to other countries.

Canning

Two individuals in England are given credit for applying and improving Appert's invention, Bryan Donkin and Peter Durand. Bryan Donkin, an associate of John Hall's at his Dartford Iron Works, realized in 1811 that iron containers could be used instead of the fragile glass, and in 1812 the factory began to produce canned food such as meat. In 1810, Peter Durand patented the use of metal containers, which were easier to make and harder to break than glass jars. (The glass jars used by Appert frequently broke.) He covered iron cans, which were prone to rust, with a thin plating of tin (which is not adversely affected by water), and invented the "tin can". By 1813, Durand was selling canned meat to the Royal Navy. The British admiralty bought these foods as part of the medical stores for distribution to sick men as well as to supply expeditions. By 1819 canning had arrived in the United States, but no one wanted canned food until the Civil War started. In 1821, the William Underwood Company in Boston introduced commercial canning in the United States. For a long time, people regarded canned foods with suspicion, and for good reasons.

In the middle of the nineteenth century, the foods produced by the canning industry were as likely to spoil as not because of inadequate heating techniques). Then, beginning in 1868, first in the United States and later in Europe, handmade cans were replaced by machine-cut types. The new technology made it possible for giant meat-canning firms like P.D. Armour to emerge in Chicago and Cincinnati. The product, however, was packed in big, thick, clumsy red cans and was not very appetizing.

The American Gail Borden was a pioneer in food canning. In 1856 he successfully produced sweetened condensed milk in cans and was granted a patent on the process. With financial support, the New York Condensed Milk Company was established in 1857. The demand for condensed milk was at first limited, but during the American Civil War it was introduced on a large scale. The Civil War contributed significantly to the popularization of canned foods in general. The army had to be fed and the government contracted with firms to supply food.

Under difficult circumstances, people learned that canned foods such as condensed milk can be tasty and nourishing. The invention of practical can openers at the end of the nineteenth century made cans easier to open, making them even more convenient for consumers. For many years, however, the flavour of most canned food left much to be desired. On the other hand, it should be realized that products such as canned peas and salmon were usually sold to people living on the American prairies or in the urban slums in Great Britain, most of whom had never eaten the fresh product.

In addition, losses due to spoilage caused by microorganisms remained high. It was not until the end of the nineteenth century that research carried out at Massachusetts Institute of Technology made a substantial contribution to improving the keeping quality, nutritional value, and taste of food products preserved in cans and glass. In the early twentieth century, the heavy cans were replaced by those made of lighter materials, and manufacturers could stress that their products were hygienically processed and, therefore, safer to eat than the traditionally unpackaged products that had been sold in bulk.

As food technology advanced, numerous chemical additives were developed to control or speed up food processing and to increase the keeping quality of canned foods. Originally, the nutritional value of food preserved by canning was not high, mainly due to the length of time required by the heating techniques. From the 1920s onward, however, the nutritional value of canned foods gradually approached that of the fresh product, thanks to modern food technology.

Finally, in the 1960s, Reynolds and Alcoa companies succeeded in making all-aluminium cans out of one piece of metal, thereby solving the problem of the weight of the cans; only the lid needed to be attached. At the same time, the invention of the rip-off closure and the pop-top lid on aluminium cans made them even more convenient, and made can openers unnecessary. For consumers, the choice between fresh or canned food became largely a question of taste, convenience and preference.

Glass

Despite its fragility and high production costs, glass had an advantage over cans: glass is chemically inert. In a metal can, iron, tin, and even lead may interact with the water of the preserved food due to chemical or galvanic reactions (although that problem had been solved when iron was replaced by lighter material). The problem of lead contamination had been removed in 1904 when the production system of the Sanitary Can Company in New York made soldering of the can unnecessary.

Glass became a relatively cheap and convenient form of packaging in1903 when Michael J. Owen in Britain invented a semiautomatic machine for producing both jars and bottles. In the nineteenth century a major problem with glass containers had been finding a way to close a relatively expensive container without making the bottle or jar useless after it had been opened. Glass bottles could be closed with a cork, but closing bottles and jars that had wide mouths remained a problem. Numerous ingenious inventions and innovations sought convenient ways to open and close glass containers (and cans as well). The breakthrough came with the invention of the zinc cap for the shoulder-seal jar. The most significant inventions were the Mason Jar in 1858 (named for its inventor, John Landis Mason), a glass jar with a thread at the neck that could be closed by screwing on a metal cap, and the Crown Cap for bottles, invented by William Painter in 1898.

In rural households in Europe from the 1890s until about the 1950s, food preservation in jars of glass and bottles by means of Appert techniques was common, and small portable canning machines made it possible to use the new food preservation techniques in the 1930s and 1940s. As the technology of food preservation improved, however, homemade food preservation by means of salting and pickling in pots and jars of glass gradually decreased. With the invention of the home freezer, it largely disappeared.

FOOD PACKAGING

Food packaging is packaging for food. It requires protection, tampering resistance, and special physical, chemical, or biological needs. It also shows the product that is labelled to show any nutrition information on the food being consumed.

Food Wrapping, Paper, Cartons, and Plastic

Paper and cardboard cartons emerged at the end of the nineteenth century as material for wrapping and packaging food. For a long time the price of materials for food packaging—tinplate, glass, and, to a lesser extent, paper— remained high and was often more costly than the food itself. Technological innovations made it possible to produce packaging material cheaply.

Paper became important for wrapping food when it could be produced from wood pulp, but paper and cardboard cartons were not yet suitable for packaging fluids. In the 1880s in the United States, paper and cartons could be made impermeable to fat and fluid by coating them with a thin film of paraffin.

In the 1930s, cellophane became an important material for food packaging, but it was gradually replaced by the expanding possibilities of polyethylene and other forms of plastic. Another breakthrough was the invention of the Tetra Pak in Sweden in 1952, which increased the capabilities of carton containers for packaging milk, fruit drinks, and other liquids. The carton container coated with polyethylene became a serious threat to the market for glass and cans.

In the 1940s, food packaging entered the era of fully disposable packaging. The convenience of the microwave was further enhanced in the 1980s with the development of special packaging materials. The demand for ready-to- eat fresh vegetables and fruits stimulated the development of Modified Atmosphere Packaging (MAP).

Labels and Brand Names

Closely associated with the history of food packaging is the development of food labels and brands. In the first half of the nineteenth century, food manufacturers realized that their products would sell better if a brand name was attached to them, a name with prestige that potential customers could easily recognize. Initially, labels with information about the contents were put on glass containers or cans.

Gradually, the label and the packaging as a whole became a means for promoting the food product. In most industrialized countries, legislation regulates the information that must be provided on packaging for consumers' protection.

Since the beginning of the nineteenth century, food packaging has been closely associated with industrialization and urbanization. Originally, food packaging in glass and cans was primarily meant to preserve food, but convenience became the most significant aspect of food packaging in the twentieth century. The retail revolution, when supermarket chains supplanted family-owned grocery stores, made food packaging an indispensable part of urban food culture. On the other hand, it created problems of waste disposal, a much-discussed concern of critical consumers.

Functions of Food Packaging

Packaging has several objectives:

- **Physical Protection:** The food enclosed in the package may require protection from, among other things, shock, vibration, compression, temperature, etc.
- **Barrier Protection:** A barrier from oxygen, water vapour, dust, etc., is often required. Permeation is a critical factor in design. Some packages contain desiccants or oxygen absorbers to help

extend shelf life. Modified atmospheres or controlled atmospheres are also maintained in some food packages. Keeping the contents clean, fresh, and safe for the intended shelf life is a primary function.

- **Containment or Agglomeration:** Small items are typically grouped together in one package for reasons of efficiency. Powders, and granular materials need containment.
- **Information Transmission:** Packages and labels communicate how to use, transport, recycle, or dispose of the package or product. Some types of information are required by governments.
- **Marketing:** The packaging and labels can be used by marketers to encourage potential buyers to purchase the product. Package design has been an important and constantly evolving phenomenon for several decades. Marketing communications and graphic design are applied to the surface of the package and (in many cases) the point of sale display.
- **Security:** Packaging can play an important role in reducing the security risks of shipment. Packages can be made with improved tamper resistance to deter tampering and also can have tamper- evident features to help indicate tampering. Packages can be engineered to help reduce the risks of package pilferage: Some package constructions are more resistant to pilferage and some have pilfer indicating seals. Packages may include authentication seals to help indicate that the package and contents are not counterfeit. Packages also can include anti-theft devices, such as dye-packs, RFID tags, or electronic article surveillance tags, that can be activated or detected by devices at exit points and require specialized tools to deactivate. Using packaging in this way is a means of retail loss prevention.
- **Convenience:** Packages can have features which add convenience in distribution, handling, stacking, display, sale, opening, reclosing, use, and reuse.
- **Portion Control:** Single serving packaging has a precise amount of contents to control usage. Bulk commodities (such as salt) can be divided into packages that are a more suitable size for individual households. It also aids the control of inventory: selling sealed one- litre-bottles of milk, rather than having people bring their own bottles to fill themselves.

Food Packaging Types

The above materials are fashioned into different types of food packages and containers such as:

Packaging Type	Type of Container	Food Examples
Aseptic processings	Primary	Liquid whole eggs
Plastic trays	Primary	Portion of fish
Bags	Primary	Potato chips
Boxes	Secondary	Box of Coca-Cola
Cans	Primary	Can of Campbell's tomato soup
Cartons	Primary	Carton of eggs
Flexible packaging	Primary	Bagged salad
Pallets	Tertiary	A series of boxes on a single pallet used to transport from the manufacturing plant to a distribution centre
Wrappers	Tertiary	Used to wrap the boxes on the pallet for transport

Primary packaging is the main package that holds the food that is being processed. Secondary packaging combines the primary packages into one box being made. Tertiary packaging combines all of the secondary packages into one pallet.

There are also special containers that combine different technologies for maximum durability:

- Bags-in-Boxes (used for soft drink syrup, other liquid products, and meat products).
- Wine box (used for wine).

Packaging Machines

A choice of packaging machinery includes technical capabilities, labour requirements, worker safety, maintainability, serviceability, reliability, ability to integrate into the packaging line, capital cost, floorspace, flexibility (change- over, materials, etc.), energy usage, quality of outgoing packages, qualifications (for food, phamaceuticals, etc.), throughput, efficiency, productivity, ergonomics, etc.

Packaging machines may be of the following general types:

- Blister, Skin and Vacuum Packaging Machines.
- Capping, Over-Capping, Lidding, Closing, Seaming and Sealing Machines.

- Cartoning Machines.
- Case and Tray Forming, Packing, Unpacking, Closing and Sealing Machines.
- Check Weighing Machines.
- Cleaning, Sterilizing, Cooling and Drying Machines.
- Conveying, Accumulating and Related Machines.
- Feeding, Orienting, Placing and Related Machines.
- Filling Machines: Handling liquid and powdered products.
- Package Filling and Closing Machines.
- Form, Fill and Seal Machines.
- Inspecting, Detecting and Checkweighing Machines.
- Palletizing, Depalletizing, Pallet Unitizing and Related Machines.
- Product Identification: Labelling, marking, etc.
- Wrapping Machines.
- Converting Machines.
- Other speciality machinery.

Reducing Food Packaging

Reduced packaging and sustainable packaging are becoming more frequent. The motivations can be government regulations, consumer pressure, retailer pressure, and cost control.

(Reduced packaging often saves packaging costs.) In the UK, a Local Government Association survey produced by the British Market Research Bureau, compared a range of outlets to buy 29 common food items, found that small local retailers and market traders "produced less packaging and more that could be recycled than the larger supermarkets".

Trends in Food Packaging

Numerous reports of industry associations agree that use of smart indicators will increase. There are a number of different indicators with different benefits for food producers, consumers and retailers.

Temperature Recorders

Temperature recorders are used to monitor products shipped in a cold chain and to help validate the cold chain. Digital temperature data loggers measure and record the temperature history of food shipments.

They sometimes have temperatures displayed on the indicator or have other output (lights, etc.): The data from a shipment can be downloaded (cable, RFID, etc.) to a computer for further analysis.

These help identify if there has been temperature abuse of products and can help determine the remaining shelf life. They can also help determine the time of temperature extremes during shipment so corrective measures can be taken.

Time-Temperature Indicators

Time-Temperature Indicators integrate the time and temperature experienced by the indicator and adjacent foods. Some use chemical reactions that result in a colour change while others use the migration of a dye through a filter media. To the degree that these physical changes in the indicator match the degradation rate of the food, the indicator can help indicate probable food degradation.

Rfid

Radio Frequency Identification is applied to food packages for supply chain control and have shown a significant benefit in allowing food producers and retailers create full real time visibility of their supply chain.

VACUUM PACKAGE FOOD AT HOME

There are numerous types of equipment being marketed for vacuum packaging food at home. They vary greatly in technological sophistication and price, and usually are called vacuum packaging machines or vacuum sealers. These machines may extend the storage time of refrigerated foods, dried foods and frozen foods. However, vacuum packaging is not a substitution for the heat processing of home canned foods. Vacuum packaging is also not a substitution for the refrigerator or freezer storage of foods that would otherwise require it. In fact, vacuum packaging can add to the concerns associated with storing of these perishable foods (which are foods not stable at room temperature and requiring cold storage).

There are many precautions that must be taken when vacuum packaging perishable foods for refrigerator or freezer storage. You must assume that the perishable food carries the risk of potential pathogenic contamination. And, when frozen food is ready to be thawed and used, steps to minimize the risks from microorganisms in food must still be followed. Again, perishable foods must still be refrigerated or frozen for storage after packing in a vacuum or partial vacuum environment.

Producing a vacuum means removing air from the contents of a package. Oxygen in environmental air does promote certain reactions in foods which cause deterioration of quality. For example, oxidative rancidity of fats in food and certain colour changes are promoted by the presence of oxygen. Therefore, removal of oxygen from the environment will preserve certain quality characteristics and extend the food's shelf life based on quality. However, removal of oxygen from the surrounding environment does not eliminate the possibility for all bacterial growth; it just changes the nature of what is likely to occur. In fact, what is most likely to be eliminated is growth of spoilage bacteria. The bacteria that normally spoil the quality of food in noticeable ways (odour, colour, sliminess, etc.) like to have oxygen in the environment. If able to multiply on foods, these spoilage bacteria can let you know if a food is going bad before it reaches the point it makes someone sick. In an almost oxygen-free environment like vacuum packaging produces, the spoilage bacteria do not multiply very fast so the loss of food quality is slowed down.

Some pathogenic (illness-causing) bacteria, however, like low-oxygen environments and reproduce well in vacuum-packaged foods. In fact, without competition from spoilage bacteria, some pathogens reproduce even more rapidly than in their presence. These bacteria often do not produce noticeable changes in the food, either. In the vacuum-packaged environment, food may become unsafe from pathogenic bacterial growth with no indicators to warn the consumer; the bacteria that would also normally be multiplying and spoil food in ways to make it unappealing (odour, sliminess, etc.) are not able to function without enough oxygen.

For example, C. botulinum (a very dangerous pathogen that causes the deadly botulism poisoning under certain conditions) grows at room temperature in low-acid moist foods if the package presents anaerobic (lacking in oxygen) conditions—if the bacteria are present, of course. Without the competition from spoilage bacteria, reproduction is even easier. Refrigeration at 38-40 °F becomes a critical step for storage of low-acid vacuum-packaged foods that aren't otherwise stable (don't keep) at room temperature (e.g., canned properly). The actual temperature of the refrigerator and the temperature at which it keeps the food are essential to maintain safety of this product. If the food were not packaged under vacuum, the oxygen in the environment would offer some protection against C. botulinum growth and toxin development in the package.

The removal or reduction of oxygen in the storage environment is indeed helpful for extending the storage quality of non-perishable dry foods such as dried nuts or crackers. Products like this are low enough in moisture that bacterial growth is prevented. Vacuum packaging can also be safe for food that will be stored frozen. However, proper thawing under conditions that minimize bacterial growth—like refrigeration—would be essential. If the package stays closed during thawing, you still have a vacuum environment where pathogenic bacteria can be active if the temperature is warm enough.

There is no advantage to combining the use of a vacuum packaging machine with boiling water or pressure canning of foods. Jars processed in either canner develop sufficient vacuums for safe, stable storage at room temperature. They also have the added advantage of a heat process that kills pathogenic bacteria able to grow in that food at room temperature.

So is a vacuum packaging machine needed or are there advantages to owning one? One would need to ask if the amount of the investment is worth the uses for the appliance. Traditionally recommended freezing procedures and packaging methods, if carried out carefully, will produce high quality products with reasonably lengthy storage times. Storing crackers, nuts and other dried foods in air-tight storage containers will also keep them of high quality for a reasonable period of time for normal usage.

And, perishable foods still need to be treated carefully to prevent pathogens from making them unsafe. Remember, removing oxygen from a food's environment does not just solve some food storage problems—it could cause others.

Consider how carefully safe food handling practices will be followed at all times, since vacuum packaging creates very good conditions for some pathogens to be a problem if any mistakes are made. For example, perishable food being vacuum packaged should not be out of refrigeration very long – no longer than 2 hours total time above 40 °F. Food that needs to be refrigerated without vacuum packaging still needs to be refrigerated! While food is being packaged and prepared or used later, extremely clean hands, and clean and sanitized equipment and work surfaces are essential. Food should be dated and still used within reasonable storage times unless frozen. Raw meats, poultry and seafood should be cooked thoroughly to recommended temperatures, measured with a food thermometer, before eating. Any food showing signs of spoilage should be discarded—when in doubt, throw it out!

PACKAGING RESEARCH

According to the World Packaging Organization (WPO), globally the packaging material and machinery industry is estimated to be worth $US 500 billion per year, representing between 1-2 per cent of the GDP in industrialised countries. An estimated 100,000 packaging manufacturing companies employ in excess of 5 million people and, in principle, serve all business sectors manufacturing and/or trading physical products.

Packaging technology has gone through a fast and significant development in recent decades; however, the smartest developments are yet to be seen. Today's modern society depends to a large extend on the availability and use of modern packaging technology, comprising a vast variety of modern materials, high tech applications and smart operations. Modern packaging technology aims to meet a vast range of requirements ranging from providing food safety, via low cost storage and distribution, self-selling marketing, convenient consumer use to responsible waste management practices.

Thanks to modern packaging technology products can be economically distributed over large geographical areas or stored over time without unacceptable quality loss. Packaging is more than a clever way of combining materials. Adding value through the development of partnership relations in the supply chain seems to be the credo for the next decennium. Good packaging facilitates a subtle cooperation between product, packaging process and material with the objective of fulfilling needs of all stakeholders along the supply chain including the post-consumer waste manager. Value chain management, product stewardship and life cycle management are considered key attributes that will drive the development of future, sustainable packaging systems. Such systems will need to go far beyond the current waste minimisation driven principles of reduce, re-use, recycle, and recovery. Packaging systems that will minimize impact on the environment, will seamlessly meet social requirements and expectations, and will be economically effective are the business winners of the future.

Drivers for Development

Today's companies in the packaging supply chain are faced with acknowledging, understanding, addressing and managing a range of issues affecting the sustainable use of packaging. Issues include the use of renewable and non-renewable resources, recyclability, regulations, and material and transport costs.

Ongoing demographic and life-style changes, technology changes, environmental issues (in particular as recognized by legislation and/ or voluntary agreements in numerous countries), consumer dynamics, and supply chain demands are important factors of influence for the packaging supply chain. responding to such issues requires pro-activity, progressivism and agility from packaging manufacturers as well as users.

Despite the industry becoming more progressive and pro-active in its approach and seeking shared responsibility, the majority of the actions are still undertaken on the basis of the traditional 4-R waste management hierarchy (Reduce, Re-use, Recycle, Recover, Dispose) rather then evaluating and assessing the life cycle impacts and developing strategies to reduce impact. As a result "down gauging" and "recyclability" are still the main drivers in avoiding environmental impact.

There is little doubt that this approach will lead to a reduction of impacts in the short term. It may take the existing "waste fat" out of current packaging systems but does not take into account the need to reduce overall environmental impacts in a substantial way. It also fails to address the increasing need for packaging systems that meet requirements from new distribution systems, increasing demands for product convenience, increasing consumer differentiation and so on.

In the longer term this approach will not be sufficient and will fail to provide adequate solutions. Numerous problem areas will emerge that will require a rigourous overhaul of the use of packaging systems in order to meet ongoing commercial demands.

Particularly for fast moving consumer goods, such as food products, the packaging is one of the key product components that can provide a commercial advantage over competing products. Hence, the packaging is of significant commercial importance for the economical sustainability and growth of businesses. There is little value in arguing the need for less packaging while economic growth is predominantly driven by diversification of markets and subsequent product variations. Key challenges for future business growth and development are:

- The ability to meet supply chain and market requirements in terms of distribution efficiency, marketing power, consumer safety and convenience, and environmental performance.
- To maintain high levels of flexibility for creating commercial advantage through value added packaging systems.
- To maximise the triple bottom line performance in order to satisfy both commercial stakeholders (shareholders, customers) and community stakeholders (government, consumers, NGOs).

These challenges cannot be successfully tackled with the traditional 4-R approach. A holistic, integrated and collaborative initiative involving the entire supply chain is essential to be able to create step change improvements. The focus should not be on how the supply chain can reduce the amount and increase the recycling of packaging used but on how it can sustainable satisfy the economic, social and environmental requirements for packaging related to the production, distribution and consumption of products in order to further enhance the well-being of our society.

What Makes a Packaging Research

Of course, in principle a packaging (system) is just a clever way of constructing a container out of a selected material or combination of materials. A wide variety and choice is available, and selection is not an easy job.

A range of parameters, varying from product characteri-stics to consumer (client) requirements and trends, affect this selection. These parameters can be grouped in three categories as is illustrated in fig.

- Parameters in the micro or product environment.
- Parameters in the ambient or distribution environment.
- Parameters in the macro or market environment.

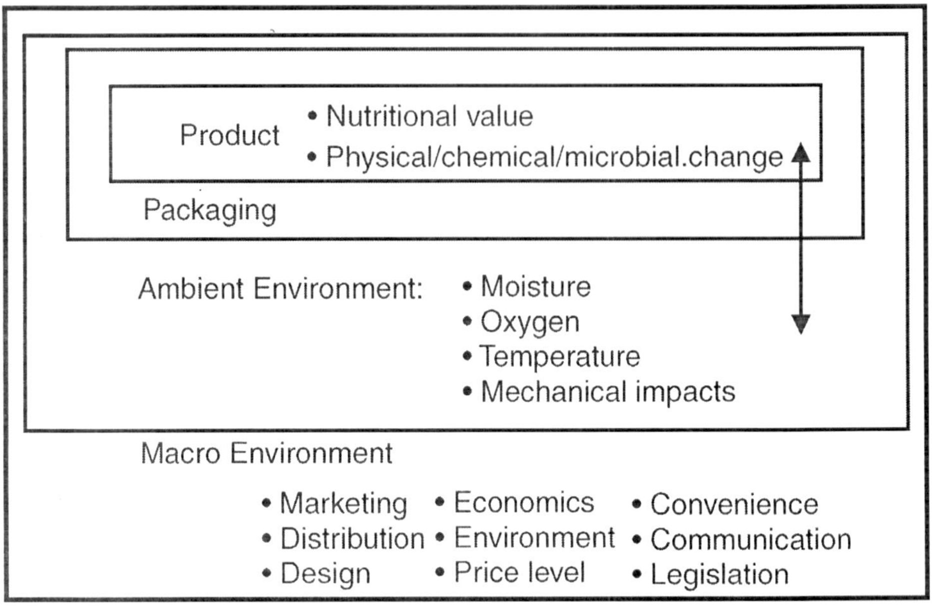

Fig: Interaction of a Packaged Food Product with the Environment.

The parameters in the macro environment are constantly subject to change and have, to a certain extent, an effect on the ambient environment (e.g., a change in distribution method can have an impact on mechanical impacts exerted on the packaging system). Because of this dynamic environment, packaging systems are continuously due to optimization, a permanent search for the optimum between functionality and cost.

This value analysis includes relating the packaging system's technical, economical and environmental performance to requirements from product, manufacturing and packaging process, warehousing and distribution, retailing and marketing operations, consumer demands and behaviour, and post- consumer waste management.

Meeting this complex of varying and often opposing demands is obviously not an easy task and requires a thorough understanding of issues involved and ability to balance them in anticipation on the pull of a changing market. Packaging research and education can and will support the packaging chain in their efforts to evaluate the complexity of demands and create adequate solutions.

Research in the packaging area can principally be distinguished into three main areas:

- Strategic Research
- Applied Research
- Fundamental Research.

Strategic research has a focus for new approaches in the packaging domain. It aims at identifying new pathways for advancing the future of packaging. Strategic research is essential to identify and understand future issues, to identify potential solutions (being it technological, organisational or managerial), and to design routes for implementation.

The packaging domain cannot advance without a substantial strategic research being undertaken. As in every other discipline novel approaches are essential to achieve effective future packaging solutions.

However, the extensive complexity of the field due to its multi-disciplinarity and material variety, its range of stakeholders, and its broad mix of functions, makes strategic research indispensable for the packaging domain. On an individual member basis and, even more relevant, by collaboration between members, IAPRI is well positioned to undertake this type of research. By combining academic with industry focussed research strengths, IAPRI is able to provide unique sets of research skills to assist both industry and government stakeholders in the strategic advancement of packaging.

Applied research is considered the historical scene of packaging research and has often focussed on specific problems concerning packaging intensive products. The challenge ahead lies in the conversion of disciplinary and/or technological advances achieved in other areas (e.g. microelectronics) to the packaging field. Particularly in advancing packaging towards active, smart and intelligent systems able to interact at different points and with various stakeholders along the supply chain, significant applied research is required.

Often this type of research involves development of "proof of concept" and "route to market" and is therefore likely to be undertaken in close cooperation with commercial entities. Most IAPRI member organisations are well experienced in conducting this type of research.

However, each member will have limitations in its scope of research for which reason collaboration between two of more members might be preferable to cover a particular applied research project. Fundamental research focuses on developing the underlying sciences for packaging material applications and technologies. This area belongs historically to the discipline areas.

Fundamental research in the packaging domain historically has focussed on understanding material and packaging system behaviour. Interaction of packaging materials in contact with product (e.g., food or dangerous good) is an example of such research.

Mathematical modelling of the dynamic behaviour of packaging cushioning materials is another example. Fundamental research is often the domain of research students and is an important part of generating research staff for packaging research organisations. Most IAPRI members, being either University entities or having collaborative links with relevant university entities, are involved in this kind of research.

Current and Future Packaging Technologies

Since packaging is an essential part of the modern food supply chain, it is worthwhile to consider the role of packaging in food innovation and the impact modern trends in packaging science will have on the future food industry.

Most, if not all, changes in the procedures of food processing and distribution have arisen from or been accompanied by changes in packaging. An early example is thermal processing. Although attributed to Nicholas Appert in the 1790s, it was not until Peter Durand adapted the tinplated steel can to withstand thermal processing that it became the widely practiced food process we see today.

Few foods arrive in our home un-packaged. Even so-called "fresh fruits and vegetables" need to be placed into a shopping bag; often more than one package to ensure its safe trip home in the boot of the car. While packaging is critical in delivering safe food to the consumer it represents about 25 per cent of the total cost of a food. This puts manufacturers under considerable pressure to reduce costs while ensuring a safe supply of food.

The food packaging industry has been efficient in its adaptation of developments in material science to design packaging to protect foods and deliver benefits to the consumer in terms of convenience, cost, communication and choice. Innovation has been the essential ingredient in the modern packaging landscape.

This article discusses the drivers that have made major changes in food packaging and speculates on developments that will deliver future packaging. Current trends in packaging provide a useful base from which to explore opportunities that packaging offers to future consumers. The trends that will be discussed are in packaging materials, package size, environmental impact and in the intrinsic role of packaging.

Packaging Materials

Most commonly used food packaging materials are derived from petroleum products. The recent increase in the price of petroleum, which is predicted to continue for some time, adversely affects packaging manufacturers. Wherever possible, the amount of packaging per unit of food needs to be reduced. The polyolefins, polyethylene and polypropylene, dominate food packaging because of their strength, inertness and ease of production. The development of metallocene catalysed polyethylene has enabled manufacturers to reduce the gauge of the films which will in part address the increasing costs and environmental waste.

Metallocene based polymers have other benefits such as easier processing, better clarity, fewer taints as well as ease of use and greater seal strength. Metallocene catalyzed polypropylene, which has a much greater potential to improve the properties of polypropylene films, which has come onto the market much more slowly than polyethylene, offers food manufacturers greater flexibility and heat stability than current polypropylene films.

The current dominance of polyethylene terephthalate (PET) for beverage bottles could be challenged by these polymers. The poor gas barrier properties of polypropylene, which has limited its penetration into the beverage market, is the focus of intense research world wide.

The use of nanocomposites to improve barrier properties without compromising clarity offers a way to increase polypropylene's penetration. Similarly active packaging technologies such as ZerO2 are innovations that can potentially provide excellent barrier properties by effectively removing any oxygen migrating through the polymer.

Packaging Size

Despite the increasing cost of packaging materials the changing consumer demographic has increased the demand for individual-serve packaging. Simple maths shows that such a trend will increase the package/ food ratio. Packaging size has been decreasing for many years and will continue to do so because consumers demand convenience. Having to empty part of the contents of a package before heating is not convenient.

This creates an opportunity for innovative manufacturers to supply food in packaging that eliminates this chore. The recent appearance of self-venting microwaveable packaging for shelf stable foods exemplifies how packaging innovations allow food manufacturers to capture benefit from changing demographics.

Environmental Impact

An important consideration of any technology is the environmental impact. Packaging has been such a key factor in the evolution of the food supply chain that its environmental impact should come under scrutiny.

Environmentalists and consumers are concerned about the impact of large quantities of waste packaging material on our water systems and land fills. Since no real alternative to packaging is likely it is important that the environmental impact of packaging is minimized.

This is an opportunity for food and packaging manufacturers to meet the consumer and regulatory demand. Since 1999 the Australian industry has adopted a National Packaging Covenant as the main vehicle to address the environmental impact of packaging. It is based on the principles of shared responsibility through the supply chain. In 2005 the Covenant was revised to incorporate a national recycling target of 65 per cent for packaging and no further increases in packaging waste disposed to landfill by the end of 2010. These targets offer further opportunities for packaging innovation such as bio-based polymers.

Bio-based Polymers

Biodegradable polymers like polyglycolic acid, polylactic acid (PLA), and polycaprolactone do not yet have all the properties to replace common polymers. Improvements in polycaprolactone have been achieved by blending with clay based nanocomposites. PLA based polymers include a polyester family of compostable packaging material, which potentially offers consumers good performance and cost effectiveness. One of the limitations to the commercial success of active and intelligent packaging has been their integration into common packaging materials. Polyolefins do not readily lend themselves to the chemistries that are involved in smart packaging. The trend to bio-based packaging technologies which are much more amenable will lead to future active and intelligent packaging developments.

Functional Packaging

Recent developments in the developing functional foods market have extended into the packing of the food product. Rather than incorporating the delicate and expensive functional ingredients into the food itself, developers have begun to package the functional ingredients in the packaging itself. Examples of such innovation include drinking straws that release the ingredient as you drink through them and bottle caps that have a sealed dose of functional ingredient that is incorporated into the drink immediately prior to consumption.

Intrinsic Role of Packaging

The role of packaging is changing. The basic and essential role of packaging is to protect and preserve the safety and nutritional quality of food. However, packaging is increasingly required to inform the consumer of the properties of the food and its package.

The date code tells consumers how long they have before the food deteriorates, the label informs the consumer of the amounts of energy, fat, protein, carbohydrate and sodium content as well as potential allergens. Information on the ingredients, serving instructions and country of origin is also included. The package is now evolving to be a vital point of communication with the customer and is becoming integrated into the marketing function.

Electronics

As the cost and size of electronic components continues to decrease the use of wireless devices such as RFID tags will become commonplace and the opportunity to incorporate other functions such as temperature measurement and real-time shelf life information becomes possible.

Many sensory attributes could be monitored and displayed for the consumer. The packaging landscape has undergone dramatic changes over the past 50 years, and these changes are likely to continue for the next fifty. Those companies that fail to integrate these innovations into their business plans risk failure.

Nanocomposite Polymer Films Containing Carvacrol for Antimicrobial Active Packaging

Active food packaging is an innovative solution to meet the continuous changes in current consumer demands and market trends. Active food packaging extends shelf life and improves safety of the food by scavenging of oxygen, moisture or ethylene, and by promoting emission of ethanol, flavours, and antimicrobial agents.

Antimicrobial packaging is attracting increasing attention from the food and packaging industry, since the use of preservative packaging films offers several advantages compared with the direct addition of preservatives into food products. The incorporation of antimicrobial agents into polymeric films allows industry to combine the preservative functions of antimicrobials with the protective functions of the pre-existing packaging concepts.

Antimicrobial activity can be achieved by including pads containing volatile antimicrobial agents into packages, incorporating antimicrobial agents directly into polymers, coating antimicrobials onto polymer surfaces, immobilizing antimicrobials by chemical grafting, using polymers that are antimicrobial by themselves.

A wide number of generally recognized as safe (GRAS) antimicrobials, such as silver substituted zeolites, enzymes, antioxidant phenolics, are used for food packaging applications. In recent years there has been a growing demand for the use of natural additives, including natural extracts such as essential oils, which are categorized as GRAS by US Food and Drug Administration.

The antimicrobial activity of several essential oils and the efficiency of their incorporation into plastic matrices, such as polypropylene (PP) and polyethylene (PEVethylene vinyl alcohol copolymer (EVOH) have been already reported. Carvacrol, which is present in high concentrations in thyme and oregano oil, exhibits a significant in vitro antibacterial activity. This phenolic compound has also antifungal, insecticidal. antitoxigenic. and antiparasitic activities.

Besides bacterial contamination, oxidation of food constituents as well as spoilage by moulds in presence of oxygen can cause food deterioration. In order to hinder the oxygen permeation, the use of nanocomposites represents a powerful tool for packaging industry.

It is known that the addition of nanosized lamellar clays with large aspect ratio into a polymer matrix is expected to improve polymer barrier properties at relatively low filler loadings. Since the pioneering studies carried out by Okada et al., an impressive number of articles dealing with the characterization of the physical properties of polymer-clay nanocomposites have been reported, some of them related to materials suitable for food contact.

Although the observed decrease of permeability is generally ascribed to the high aspect ratio of the clay layers which should increase the tortuosity factor, the influence of nanoparticles on the crystallization rate and extent of the polymer melt also plays a role.

Since crystals are generally impermeable to the transport of low molecular weight substances, the combination of higher crystallinity and impermeable clay elements may result in improved barrier properties for these materials. On the other hand, the small clay loading does not affect the processability and does not substantially increase the density of the polymer. Furthermore, due to the fine particle size of the filler, the film clarity for all practical purposes is not reduced.

This work represents a preliminary study aimed to develop antimicrobial films of low-density polyethylene (LDPE) containing carvacrol. As reported in literature, one drawback of PE liners in barrier packages for, e.g., aseptically processed juices, is the loss of flavour/aroma due to the scalping effect of the polymer membrane. Nanoparticles [i.e., organo-modified montmorillonite (MMT)] were used to improve the barrier properties of packaging films and to protect the volatile and heat-sensitive carvacrol from degradation. In this frame, the nanoclay filler is believed to positively interact with carvacrol dispersed into clay galleries, thus preserving the antimicrobial activity of the doped film.

MINIMUM PACKAGING TECHNOLOGY FOR PROCESSED FOODS

Modern food packaging technology brings traditional foods into a global arena which increasingly emphasizes their commercial and economic aspects. This means that food and packaging technologists become involved in the entire food supply system. This system ranges from the sea, village farm, plantation, to the markets and consumers in towns and cities, not only in their own country, but also in distant overseas markets.

The surplus foods grown in the village have a need to be more carefully harvested, protected from spoilage and damage, packaged, and transported by various means to these markets. Unless the goods are sold with minimum spoilage and at their peak flavour, appearance, and nutritional value and presented in an attractive way, they may not be eaten at all. This is a worse situation than if the crop had never been grown and can represent serious loss and waste to a community. In addition, careful emvironmental conside-rations need to be given to minimum packaging forms to avoid pollution problems and ensure sustainabilty. Very little investment has been made so far in developing traditional technologies or in applying scientific knowledge in most of the developing countries; meanwhile the more expensive products of imported technologies have further slowed the development of indigenous technologies.

It has been increasingly recognized that the time has come when these traditional technologies must be upgraded through scientific application of packaging principles and then integrated with other packaging functions such as marketing and advertisement. Technologies are called traditional if, unaffected by modernization, they have been commonly applied over a long period of time. In general, traditional technologies tend to be cheap, easy to produce, apply, maintain, and repair. They are generally labour-intensive, which can be economically beneficial, but as far as food packaging technologies are concerned, the final products are often hygienically sub-standard and they usually have a short shelf-life. Many traditional foods have nonetheless remained unchanged in process or package for centuries, due to the fact that they developed in a particular location and are deep rooted in the natural, cultural, religious, and socio-economic environment. Some have disappeared without a trace as a result of modern influences, while others have expanded on a global scale, becoming household products, e.g., soysauce, now a multimillion dollar industry. The reasons for this phenomenon need to be examined.

TRADITIONAL FOOD PACKAGING TECHNOLOGIES

Food Systems

Population drift from rural to urban areas has caused drastic changes in the food supply network from farm to the consumer in many emerging nations. One traditional belief which can no longer be sustained is the old saying that, "There are always fish in the rivers and lagoons, and rice, taro, or sweet potato in the fields; therefore let there be no concern for the next meal."

It is more likely that the farmer has gone to the city or even overseas, and is earning a labourer's wage to keep his family in food during the off-season. So food is now brought to the market by many and various means, and redistributed to these new consumers. There are new vistas for traditional food markets where the technologies are tested beyond their limits.

Given the circumstances in which many developing countries are today, the challenge for their traditional technologies is that often they do not contribute sufficiently to meeting socio-economic imperatives. This is true also of those food technologies where many of the processing methods have remained unchanged for centuries, and are becoming inadequate to cope with modem needs, because they are too labour-intensive and depend now too much on natural environmental conditions.

It is now clear that there is a need to lessen the dependence on nature, reduce the drudgery, shorten the time of the work involved and upgrade the preparation, quality, packaging, presentation, and shelf-life of these traditional foods and their packaging.

Women and Food Processing

Women play a major role in most traditional food processing and packaging. They dry leaves, pulses, and cereals, make curds and cheese, smoke meat and fish, ferment, grate, dry sweet potato and carry out a wide range of food preservation and packaging processes.

It is indispensable, therefore, that women view the proposed technology improve-ments as capable of reducing their labour, without diminishing their role and status, or, in the case of marketable products, their profit. It should be borne in mind that the upgrading of traditional food and food packaging technologies is a sensitive area, for which reason the subject should be approached with caution and due regard paid to the social, economic and cultural factors involved, in addition to the gender issues.

Further sensitivity needs to be applied to the small business operation in the preparation and packaging of traditional foods. Programmes for mass production of a particular food, many have dire consequences for the small business operator.

In the consideration of the structural characteristics of traditional food industries, in particular the application of new food technologies and the use of labour saving continuous large-scale processing, the task needs to be approached thoughtfully.

Upgrading of Food Packaging

Upgrading of traditional food packaging technologies in many cases, introduces exogenous factors, i.e., the importation of technology from abroad. Whether or not adapted to local circumstances, the use of imported packaging technologies in many developing countries remains restricted to modern technologies; even when these are locally developed, they are more complex to use, repair, and maintain. They are also expensive and tend to rely on imported components and non-renewable sources of energy.

FOOD PRESERVATION PRINCIPLES AND THEIR INTEGRATION WITH FOOD PACKAGING

Food Unit Operations

Before food can be packaged, there are many unit operations involved after harvesting the raw materials, including cleaning, grading, disposal of unwanted material, then stabilization of the enzymatic, biochemical and microbial spoilage. If a study of the preservation and packaging of foods is undertaken, a key question is, "What factors cause spoilage and deterioration in foods". The main factors are micro-organisms (bacteria, yeast, and moulds), as well as enzymes, temperature, and biochemical changes in the foods. Food preservation techniques are designed to prevent these spoilage changes and impart a keeping quality or shelf-life to the processed foods.

Packaging is an integral part of the processing and preservation of foods and can influence many of these factors. It can influence physical and chemical changes, including migration of chemicals into foods. The flavour, colour, texture as well as moisture and oxygen transfer is influenced by packaging.

The effects of temperature changes and light can be modified by packaging materials. Let us consider the more important methods of preservation of foods used by food industries today and how they integrate with the food packaging used in their processing.

- **Cold Preservation:** Used to slow down or inhibit chemical and biological processes in bacteria and spoilage agents in the foods.
- **Fermentation Preservation:** Used to slow down spoilage factors through the production of alcohol or acids which assist in preservation. This technique is often combined with pasteurization.
- **Reduction of Available Water:** Many spoilage factors require the presence of moisture in order to operate. When this available water is removed or reduced then better preservation can be achieved.
- **Pickling or Curing Preservation:** These methods can be used together with smoking and with refrigeration as a combined form of preservation.
- **Chemical Preservation:** Used to inhibit the spoilage factors and to complement other food preservation techniques.

- **Gas Environment Control:** Used to inhibit post-harvest deterioration, often used together with refrigeration.
- **Combination and Assorted Methods:** Several food preservation techniques may be effectively combined to reduce spoilage factors to acceptable levels. These include combinations of those listed, together with the following techniques.

The Influence of Packaging on the Environment

Packaging in the modern world has a considerable impact on the environment. Food packaging makes up two fifths of the household waste. Packaging also accounts for an increasing share of the costs of the food processing industry, rising from about 4 per cent in 1947 to 10 per cent in 1987, and continuing to rise.

Despite new materials which have reduced packaging weight, the total and relative costs of food and beverage packaging are increasing. On average, the cost of packaging materials represents about one-fifth of material costs, however, in 10 out of 40 food industry sectors, packaging costs exceed the costs of the edible food stuff ingredients. In most countries packaging continues to be driven by consumer demand, with regulatory bodies playing a limited role.

In Europe, however, legislation and taxes on packaging have been established to encourage reduced packaging waste and more sustainable packaging practices.

Case Studies of Some Traditional Foods and Their Packaging

China is one example of an ancient civilization in which the different national minority groups have developed their specific food cultures. These traditional foods are a valuable cultural heritage to the Chinese people.

There are examples of foods which have been introduced by culture transfer and become traditional in time. The processing of rice, wheat, soybean, and sesame was introduced to Japan from ancient China, translated first to the centres of power and religion, later to the regions. Hence, such technology transfer is not a new phenomenon.

There is a vast difference, however, between the early, more leisurely adoption of transferred food cultures and the explosion of new technology at present threatening to overwhelm traditional food processing and packaging techniques and to suppress the original characteristics of the traditional products. The attraction of traditional foods is related to their wide variety and diversity. For example, in Japan there are approximately 500 varieties of "Tsukemono", a fermented pickle. This attraction may be lost when new technology is applied without careful thought.

Another aspect of traditional foods is the way many of them have simply disappeared without trace, whilst others have expanded on a global scale and have become household products in most countries. One such example is soysauce. Its wide acceptance and commercial expansion may be the result of a wider influence, with regard to meat-like flavours in diets where meat is absent, either by choice or through circumstance. It is found, packaged in a multiplicity of forms, in almost every country.

The question is posed whether there are other traditional foods, which by careful upgrading and packaging can follow the example of soysauce in becoming widely accepted. Also that these foods can begin to generate higher incomes for small business operators. Some examples of traditional foods with potential for expansion are from the following countries:

Indonesia

This is a vital source of protein in Indonesia, serving as a meat substitute. It is a product of a solid substrate fermenta-tion, using the mould, Rhizopus oligosporus, as the active organism. The soybeans are soaked, dehulled, partly cooked, and inoculated, then incubated for 1-2 days. This enables the mould to form fibrous mycelia which knit the soybeans together in a compact cake which can be sliced and cooked.

The traditional form of packaging for tempeh has been banana leaves as a wrapping material. Now a number of tempeh cottage industries are using the tray or the plastic bag technique. The tray of inoculated beans is covered with banana leaves and wax paper, then incubated. The final product is sliced and wrapped in banana leaf, or plastic (polyethylene) bags. A more recent technique is to incubate the tempeh directly in perforated plastic bags or tubes with perforations at 0.25 to 1.3 cm intervals to allow a controlled access of oxygen. The tempeh can be sold directly in this packaging.

Thailand

In Thailand, fermentation is a favourite means of food processing and over 44 commercial, traditional fermented foods have been identified. These foods are highly acceptable country-wide and are essential components of diets.

They are used as condiments and supply specific flavours as well as being sources of protein, calories, and vitamins. The level of traditional fermented technology of the small and medium food manufacturers are generally at the household or slightly larger (backyard) level. The problems faced are maintenance of quality standards, efficient fermentation on an industrial scale and new product and package development.

Phak Sian Dong

It is a Thai native fermented vegetable (Gynandropsis pentaphylla). It is pickled in a.liquor which is prepared with coconut juice and salt added, or rice water and salt. The "Phak Sian" is wilted in the sun to lower moisture. The fermentation takes only 36-48 hrs. and the shelf-life is only 2-3 days if no further processing is applied. If the process and the packaging were upgraded, this product could give a longer shelf-life.

Pakistan

Roti: An operation for the production of semi-levened bread was set up as the "Roti" Corporation of Pakistan. The Corporation was charged with producing good quality, semi-leavened bread under hygienic conditions, modern packaging, and distribution. Sixteen plants were set up with a capacity of 35,000 "Rotis" per shift, a total of nearly two million "Rotis" per day. The project had difficulties because:

- The taste and texture were different from traditional "Roti".
- The Roti crumbled on rolling.
- People wanted fresh "Roti" bread.
- Women were dislodged from their work at home.
- The overheads and packaging made "Roti" more expensive than home made ones.

Diversification was the only solution to the economic recovery of the plants.

Yoghurt or "Dari"

A most common dairy product in Pakistan consumed widely in the hot months of the year. Traditionally "Dari" has been prepared by unqualified milk retailers in broad earthenware dishes ("Konondas"). The milk is boiled and cooled to around 38°C then cultured with yoghurt from the previous batch. After 6-8 hrs. it sets, then it is cut and sold fresh. The quality is never uniform.

The product and the process have been upgraded since, with upgrading of the quality control and the packaging. Now the milk is correctly processed, analysed, standardized, pasteurized, inoculated, incubated, and packaged in sanitary polystyrene containers, then refrigerated. The retail cost is relatively higher, but kept minimal by recycling the containers which are washed, sanitized, and reused.

THE IMPORTANCE OF FOOD PACKAGING IN FAO PROGRAMMES

In fruit and vegetable processing, technical projects cover the entire food chain from the harvesting of horticultural produce through storage, processing, packaging, and marketing. Roots and tubers projects range from storage, post- harvest loss reduction, through flour production and bakery products development.

In vegetable oils, assistance has been provided by FAO in the processing of oilseeds, palm and olive oil extraction, small-scale processing and refining of edible oils. Other food processing activities range from advisory work on agro-industrial development, coffee processing, coconut processing, cocoa and chocolate projects, soybean and cashew nut processing.

Other examples include:

- Development of handling and packaging systems for soft fruits in an Asian country.
- Upgrading of dates processing and packaging in the Near East Region.
- Introduction. of modern packaging methods for highland vegetables and fruits in an Asian country.
- A coordinated programme of food packaging activities for the Asia and Pacific region covering commodities, packaging materials, equipment, and quality aspects of packaging.
- Projects on the processing and packaging of cereals, including rice, wheat, sorghum, millet, maize, and quinoa have been implemented, and there has been technical backstopping by FAO in many countries for these staple foods.
- Feasibility studies are taken to the pilot processing industry stage. Related technical research, training, and extension programmes have been supported in a dozen countries.

The importance of food packaging in the FAO programme is evidenced by the number of projects undertaken so far. Food packaging is seen as a vital link in the overall chain of food production, processing, marketing, and consumption.

In the Asia and Pacific Region, FAO has been involved in over 40 projects which involve the upgrading of traditional food technologies.

Food packaging is an integral part of the processing and preservation of these staple foods and can also minimize many of the potential spoilage changes, imparting improved keeping quality, and increased shelf-life to the processed and packaged food. These and other activities and ideas are being proposed in recognition of the importance of food packaging in the containment, transportation, distribution, marketing, and consumption of high quality traditional foods.

The mandate of FAO for the improvement of food processing and packaging has placed considerable emphasis on the upgrading of traditional food technologies, particularly for staple foods.

NOVEL IDEAS IN FOOD PACKAGING

Modern society now consists of millions of impatient multitaskers—generations of individuals who want to maximize their time by engaging in two tasks or more simultaneously. This global trend of on-the-go access, convenience, and immediate gratification pervades not only the industries of technology, communications, and entertainment but the food industry as well.

In the 19th century, pioneers such as Nicholas Appert, Louis Pasteur, Samuel C. Prescott, and William L. Underwood developed food packaging and preservation concepts that maintain relevancy today. Twentieth-century inventions such as glass bottles, cellophane wrap, aluminum foil, and plastics shepherded greater utility and flexibility in food packaging.

Other 20th-century packaging developments such as packages incorporating antimicrobials and oxygen scavengers established new precedents for prolonging shelf life and protecting food from environmental influences. Nevertheless, omnipresent global trends such as increased industrial processing of food, greater importation and exportation of food products, and less time for preparation of fresh foods compel the food and beverage packaging industry to investigate newer, more advanced packaging solutions.

Thus, while protecting and preserving food were once perceived as the principal roles of food packaging, facilitating convenience has quickly emerged as equally important. Other elements of increasing importance in food packaging include traceability, tamper indication, and sustainability. Many new and exciting developments in food packaging fulfil these roles and more. A new Scientific Status Summary issued by the Institute of Food Technologists discusses recent innovations in food packaging materials. Written by Aaron Brody, Betty Bugusu, Jung Hoon Han, Claire Koelsch Sand, and Tara H. McHugh, the Summary is titled "Innovative Food Packaging Solution."

Active and Intelligent Food Packaging

Beyond passively delaying environmental elements from affecting food products, active and intelligent food packages use more dynamic techniques to contain and preserve food. For example, two common issues in maintaining the quality of packaged food are oxygen and moisture control.

Oxygen in packages aids the growth of aerobic microbes and moulds. Oxidative reactions in packaging also result in unintended odours and flavours and changes in colour or nutritional quality. Similarly, moisture in food packages may cause powdered products to form lumps or crisp products to soften as well as supporting the growth of microbes.

Conversely, too little moisture can result in dehydrated foods. Active packaging incorporates components that address these issues. Oxygen scavengers remove oxygen from food packages, thereby impeding the growth of microbes and preserving the intended flavour and odour of foods. Carbon dioxide emitters suppress microbial growth in products such as meat, poultry, and cheese.

Moisture-control agents suppress water activity, serving to remove fluids from meat products, prevent condensation from fresh produce, and curb the rate of lipid oxidation. Lastly, maintaining humidity in packages is accomplished by humidity controllers, which can either diminish the loss of moisture from foods or reduce excess moisture in the interstices of package closures.

Other tools in the array of active packaging components include antimicrobials and ethylene absorbers. While active packaging incorporates robust ways to control oxidation, microbial growth, and moisture, intelligent packaging designs facilitate the monitoring of food quality. Time temperature indicators (TTIs), ripeness indicators, biosensors, and radio frequency identification (RFID) are all examples of intelligent packaging components. Most of these smart devices have not had widespread commercial application, but two are gaining more notoriety: TTIs and radio frequency identification.

TTIs can play a critical role in indicating the freshness and safety of a product. They monitor and communicate which food products are safe to eat, which becomes extremely important when food is stored in less than optimal conditions such as extreme heat or freezing. In the case of foods that should not be frozen, a TTI would indicate whether the food had been improperly exposed to cold temperatures. Conversely, a TTI could specify whether foods sensitive to heat had been exposed to unnaturally high temperatures and the duration of exposure. Radio frequency identification provides wireless monitoring of food packages through tags, readers, and computer systems. Its uses within the food industry are numerous and range from facilitating the traceability of food to improving the efficiency of supply chains.

Table: Oxygen Transmission Rate

Film	OTR	WVTR	Specification (μm)
PET	110	15	12
PET/PE	0.93–1.24	0.248–0.372	12/50
PET/PVDC/PE	0.33	0.132	12/4/50
PET/PVAL/PE	0.13	0.26–0.39	12/3/50
PET/EVOH/PE	0.06	0.134–0.268	12/5/50
PET/Al–met/PE	0.06–0.12	0.006–0.03	12/–/50
PET/Si0x	0.006–0.06	0.0024–0.06	12/–
PET/Al–foil/PE	0	0	12/9/50

PE = polyethylene low density; PET = polyethylene terephthalate; PVDC = polyvinylidene chloride; PVAL = polyvinyl alcohol; EVOH = ethylene vinyl alcohol; Al-met = aluminum metallization; $Si0_x$ = silicon oxide; Al-foil = aluminum foil.

But perhaps the ultimate benefits of RFID in food packaging are that it speeds stock rotation and improves tracking. RFID systems are beneficial for many food manufacturing operations and supply chains. Developing an intelligent food packaging application for food quality and safety would require RFID to become more established in the food industry and the integration of food science. Retail chains such as Wal-Mart and Home Depot already use RFID, so its prominence is likely to increase. Because RFID systems provide safety and security benefits by tracking the origin of food supplies, retailers are considering ways to integrate this technology into the management of their supply chains.

Controlling Volatile Flavours and Aromas

The loss of volatile flavours and aromas is a packaging issue that stems from the mass transfer of components between and within food and its packaging. For example, direct contact between the food and its packaging results in the migration of packaging components into food and the unintended absorption of volatile food flavours by package materials is known as flavour scalping. Most incidences of migration occur in plastic packaging systems, and polyethylene materials are responsible for most of the flavour scalping in foods. Both migration and flavour scalping are unfavourable because they deteriorate food quality and reduce consumer confidence in packaged food items.

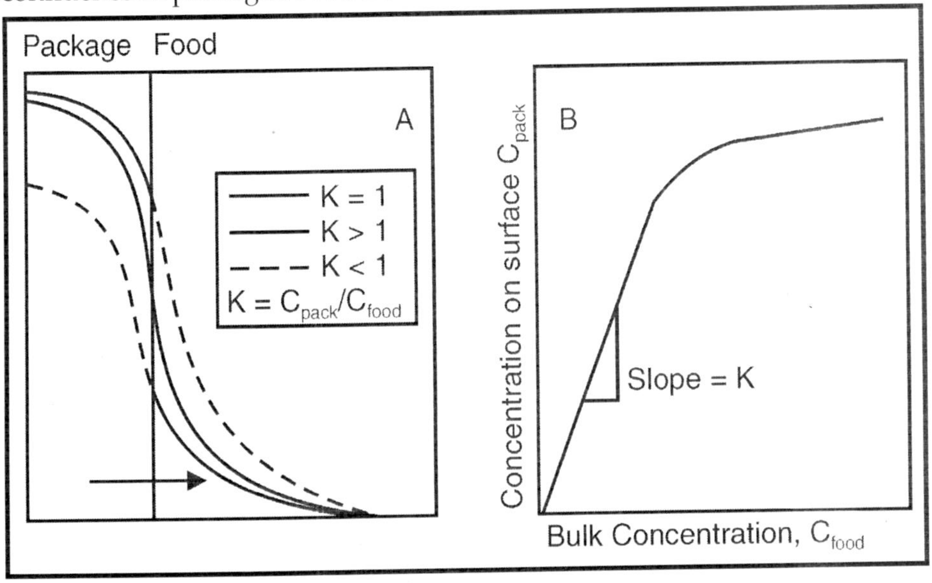

Fig: Effect of Interfacial Partitioning of Molecules on Mass Transfer Between Food and Packaging Materials.

A: Migration of package constituents into foods. B: Scalping of food flavour into packaging materials. K is a partition coefficient of a migrant.

The solution to these issues is packaging components that incorporate absorption and barrier controls. Flavour and odour absorbers usurp unwanted gaseous molecules such as volatile package ingredients, chemical and microbial metabolites, respiration products, or rancid flavours and odours.

Flavour and odour absorbers utilize the same transfer mechanism as flavour scalping to remove unintended characteristics in the forms of sulfurous compounds, amines from protein degradation, aldehydes and ketones, and bitter taste compounds.

High-barrier packaging reduces absorption, desorption, and diffusion of gases and liquids to maintain food quality. It also assists in preventing oxygen and water vapour from penetrating packages. Polymer blending, lamination, and metallization are all ways to enhance the barrier properties of packaging materials.

Other innovative tools for improving the barrier property of packaging material include transparent vacuum-deposited or plasma-deposited coating of silica oxide PET films and composites of plastics with nanoparticles.

Evolution of Foodservice Packaging

Other innovative trends in food packaging are occurring in foodservice. As consumers continue to spend heavily on foodservice products, the role of packaging in ensuring food safety and providing convenience can only increase. Packages designed for tracking and shelf-life extension reduce the risk of food-borne illness in the foodservice industry, but heating issues continue to be tricky.

New packaging products, such as the CuliDish, are helping to address these issues. The CuliDish's design allows simultaneous microwave heating of food that requires high heat and food that does not (such as salads) in the same tray. Such innovations in the area of heat and heat retention will reduce the safety risk associated with improper cooking. Food consumers prepare and eat only 60 per cent of meals at home, and 20 per cent of consumers eat while in transit to another location. As a consequence, many of the innovations in foodservice packaging are to accommodate meals eaten in transit and multi- component meals—both of which are trends of convenience.

The high demand for on-the-go meals has led to a significant increase in the variety of foods packaged for in-transit dining. Edible films and wraps have emerged on numerous foods, and package designs using modular folding cartons with flip-off lids or pouches with seatbelt flaps have been created for those who dine while driving. Multi-component packaging accommodates the multi-unit meals that are available at quick-service restaurants.

This type of packaging simplifies foodservice preparation, lessens waste, and makes consumption of multi-unit meals easy. Multi-component packaging is available in many forms: Les Petits Grande has reusable trays that clip together to form one larger serving tray, KFC uses triple-dip-strip cartons that allow consumers to dip chicken strips in three different sauces, and numerous coffee houses employ trays for holding more than one cup of coffee.

Green Packages

One of the key trends within food packaging is sustainable packaging. The Sustainable Packaging Coalition—an international consortium of more than 200 industry members—characterizes packaging as sustainable if it meets the following criteria:

- It is beneficial, safe, and healthy for individuals and communities throughout its life cycle.
- It meets market criteria for performance and cost.
- It is sourced, manufactured, transported, and recycled using renewable energy.

- It maximizes the use of renewable or recycled source materials.
- It is manufactured using clean production technolo-gies and best practices.
- It is made from materials healthy in all probable end-of-life scenarios.
- It is designed to optimize materials and energy.
- It is recovered effectively and used in biological and/or industrial cradle-to- cradle cycles.

A package's sustainability is determined by the source of its packaging material. Consequently, corporations and environmental groups are working collaboratively to reduce the effect of packaging on global sources.

Nanotechnology in Food Packaging

Some of the most exciting developments in food packaging involve nanotechnology; the science about very small materials is poised to have a big impact in food packaging materials. Nano-sized innovation could produce remarkable new packaging concepts for barrier and mechanical properties, pathogen detection, and active and intelligent packaging.

At the forefront of nano-sized development in food packaging are nanocomposites. Nanocomposites are materials that are made up of nanoparticle components. Toyota was the first company to commercialize nanocomposite materials, using nano-sized montmorillonite clay to increase mechanical and thermal properties of nylon. In food packaging, montmorillonite clay is being explored as the nano-component in a variety of polymers: polyethylene, polyester, nylon, and starch.

Nanocompositeplasticfilmsblockoxygen,carbondioxide,andmoisture from reaching food, so when used as packaging, the material extends the shelf life of food. Nanocomposite food packages are also light, strong, and heat resistant. In addition, research into the development of biodegradable nanocomposite packages is under way. While nanocomposites hold promise in food packaging through improved barrier properties, another type of nanomaterial shows great potential in managing microbial growth. Researchers have discovered that carbon nanotubes exert powerful antimicrobial effects: Direct contact with aggregates of carbon nanotubes proves to be fatal for Escherichia coli. The theory is that the long, thin nanotubes puncture E. coli cells, causing cellular damage. Another nano-sized solution with positive indications for the future is nanosensors. When integrated with food packaging, nanosensors can detect chemicals, pathogens, and toxins in food.

Forexample,biosensorshavebeendevelopedthatdetectStaphylococcus enterotoxin B, E. coli, Salmonella spp, and Listeria moncytogenes.

Nanosensors can also detect allergen proteins to prevent adverse reactions to foods such as peanuts, tree nuts, and gluten. Nevertheless, progression in this area moves cautiously because the effects of nano-sized materials on humans are still under investigation.

The Bottom Line

Since its inception in the 18th century, food packaging has made great advances in active and intelligent packaging solutions. These advances have led to improved food quality and safety. While most packaging innovations have been the result of global trends and consumer preferences, some innovations have stemmed from unexpected sources, such as the emergence of nanoscience. Undoubtedly, new packaging solutions will focus more on food safety (controlling microbial growth, delaying oxidation, improving tamper visibility), product quality (managing volatile flavours and aromas), convenience, and sustainability. These are the most important factors in a fast- paced world where borders are rapidly diminishing and customer bases are increasingly global.

MILK CARTON

Milk cartons are water tight paper containers used for packaging milk for retail distribution. One of the most common supermarket items, and found in nearly every home, the milk carton is nonetheless a precision product, manufactured according to exacting standards. Up until recent times, milk was not usually available as a retail item. Once milk is removed from the cow, it spoils quickly in heat, and is vulnerable to contamination. Until 20th century, the most economical and hygienic way to store milk was to leave it in the animal.

In Europe, a town cow keeper would bring his or her cow directly to the doorstep of the customer, and milk the animal there into a household container. In some places, milk was sold from a shop next door to the cow stall. In either case, the milk could not be safely stored for anything but a small amount of time. A large metal milk container was developed in Europe between 1860 and 1870. Called a churn, the lidded metal container could hold about 21.12 gal (801) of milk.

Milk in churns was shipped by rail from farming areas into towns, where the demand for milk was high. Milk in metal churns was also dispensed door to door. Instead of the cow keeper bringing the cow, now the milk was ladled out of the churn into a smaller household bucket or can. The glass milk bottle was invented in 1884.

This offered convenience to milk consumers, since the sterilized bottles could be kept sealed until needed. Milk that was pasteurized (quickly heated to above boiling, then cooled) was resistant to bacterial contamination and spoilage for several days. Bottled milk became prevalent across the United States and Europe through World War II, though glass containers are rarely seen now.

The first paper milk carton was introduced in 1933. Wax was applied to the paper, to make it waterproof. In 1940, polyethylene was introduced as the waterproofing material. Refillable glass bottles reigned for a long time after milk cartons were introduced, but by 1968, over 70 per cent of milk packaged in the United States went into paper cartons. The manufacture of milk cartons is actually a two-step process, at two different locations. The carton manufacturer cuts and prints the carton, which is shipped in a "knocked down" or flattened form to the milk packager. The packager completes the process by forming, filling, and sealing the carton.

Raw Materials

Milk containers are made from paperboard coated with a waterproof plastic, generally polyethylene. The wood pulp that is used to make paperboard for milk cartons is a blend of softwood and hardwood. Softwood is usually a type of pine, though the actual trees used vary depending on the location of the paper mill. Softwood produces long wood fibres that provide strength to the paperboard. Hardwood comes from deciduous trees such as oaks. Hardwood has shorter fibres that make for a better printing surface. Pulp for milk carton board is usually 60 per cent hardwood and 40 per cent soft.

Several other chemicals are used to make milk cartons. One is oxygenated chlorine, which bleaches the wood pulp. Other chemicals specific to each manufacturer are added to the paper to add strength. Chemical pigments in the ink are used for the printing process as well.

The Manufacturing Process

Making the Paperboard: The heavy paper used for milk cartons is categorized as a type of paperboard. It is typically made on a Fourdrinier machine, one of the oldest and most common types of papermaking equipment. The process begins with wood chips. The chips are heated and bathed in chemicals that soften them and break them into small bits of wood fibre. The pulp is bleached in a bath of oxygenated chlorine. The pulp is then washed and passed through several screens, to remove debris. Next, the pulp is fed through a machine called a refiner, which grinds the wood fibres between rotating disks.

The refined pulp flows into the headbox of the Fourdrinier machine. In the headbox, a mixture of water and pulp is spread across a continually moving screen. The water drains away below through the openings in the screen, leaving a mat of damp wood fibre. The mat is drawn through huge rollers that squeeze out additional water. Next, the paperboard is dried, by passing it over steam-heated cylinders.

Applying Waterproof Coating

The dried paperboard next moves through the rollers of an extruder. As the paperboard is pulled through the rollers, the machine extrudes a small amount of molten polyethylene. The polyethylene clings to both sides of the paperboard in a thin film. Several grades of polyethylene may be combined in the extruder, and the machine actually lays down multiple layers of film in one pass.

The different layers accomplish different tasks, such as reducing moisture penetration, reducing oxygen penetration, and aiding in essential oil retention. As the paperboard comes through the extruder, it passes over a chilled roller, which cools both surfaces.

The paper now has an extremely glossy, waterproof finish. It is wound into a large roll, to be transported to the printing area. The roll is typically 120 in (3.05 m) wide, too big to fit onto the printing and cutting machine. The large roll is slit into narrower rolls, the width determined by the desired dimensions of the finished carton.

Printing and Cutting the Blank

Printing is usually done by the flexo-graphic method, which uses rubber printing plates attached to steel shells. Workers load the roll of polyethylene- coated paperboard into the press. The press prints the words and images of the milk carton onto the paperboard.

A typical milk carton might be printed in anything from one to seven colours. All of the colours are printed at one pass through the machine. Next, the same machine scores the paperboard along what will be the edges of the carton, where the box will fold later.

A die lowers, and stamps out the carton. If you cut open an empty milk carton down one side and across the bottom and unfold it, you can see the shape of the cut piece. This flat, scored, and printed piece is called a blank. The high-speed printing and cutting equipment turns out hundreds of blanks per minute.

Sealing the Blanks

Workers at the carton plant next load the blanks into a sealing machine. The machine takes the flat blank and folds it laterally, creating an overlapping side seam. The seam is then heated and squeezed together. The heated polyethylene bonds and the seam are strong and watertight without any additional glue.

Thousands of blanks per minute shoot through the sealing machine. This is the final step at the carton manufacturer. The rest of the process is completed at the dairy. The sealed and folded blanks are loaded into corrugated cartons, and they are shipped.

Forming and Bottom-sealing

Dairies use specialized machinery to transform the blanks into open containers. Workers first load the blanks into a chute leading into the forming machine. The blanks are pulled by suction down onto mechanical arms called forming mandrels. The forming mandrels snap the carton open along its scored lines, and overlap the two bottom flaps.

The mandrels are aligned like spokes on a turning wheel. As the carton on the mandrel reaches the top of the wheel, the bottom of the carton is pressed against a hot plate that descends and seals the bottom seam. As the wheel continues to rotate, the bottom-sealed carton moves down, and is pulled by suction off the forming mandrel and set down on a conveyor belt.

Filling and Top-sealing

The conveyor belt moves the carton to the filling area. Milk from the dairy's storage area descends by pipes to the filling machine. A pre-measured amount of milk fills a chamber above the carton. Then the milk is released through a spout into the carton.

The filled carton passes along on the conveyor belt to the top-sealing machine. The top-sealing machine lowers onto the carton and pinches the top together along pre-scored lines. The shape of the conventional milk carton is called gable-topped. The top-sealer forms the gable, and heats and presses the top seam together. As in all the other seams, the polyethylene bonds to itself, and no additional glue is needed.

Stamping the Date

All milk cartons must have a date stamped on the top, indicating how long the milk will stay fresh. At the next stop along the conveyor belt, the filled, sealed carton passes under a stamping machine, which impresses the date along the tope edge of the carton. At a big milk-processing plant, the whole operation, from folded blank to date-sealed finished product, takes only a few seconds. After the date is stamped, the finished milk carton moves off the conveyor, and is packed either automatically or by hand into a packing case, for shipment to market.

Quality Control

Manufacturers make quality checks at every step along the manufacturing process. The pulp must be inspected to make sure it is the proper colour and density, and has the desired fibre characteristics.

As the pulp is a blend of long and short fibres, from soft and hard-wood trees, batches may differ according to the kind and proportion of trees used. The paperboard must pass numerous quality checks, for different reasons. The Federal Drug Administration (FDA) requires that milk cartons meet strict standards for hygiene and safety.

For instance, the FDA must approve any chemicals added to the paperboard and the manufacturer must be able to prove it is meeting its regulated requirements.

The width, thickness, and fibre mix of the paperboard is continually monitored by instruments attached to the paper-making machine, and the board is checked for contaminants as well. At the dairy or milk processing plant, forming and filling of the cartons is done under exacting standards for hygiene and safety.

By-products/Waste

The manufacturing process for milk cartons is extremely efficient, and there is very little waste. However, most used cartons are thrown in the trash and end up in landfills. It is possible to recycle them, though, if the appropriate recycling facilities exist. A milk carton recycler collects empty cartons from large users such as schools and hospitals. Then the recycler shreds the cartons, sanitizes them, and ties the shreds into bales. A pulp mill buys the bales from the recycler.

At the mill, the polyethylene coating is separated from the paper, and strained off for re-use by a plastics manufacturer. The shredded cartons are then reprocessed into pulp, and can be used to make high grades of printing and writing paper.

The Future

Milk carton manufacturing has not changed dramatically for many years, because the process is already highly streamlined and efficient. An increasingly popular modification to the traditional gable-topped carton is the addition of a plastic pour spout, but this requires only minor changes in the manufacturing process. As milk consumption falls in the United States, future changes might be in the graphic design of the cartons, as dairies compete harder for customers. Because the gable-topped cartons are very cost-effective to manufacture, packagers are searching for other products that can be sold in them. However, the polyethylene coating for milk cartons is not appropriate for every liquid. For instance, wine and motor oil have different characteristics than milk, and so need different waterproof barriers. Chemists and design engineers are currently researching new plastic coatings, so that other liquids besides milk can use paper cartons.

□

3

Understanding the Food Biotechnology

INTRODUCTION AND OBJECTIVES

Current and potential future benefits of biotechnology are numerous. They include new and more effective pharmaceuticals, more accurate methods of diagnosing disease, improved waste management techniques, new methods of production and improved food quality and safety. For people in Asia – whether they are wheat farmers on the Ganges Plain of India, rice farmers on the terraces of Bali, cotton growers in China or inhabitants of fast-paced cities like Singapore or Tokyo – the implications of biotechnology will be significant.

In the area of food and agriculture, the effects of biotechnology are likely to have many facets including better crop yields, reduced use of chemicals for plant disease and pest control, less environmental degradation, as well as the development of innovative food products, such as foods with improved nutritional value or better food quality and safety. Biotechnology is not seen as a panacea for all the region's food production problems. The supply of food is a complex process and biotechnology offers one part of a multi-faceted strategy to meet the growing demands for more and better quality foods. The Asian Food Information Centre and the International Service for the Acquisition of Agribiotech Applications have joined together to develop Food Biotechnology: A Communications Guide to Enhance Understanding Biotechnology. The Guide is intended to provide leaders in the scientific, medical, food and agricultural communities and educators involved in these areas, with a helpful resource kit. This resource is intended to provide context and to improve understanding of the practice and issues associated with modern biotechnology.

The kit aims to provide the most scientifically sound and up-to-date information about biotechnology products and processes. The resource provides an overview of regional production and regulations regarding crop biotechnology and includes findings from research conducted in Asian countries on consumer understanding and awareness of biotechnology. A presentation outlining the basic science of biotechnology is included in PowerPoint format with an accompanying commentary.

This could be used as a draft for presentations on Food Biotechnology or as a starting point for presentations in other languages. Future resources are planned which will provide information relevant to other areas of modern agricultural biotechnology. Given the diversity of communities in Asia with respect to race, religion, and social and economic status, it is especially important that any communication be based on an appreciation and respect for one's audience. It is also important to establish a baseline for the level of the understanding of food biotechnology present in your audience.

STATUS OF FOOD BIOTECHNOLOGY IN ASIA

Countries in Asia have a long history of productingfoods using biotechnology including soy sauce, tempeh and natto, belacan, cincaluk, budu and ngoc nam, tapai, toddy and sake. Foods such as pickles, vinegar, bread, yoghurt and cheese are also the products of biotechnology. More recently, countries in Asia have begun working in the area of crops produced from modern biotechnology or genetic modification. The current status of various countries and the regulations governing this area are listed below.

Table: Current Status of Biotechnology Crops in Asia

Country Experiments	Contained Experiments	Field Pre-commercialization/	Large Scale Commercialization
China	+	+	++
Australlia	+	+	++
India	+	+	++
Indonesia	+	+	+
Philippines	+	+	++
Thailand	+	+	–
Vietnam	+	–	–
Korea	+	+	–
Japan	+	+	+
Malaysia	+	+	–
Singapore	+	+	+

China, Australia, India, and the Philippines are the only countries in the region that have full-scale commercialisation of biotechnology crops. In China, genetically modified cotton, sweet pepper, tomato, and petunia have been approved for commercialisation. In 2003 area in China cultivated with biotechnology crops were close to 3 million hectares. Australia grew approximately 300,000 hectares in 2003. There is a considerable amount of research taking place around the rest of Asia, however, and most countries have R&D programmes on genetically modified crops and other areas of food biotechnology.

AGRICULTURAL BIOTECHNOLOGY AND FOOD SAFETY

When a consumer buys food s/he expects it to be safe and have the same quality characteristics that s/he is accustomed to, and familiar with. Consumers have the right to know that this is the case and if there is anything different about that product. The Food and Agriculture Organization and the World Health Organization of the United Nations advocate the concept of 'substantial equivalence' as the most practical approach to address the safety evaluation of foods or food components derived through modern biotechnology. This approach states that 'if a new food or food component is found to be substantially equivalent to an existing food or food component, it can be treated in the same manner with respect to safety.' So what kind of tests are used to determine if the food is as safe or safer than existing foodstuffs? Researchers must prepare comprehensive data to support the safety and wholesomeness of new crop varieties developed through biotechnology.

This process requires years of laboratory and field testing before a product can be brought to the market. To provide assurance that foods derived through biotechnology are as safe as those produced by traditional breeding programmes, the safety assessment strategies involve several key steps. These steps include molecular characterisation of the genetic modification, agronomic characterisation, nutritional assessment, toxicological assessment and safety assessment.

For example, typical questions that must be addressed are:

- Does the genetically modified food have a traditional counterpart that has a history of safe use?
- Has the concentration of any naturally occurring toxins or allergens in the food changed?
- Have the levels of key nutrients changed?
- Do new substances in the genetically modified food have a history of safe use?

- Has the food's digestibility been affected?
- Has the food been produced using accepted, established procedures?

Even after these and other questions about the biotechnology derived foods are answered, there are still more steps in the approval process before the crop can be commercialized. In fact, genetically modified foods are the most studied food products ever produced.

- **Safety assessment:** Molecular characterisation – for new plant varieties produced through modern biotechnology, the source of the gene introduced into the plant is first identified. The transformation system used to insert the gene is defined, as well as the number of copies of inserted genes and the integrity and stability of the genetic insert.
- **Agronomic traits:** Usually the starting points for evaluating substantial equivalence. For example, in the case of potatoes, the traits commonly examined are yield, tuber size and distribution, dry matter content and disease resistance.
- **Nutritional assessment:** Involves key nutrients including fats, proteins, carbohydrates and essential vitamins and minerals.
- **Toxicology assessment:** Toxicants and anti-nutrients are compounds known to be naturally present in some crops that could have an impact on health if their levels increased. For example, solanine glycoalkaloids in potatoes or trypsin inhibitors in soybeans). The levels of anti-nutrients in crops produced through biotechnology are compared to conventionally produced varieties grown under comparable environmental and agronomic conditions.
- **Safety assessment:** When a crop produced through biotechnology is shown to be substantially equivalent to a conventional crop, the safety assessment focuses on the introduced trait and the expressed protein product.

The overall goal of these tests is to determine whether the plant is substantially equivalent to food derived from a conventional source that has a history of safe use. A substantial equivalence evaluation focuses on the product rather than the process used to develop the product. If the new product is substantially equivalent to the conventional food or feed, then the product derived through biotechnology is considered to be as safe as the conventional counterpart. If the food produced using biotechnology contains a new trait, which changes the levels of nutrients or antinutrients, such as a higher level of a vitamin or a lower level of an allergen, the assessment focuses on demonstrating the safety of the new trait.

Allergens

One of the public's biggest concerns related to genetically modified foods is that an allergen could be accidentally introduced into a food product. The DNA inserted into a plant is safe and no case of allergy to DNA is known, the concern is whether the protein produced by the plant as a result of the inserted DNA could cause an unexpected allergic reaction. Scientists know a lot about which foods trigger allergic reactions in adults and children. Ninety per cent of all food allergies are associated with only eight foods or food groups – shellfish, eggs, fish, milk, peanuts, soybeans, tree nuts, and wheat. These, and many other food allergens, are well characterized. To date, genes found to express any known allergenic protein have been specifically excluded from the research and development process.

Scientists have agreed that following these simple steps provides compelling assurance that no allergic effects will result from foods derived from biotechnology:

- Avoid transferring genes from foods known to be allergenic.
- Check the structure of any new proteins produced in foods derived from biotechnology against the structures of known allergens to assure that no allergenic structures exist in the new protein.
- Measure the stability of the new protein in stomach and intestinal fluids. Most allergens are stable to these conditions. Proteins which are unstable to these conditions are not likely to be allergens.
- Determine how much of the new protein will be present in the food consumed by humans. Most allergens are present in large amounts. Allergenicity screening continues to be a very important part of safety testing before a crop can enter into the food market.

Antibiotic Resistance

Some biotechnology crops contain genes for a trait called antibiotic resistance. Scientists use this trait as a marker to identify cells into which the desired gene has been successfully introduced. Concerns have been raised that these marker genes could move from biotechnology crops to microorganisms that normally reside in a person's gut and lead to an increase in antibiotic resistance.

There have been numerous scientific reviews and experimental studies of this issue and they have come to the following conclusions:

- The likelihood of antibiotic resistance genes moving from biotechnology crops to other organisms is extremely remote.

- In the unlikely event that an antibiotic resistance gene is transferred to another organism, the impact of this transfer would be negligible, as the markers used in genetically modified crops have limited or no clinical or veterinary use.

However, in response to public concerns, scientists have been advised to avoid using antibiotic resistance genes in biotechnology modified plants. Alternative marker strategies are being developed.

COMMUNICATION

Recommendations Drawn From Afic Survey Findings

The development of any educational material should be based on a sound understanding of what the audience currently knows. There is poor overall awareness and understanding of food biotechnology.

Furthermore, there is little understanding of agricultural practices in general, especially crossbreeding and cultivation techniques:

- Consumer interest is primarily focused on the potential benefits of biotechnology such as nutritional benefits and the use of biotechnology to reduce pesticide use. Therefore education activities will be most effective if consumer benefits of biotechnology foods are used as the cornerstone message or at least as an introduction to the topic.
- The terminology used is important in determining responses to the information received. Technical terminology such as "genetically engineered", "genetically modified" is perceived to be intimidating and held implication that the foods had been altered by industrial methods. The terms "genetically enhanced" and "biotechnology foods" were found to be the two most suitable forms to describe food biotechnology
- Consumers were generally unaware of the concerns debated among the inner circle of stakeholders. Providing information on these issues may not improve knowledge levels and instead create further confusion.
- In Muslim countries, information on the source of the genes was sought because consumers needed to know that modification of gene sequences did not change 'halal' status.
- Messages that drew comparison with the West were considered inappropriate, thus case studies and research results sourced from the west were not perceived as credible.
- The main source of information used for biotechnology was the media and hence educational initiatives should look to work with media.

- The credibility of communication channel is influenced by its source. Scientific and academic community, and international agencies are viewed as credible sources of information.

Key Messages on Food Biotechnology

The topic of food biotechnology continues to be complex and confusing and it is therefore important to identify the key factual messages and to state them clearly and concisely. Providing one or more supporting facts can then reinforce this knowledge. The following messages are those which have been identified through research and experience to be the points most relevant and of most interest and concern to audiences in Asia.

Key Messages

Food biotechnology can contribute to food security in Asia:

- Food biotechnology can help to produce better quality and more nutritious foods. ??Food biotechnology is not a panacea for all the region's food production problems. The supply of food is a complex process and biotechnology cannot, and does not, apply to all the issues that face the region in the area of food security. It does however offer a useful and important complementary tool in helping to address food security and quality issues in Asia.
- Biotechnology can contribute to solving the challenge of conserving non-agricultural land, whilst producing sufficient food for growing population through increased yield productivity.
- Biotechnology provides greater opportunities to grow crops where it was previously impossible, due to extreme weather or soil conditions.

Foods produced using biotechnology will have direct consumer benefits While most corn, soybeans and other crops produced through biotechnology are no different in nutrition, composition or safety than conventionally produced crops; some actually have improved nutritional profiles that benefit consumers.

Examples of im proved foods include:

- Oil crops with lower levels of saturated fats to reduce saturated fat content of the diet.
- Oil crops with lower unsaturated fat content, which require less hydrogenation and therefore produce foods with lower trans fat content.
- Potatoes with increased levels of solids that absorb less fat when frying.
- Rice, sweet potato and other staples with higher levels of vitamin A, reducing the high prevalence of vitamin A deficiency.

- Rice and other staples with higher levels of iron and zinc, which are both essential nutrients in the human diet.
- Delayed ripening traits can produce fruits and vegetables with better flavour and remain fresh for longer periods of time.
- Increased solid matter content of tomatoes and potentially other fruits and vegetables results in superior taste, quality and shelf life.
- Plus - Reduced pesticide use on crops which use biotechnology to strengthen a crop's ability to defend itself against destructive insects.

Food biotechnology is a green technology and biotechnology offers considerable benefits for the environment.

- Crops produced using biotechnology require less pesticide.
- More efficient use of herbicides leads to less damage to the environment from pollution and soil erosion.
- Biotechnology helps protect water by reducing the level of nutrients in farm run-off and conserving topsoil.
- Olant diseases that can destroy an entire crop are now largely preventable among certain crops, protecting farmers and our food supply from devastating losses.

Foods produced from biotechnology are safe:

- To date, there is no evidence that any harm has come to anyone of the millions of people around the world in the last decade who have eaten foods derived from biotechnology.
- Regulatory authorities in the region closely monitor the safety of all foods including foods produced through biotechnology.
- The Food and Agriculture Organization and the World Health Organization have established procedures to determine the safety of biotechnology products and these procedures are met or exceeded by regulatory systems around the world. Countries such as the United States. Japan, Canada, Australia, Argentina, Korea, Russia, Poland, Hungary, Romania and the European Union have all used their regulatory process to determine the food safety of at least one product of biotechnology.
- Professional organisations such as the Chinese Academy of Sciences, Australia and New Zealand Food Authority, and the Institute of Food Technologists have supported the use of food biotechnology to improve food production.

- To date all foods resulting from biotechnology have not been found any more likely to cause allergic reactions on consumption, than their traditional counterparts.

Language

In the area of communication on science and technical issues, the use of very technical language is often counterproductive. Scientific jargon, although accurate, can confuse and even alarm non-scientists, evoking negative reactions.

Food biotechnology needs to be discussed in everyday terms. It is important for people to understand that the technology is about seeds that are planted in the ground and that grow into plants just like any other plants. If normal everyday language is not used it sends the message that the technology is about experiments undertaken just in the laboratory and it gives a false impression of food biotechnology.

The understanding and acceptance of any science or technology including food biotechnology can change dramatically depending upon the language used. The preferred scientific term for defining "recombinant DNA technology" is biotechnology or green technology. In many Asian countries, the most readily understandable terms include food biotechnology or genetically modified foods. Abbreviations such as "GM food" or GMOs are perceived as jargon.

Such terminology may lead to confusion, miscommunication and even misinterpretation of the topic and related issues. A list of suggested "Words to use" and "Words to lose" has been developed to help with discussions on food biotechnology. This list was created from talking with consumers, professionals in the scientific and health community and the media

Food Biotechnology in Asia

This part helps provide the most scientifically sound and up-to-date information about food biotechnology. The PowerPoint presentation and accompanying suggested commentary notes help to provide a basic explanation of food biotechnology.

It also aims to answer many questions while clarifying common myths about food biotechnology. It can be customised to suit different audiences or requirements.

Food Biotechnology in Asia

You may have heard a lot about food biotechnology lately. If so, you may be wondering what it is and what it means to you. Biotechnology is an important tool used to improve the quality of our lives. It has been with us for years, is with us now, and will continue to be around in the future. It has already provided many benefits from life-saving medicines to more nutritious foods. This presentation will focus mainly on food biotechnology. Biotechnology as applied to the food production system builds on the knowledge gained over thousands of years of plant production. It is a process that has the potential to improve the nutrition, taste, quality and freshness of many foods today. Studies show that most people in Asia are not aware of the terms "biotechnology" or "genetic modification" and if they are, they don't know enough to explain what it means.

What is Biotechnology

Biotechnology can be a confusing term, but let's take the word apart. "Bio" means biology or the science of living things while "technology" means the tools and processes used to make products. Together, it means using biology to make new products and in this context, food crops.

Foods from Traditional Biotechnology

Some examples of foods derived from traditional biotechnology include soy sauce, fermented soybeans, shrimp paste, rice wine, and fish sauce. Even pickles, bread, yoghurt, and cheese are all products of biotechnology. Micro- organisms have been used to make such products.

Biotechnology Timeline

Food biotechnology has been evolving for thousands of years:

- 10000 BC: Crops are domesticated through farmer selection of desirable plant types.
- 8000-9000 BC: Goats and sheep are the first animals domesticated in Mesopotamia,thus beginning the selective breeding process.
- 6000 BC: Fermentation is the breakdown of sugars into alcohol or lactic acid by mircroorganisms, such as yeast. Egyptians used this important process to brew beer 6000 years ago.
- 4000 BC: Although flat bread already existed, around 4,000 BC Egyptian breadmakers found another use for yeast. They found it would cause the bread to rise.
- 1880s: For the first time in 1885, Louis Pasteur used a vaccine to artificially increase immunity against a disease – in this case rabies.
- 1920s: In 1928, Sir Alexander Fleming discovered penicillin, which paved the way for Howard Walter Florey and Ernst Boris Chain to later develop it into an effective therapy for infectious diseases.
- 1960s: Parallel improvements in varieties of rice and wheat sparked the Green Revolution and contributed to a doubling of the world's food supply of cereals.

- 1990s: Genetically improved plants are developed using the tools of modern biotechnology.

Evolution of Biotechnology

Thus the evolution of food biotechnology dates back all the way to10,000 BC. Now, we are equipped with modern tools that allow us to improve our foods even more efficiently than before.

What is Modern Biotechnology

Modern biotechnology employs the tools of genetics to enhance beneficial traits of plants, animals, and microorganisms for food production. It involves adding or removing selected genes to achieve desired traits. Selecting specific genes to add to, or remove from, plants or animals is a more precise method of breeding, offering farmers more ways to improve crop and animal production.

Analogy

This slide provides a good analogy for the differences between traditional plant breeding and modern biotechnology.

Genetically Modified Applications

Genetic modification or modern biotechnology is being used to improve many foods and it has already been adopted in commercial agricultural production in many countries.

Products Currently in the Market

In 1990 the first food products enhanced via biotechnology were introduced to the market. These products consisted of an enzyme used in food produced using biotechnology entered the U.S. marketplace. This was the FlavrSavr? tomato which stayed fresher longer than other tomatoes. This is the list of countries that have approved genetically modified food products.

Consumer Benefits

There are many current and potential applications for biotechnology, including improving taste, safety, nutritional profile and quality of many foods. Biotechnology could provide potential consumer benefits through safer, tastier, more nutritious food choices.

Future Food Products

Future products that are being developed include those that:

- **Fight the lack of micro-nutrients:** e.g. Increasing the amount of vitamin A or iron in rice. Increasing the amount of vitamin E in vegetable oils.
- **Help prevent common diseases:** e.g. Soybean and canola oil with more stearate. Potatoes with higher starch content.

- **Reduce non-food related allergies:** e.g. Modifying a plant called guayule that produces a latex, which causes fewer side effects and might be cheaper to produce than the commonly used latex from the Brazilian rubber tree.
- **Reduce toxins:** e.g. Insect resistant maize less likely to harbour mycotoxins in the corn ears.
- **Serve as edible vaccines:** e.g. Potatoes containing a vaccine against Hepatitis B virus.
- **Reduce allergens in foods:** e.g. Developing techniques to identify and neutralize the genetic material in rice, wheat, peanuts, and other foods that cause severe allergic reactions in some people.

Consumers Support GM Food

Many Asians are not opposed to the concept of biotechnology. People are enthusiastic about the potential for improved food quality and safety through biotechnology.

Asian consumers remain positive about the many potential benefits of GM food, despite unbalanced media coverage and confusion in the international marketplace. A survey coordinated by the Asian Food Information Centre in Dec 1998- Nov 1999 revealed the following: More than 80 per cent of people were prepared to try a food product made from genetically modified crops. More than half of the respondents would purchase or eat genetically modified foods if they were proven to be healthier.

Farmer Benefits

Biotechnology could offer farmers a more efficient way to produce safer products in greater numbers. Some of the benefits include: More flexibility in operations, lesshard manual labour.

Efficient pest control built into crops means farmers are exposed to less risk and more willing to invest in their farm operations.

Farmers can control weeds at any time. Finally, it makes farming more attractive to the younger generation.

Environmental Benefits

- Higher yields decrease need to convert forests and natural habitat into farmland.
- Conservation tillage aided by biotechnology: The development of herbicide resistant crops has allowed farmers to practice conservation-tillage farming. This is the practice of planting

seeds through the stubble of last year's crop, rather than plowing and disking the field. The stubble protects topsoil against loss to wind and rain and reduces chemical run-off to streams. By not plowing, farmers also conserve soil moisture, which can reduce irrigation demands in some regions.

- Improved water quality through reduced soil erosion and run-off: Soil sedimentation or siltation is sometimes a major threat to stream quality. A summary of studies found that no till farming which is facilitated by biotechnology, can reduce soil erosion by 90 per cent.
- Reduced use of insecticides and herbicides aids beneficial insects, wildlife, plants, and humans - Use of biotechnology derived plants with built-in resistance to insects and diseases could mean that substantially fewer pesticides, insecticides, and herbicides would be required, thus reducing farmers' exposure, a particular problem in many developing countries where protective gear may not always be available.
- Nitrogen fixing crops could reduce use of nitrogen fertilizers: One of the biggest challenges in agriculture is the fact that most crops, with the exception of legumes such as clover, do not naturally produce nitrogen, but require the application of nitrogen fertilizers for growth. Considered "frontier" research at present, international scientists' research is progressing to produce nitrogen-fixing rice. That is, rice that can produce its own nitrogen to enable it to grow. Currently, it is estimated that about 10 million tons of nitrogen fertilizer are needed each year for rice production worldwide, and that amount is expected to double in the next several decades. Besides the potential decreased cost to poor farmers, the massive Scientists have made progress in transferring one gene involved in the nitrogen fixing process to rice plants, and are working on achieving the same results with other genes involved.
- Biodiversity can be aided by improved plant resilience: Biotechnology can aid in preserving endangered plants through genetic enhancement of traits needed for survival. Modern biotechnology, together with other methods, such as seed banks, can help to preserve and even reintroduce native plants that are endangered. This could promote biodiversity and help to enhance food security by saving plant varieties for the future.

Economic Benefits

In the US, the Primary Benefit of Bt Corn Varieties has been Increased Yields: In 1999, it is estimated that 66 million bushels of corn were saved from the corn borer, or the equivalent production of nearly 500,000 acres.

- Net revenues are estimated to have increased by U$99 million in 1999.
- The use of herbicide tolerant soybean varieties has been a reduction in weed control costs, of U$216 million per year in 1999 and growers have also reduced the number of herbicide applications, by 19 million in 1999. In addition to the potential consumer benefits, agricultural biotechnology presents a range of possible economic benefits. Impact of Bt Cotton in China
- A sample of 283 cotton farmers in Northern China was surveyed in December 1999. Farmers that used Bt cotton reduced the use of pesticide without reducing output/ha or quality of cotton. This resulted in substantial economic benefits for small farmers.
- At least 85 per cent of the 1999 benefits from the adoption of Chinese Bt cotton varieties went to small scale farmers
- Farmers who grew most popular Bt varieties reduced their costs of production by 20-23 per cent over new non-Bt varieties.
- Small farmers- those whose farms are less than 1 ha or have family incomes less that RMB 10,000-gained almost twice as much income per unit of land from adopting Bt cotton as large, more wealthy farmers gained.
- In addition to the potential consumer, environmental and economic benefits of biotechnology, there should be worldwide benefits in meeting the food needs of the growing population in Asia. Norman Borlaug, Nobel Prize winner, "In the next 25 years, farmers in Asia must increase their yields by 50-75 per cent."

Combating Hunger

These benefits are particularly important considering about one billion people around the globe cannot count on eating every day, the World Bank. For example the populations of India and China are forecast to grow to 1.6 and 1.5 billion, respectively by 2050. The Philippine population is set to almost double over next 25 years. Simply put, the use of agricultural biotechnology can result in more food being produced on less land to feed a rapidly growing global population.

Approved Food Biotechnology is Safe

Opponents of biotechnology question its biosafety. However, many of the criticisms are not supported by evidence or fact. Government agencies involved in health, science, technology, agriculture and trade are committed to ensuring the safe application of biotechnology. A number of other health and food organisations also support the scientific basis of biotechnology. These include UN FAO, WHO, OECD, The Third World Academy of Sciences,the Institute of Food Technologists and the Australian Institute of Food Science and Technology. By May 2001, more than 3,000 leading scientists, including two Nobel Prize winners, had signed a declaration endorsing gene technology as a safe, environmentally-friendly and useful tool to help feed the developing world.

Labelling Policy

In Asia, national food standards have been developed in all countries to ensure the safety of the food supply. Standards for the labelling of foods produced through biotechnology are currently under discussion in most Asian countries and also by the United Nations agencies responsible for global food guidelines.

In Japan, food ingredients produced through biotechnology must be labelled if they make up the first five ingredients by weight. Refined products such as oils and sugars in which no protein or recombinant DNA can be detected are excluded from labelling requirements.

Korea has introduced mandatory labelling for all genetically modified foods with more than 1 per cent genetically modified content. The debate around the labelling of genetically modified foods stems from the consumers "right to know" rather than a safety issue. All foods that are allowed to be sold in the market are regulated by the country's food regulations and are considered wholesome and safe to eat.

What does the Future Hold

The future for food made using agricultural biotechnology looks promising. New foods, nutritionally enhanced to protect and promote good health, are in development. Advances in biotechnology can help further reduce toxins in plants and help to detect plant contaminants more efficiently, thus improving the safety of our food supply. Fruits and vegetables may stay fresher for longer periods of time. Current advances suggest it may be possible to eliminate a number of common allergens from many foods. The available global food supply could be increased to support the rapidly growing world population.

MYTHS AND FACTS ABOUT FOOD BIOTECHNOLOGY

1 Myth

The application of biotechnology to crops, animals and microorganisms to produce genetically modified food is radically different from traditional crop production systems.

1 Fact

Biotechnology is an evolution of traditional agricultural methods. Over the past 10,000 years, people have routinely used their knowledge of plants to improve food production. Biotechnology is the latest development in the evolution of agricultural methods. Farmers used to rely on plant breeding to add or eliminate specific genetic traits in a plant. For example, because of plant breeding, corn today looks nothing like it did one hundred years ago.

Although it typically took several growing seasons to produce a plant that expressed a desired trait, farmers were eventually able to produce crops that:

- Were resistant to drought, insect pests or diseases
- Possessed stronger stalks to withstand strong winds
- Produced higher yields

In more recent years, techniques such as irradiation and mutation of seeds to create changes which could be selected for desirable traits, as well as specialized techniques to induce crossing between distantly related plant species have been successfully and safely applied to thousands of varieties of crops without undergoing anywhere near the scrutiny which has been applied to products of biotechnology.

Genetic modification is actually a more efficient and precise way to achieve the benefits of crop improvement. Using biotechnology techniques, scientists are now able to pinpoint the specific gene responsible for a particular trait and then extract or add that gene to a specific plant.

2 Myth

Foods produced using biotechnology are brand new.

2 Fact

Foods produced using modern biotechnology have only been available since the mid-1990s. Modern agricultural biotechnology can be likened to the process that bakers, brewers, vintners and ranchers have used for centuries when they applied biology to modify genes to make bread, beer, wine and cheese.

Examples of foods and crops produced using biotechnology that have been approved for food use in the US include:

- Tomatoes with delayed ripening traits that have better flavour, remain fresh longer and withstand transport better than traditional tomatoes.
- Soybeans, canola, corn, cotton and potatoes resistant to insects, herbicides or both.
- Squash resistant to a virus that often kills the vegetable on the vine.
- Soybeans and canola that produce cooking oil with less saturated fat.
- Papaya resistant to a virus that causes significant yield losses.

All of these foods have undergone rigourous testing and have proven to be safe to eat. The record of the past 6 years of safe consumption provides further assurance that the safety evaluations of these products prior to their introduction have been effective.

3 Myth

Foods produced using biotechnology have not been established as safe and are not adequately regulated.

3 Fact

The Food and Agriculture Organization of the United Nations and the World Health Organization have established procedures to determine the safety of biotechnology products and these procedures are met or exceeded by regulatory systems around the world.

Countries, such as the United States, Japan, Canada, Australia, Argentina, Korea, Russia, Poland, Hungary, Romania and even the European Union have all used their regulatory process to determine the food safety of at least one product of biotechnology.

4 Myth

Biotechnology cannot relieve world hunger

4 Fact

Biotechnology can help alleviate hunger worldwide. In the next 50 years the global population is expected to double, reaching more than 8 billion people by 2050. Population growth and population demands for improvements in dietary choice and quality will require the world food supply to increase at least 250 per cent from its current quantity. The amount of land currently committed to food production - approximately 36 per cent of the earth's cumulative land area – cannot yield the amount of food needed by this increased population.

Although forests could be cleared to obtain needed acreage, a better approach is to find ways of getting greater crop yield from existing land. Biotechnology can increase the quantity of the harvest by addressing the factors that traditionally deplete crops such as pests, weeds, drought and wind. Plants from biotechnology are being bred to withstand these stresses and therefore increase the proportion of crops that survive and are harvested each year.

5 Myth

The application of biotechnology only benefits farmers and not consumers.

5 Fact

Biotechnology can have both direct and indirect benefits to the consumer. Products that have been introduced to the market have had enhanced flavour and freshness, better nutritional value and lower saturated fat contents. Indirect benefits include reduced use of pesticide and more sustainable tillage practices, which address costly environmental problems like water pollution. Food biotechnology could have more direct benefits to consumers in the future. It could allow the production of biodegradable packaging; alternatives to chemical pharmaceuticals; and more healthful food products fruits as delivery medium for vaccines for diseases prevalent in some less developed countries.

6 Myth

Biotechnology was responsible for concerns about the health of laboratory rats after they were fed genetically modified potatoes.

6 Fact

During a television programme in 1998, Dr. Arpad Pusztai of the Rowett Research Institute in Aberdeen, Scotland, suggested that after feeding genetically modified potatoes to five rats over a 110- day period, some showed stunted growth and had impaired immune systems. The biotechnologyderived potatoes fed to the rats contained a lectin from snowdrops, which is toxic to some insects. After publication of these results as a letter in the Lancet, Dr.

Pusztai's experiments were reviewed by six experts appointed by the Royal Society of the UK. These experts concluded that the work published in the Lancet was flawed in many aspects of design, execution and analysis and that no conclusions could be made from it.

The Royal Society found no convincing evidence of adverse effects of the potatoes and concluded that it would be unjustifiable to draw general conclusions about whether genetically modified foods are harmful to humans or not. Furthermore, the potatoes studied by Dr. Pusztai have not been approved and could not be approved in any country in the world.

7 Myth

Crops and foods produced using biotechnology will cause people to become more resistant to antibiotics.

7 Fact

The US FDA has determined there is no evidence of increased risk of antibiotic resistance in humans from foods currently in commerce that were developed using biotechnology. In past years, scientists have used genes derived from bacteria to determine whether a specific trait has been successfully added or extracted from a plant. On occasion antibiotic proteins are used as selectable markers raising concerns that the proteins will pass into the food supply and when consumed, cause people to become resistant to antibiotics.

In a thorough review of this method, the US FDA has determined its safety. It is important to note that even if antibiotic resistance were to transfer from foods developed with biotechnology to bacteria in humans, the antibiotics involved in the biotechnology processes are not important to medical or veterinary needs and any resistance created in humans or animals would still allow the use of antibiotics which are important. Nevertheless, there is now international agreement that the use of antibiotic marker genes will be phased out as soon as reliable alternative technologies are developed.

8 Myth

If foods produced through biotechnology are available in the food supply, people with allergies will not be able to identify foods to which they may be allergic.

8 Fact

The US FDA 1992 guidelines requires companies to label an end product if it contains any of the eight most common food allergens; milk, eggs, wheat, fish, shellfish, peanuts and soy tree nuts. It is good practice and standard procedure for foods to be granted approval only when regulatory authorities are satisfied that a secure mechanism is in place to protect sensitive consumers. In many countries there are voluntary or mandatory requirements for companies to label their products identifying the common allergens. There are no biotechnology-derived foods currently on the market, which contain any of the recognised common allergens. Indeed, biotechnology may one day provide allergy experts with the means to remove allergens from many foods that cause allergic reactions, by isolating and removing the allergenic component.

9 Myth

The long-term effects of foods produced using biotechnology are unknown.

9 Fact

From years of research, we know that the benefits are tremendous, with no additional risk. The scientific consensus is that the risks of food biotechnology products are fundamentally the same as for other foods. Current science shows that foods made using biotechnology are safe to consume, and safe for the environment. For this reason, a host of regulatory agencies have determined that these products are safe to introduce to the food supply. There is no such thing as "zero risk" for any food; however, foods produced using biotechnology have all met governments' most stringent food safety standards. The future is never guaranteed, but years of research and the absence of harmful evidence indicates the benefits of agricultural biotechnology far outweigh any risks. When asked about the anxiety surrounding the application of biotechnology to food in Europe Dr, James Watson, the scientist who determined the structure of DNA, likened the resistance to the initial ban on medical biotechnology. If that ban had continued, "it would have stopped us from understanding cancer and a whole host of things,' he noted. "To argue that you don't know what is going to occur is true about everything in life. People would not get married, have children, do anything..." It is also noteworthy that in some instances biotechnology increases safety of foods. For example, biotechnology-derived crops with their own natural insect protection such as Bt corn are less susceptible to attack by harmful mycotoxin moulds. Thus, stored Bt crops are less likely to develop harmful concentration of aflatoxins during storage.

10 Myth

Crops produced using biotechnology will harm the environment.

10 Fact

Biotechnology is a key element in sustainable agriculture that will benefit the environment. Benefits include reduced pesticide usage, water and soil conservation and greater safety for workers and the ecosystem. Many crops – including tomatoes, potatoes, corn and cotton - now have the internal ability to repel insects. Consequently, fewer applications of pesticide are required. A type of corn used to feed pigs will reduce the phytic acid in animal waste that causes algae to grow in water supplies. The better yields from crops using biotechnology will reduce the pressure to clear additional land for farmland.

11 Myth

The production of crops resistant to certain pests and weeds will lead to the evolution of "superbugs" and "superweeds" that are resistant to existing methods of pest and weed control.

11 Fact

No scientific study has suggested that this type of scenario could occur as a result of crops developed through biotechnology. However, many systems are in place - including crop rotation, hybrid rotation and integrated pest management - as a precautionary measure to help prevent it from occurring. Insects and weeds already evolve and develop tolerance or resistance to their environment, so biotechnology can potentially better manage this evolution of resistance.

The potential transfer of traits by pollen remains the same as ever. Considerable study is taking place to ensure that strategies are developed and implemented in each country where insect-protected crops are planted to ensure that insect resistance is managed and controlled over as long a period as possible. These strategies are being developed specifically for the agricultural conditions of each country taking into account such factors as crop rotation and alternate crop and non-crop hosts for the insects.

12 Myth

Genetically modified corn kills Monarch butterflies.

12 Fact

In May 1999, Nature magazine published a letter from researchers at Cornell University that reported findings suggesting further research is needed into the relationship between pollen from select strains of Bt corn and the Monarch caterpillar. Since that publication, many university researchers, including others at Cornell, have stepped forward to stress that the Monarch study did not represent natural conditions.

A report from the US Environmental Protection Agency indicated that the "data provide a weight of evidence indicating no unreasonable adverse effects of Bt proteins expressed in plants to non-target wildlife." Furthermore, a study from the University of Illinois indicated that Monarch butterflies were not harmed by Bt pollen in actual field conditions. As with any scientific issue, several studies are needed before conclusions can be made.

13 Myth

Biotechnology produced insect resistant corn causes allergy related illnesses in the Philippines.

13 Fact

In a news briefing in February 2004, Dr Terje Traavik, a professor of Gene Ecology at the University of Tromso in Norway announced his finding suggesting that around 50 farmers and individuals living near the insect resistant corn field in the Philippines suffered allergy related illnesses due to exposure to Bt corn pollen. Prior to his announcement, his research data and finding had not been peer-reviewed as has been the norms in scientific publications.

Dr Nina Gloriani Barzaga, a Professor of Medical Microbiology and Microbial Immunology at the University of the Philippines Manila; and Director of the Institute of Biotechnology and Molecular Biology, National Institutes of Health Philippines responded that the insect-toxin protein in the Bt corn has been assessed for allergenic potential based on established criteria and procedures. This toxin is not considered an allergen. Many university researches requested Traavik to give other scientists access to his experimental methods and data to review them.

14 Myth

Thailand papayas have been found to be widely contaminated with biotechnology produced plants and as a result Thai farmers at risk of violating US Patent.

14 Fact

Thai Department of Agriculture inadvertently distributed virus resistant papaya produced using biotechnology to local farmers. These plants had been tested in containment for testing. Conventionally bred papaya crops suffer from several diseases and pests.

The most widespread disease of papaya is caused by papaya ringspot virus, affecting papaya production and productivity in many parts of the world including Asia. Traditional means to control this disease were not very effective and the disease can be easily and widely spread through insect bites. Furthermore, there is no known papaya variety tolerant to the disease. Virus resistant papaya produced using biotechnology renders the plant resistant to the virus. These papaya varieties had been approved for food use in the US since 1997 and Canada since 2003 following safety assessment, and examinations of nutritional composition, toxicological implications and allergenic potential by authorities in those countries. Cornell University that patented the invention related to biotechnology produced virus resistant papaya will work with Thailand Department of Agriculture to develop a plan to use the papaya technology in Thailand. Cornell has no desire to charge poor farmers for use of its technology.

□

4

Fermentation as a Method of Food Processing

INTRODUCTION

Globally, there are varieties in fermented foods and beverages and so does the ingredients and recipes for making them. For instance, in Russia, a slightly sour weak beer called Kvass is made from rye flour and malt. In Australia Kefyr is made from milk with the help of a Mushroom variety. Airag is a traditional fermented drink in Mongolia. Kumyss is made in Russia and Turkey from sour and fermented milk. Tsampa is made in Tibet from tea, roasted ground barley, Yakbutter and sugar. Pulque is a traditional alcoholic drink made in Mexico and Posca was once the main beverage of the Roman Army.

In the Indian subcontinent, making and use of fermented food and beverages using local food crops and other biological resources is very common amongst the high landers of Himalaya, though the name of the products and the base material vary from region to region. The people of Indian trans- Himalayan region such as Ladakh and Lahaul-Spiti make local beverages from barley called as Chang.

While, the people in Kinnaur district of Himachal Pradesh call it Ghanti, which is made from fermented musk. In Sikkim and Darjeeling finger millet is the main substrate for their local beverages called as Kodo ko Jaanr. The high altitude residents of Uttaranchal State that comprises of two regions viz., Garhwal and Kumaon call it as Chakti in Dharchula, Wine in Munsyari and Chang in Chamoli and Uttarkashi.

The present chapter deals with indigenous knowledge of fermented foods and beverages of high altitude regions of Uttaranchal Himalaya in India. Uttaranchal is situated geographically in the eastern side of the northwestern Indian Himalaya. The study was focused on the Bhotiyas of Pithoragarh, Chamoli and Uttarkashi districts of Uttaranchal. These high landers of Uttaranchal are popularly known as the Bhotiyas, however, these people prefer to call themselves as shaukas in Kumaon region.

Traditionally, the Bhotiyas of Uttaranchal were trans-border traders, and traded between India and erstwhile Tibet. They used sheep and goat as pack animals, and to feed their animals, they had adapted themselves as transhumant pastoralists. Their traditional economy revolved around sheep and goat rearing, besides little agriculture and trade. Most of these Bhotiya communities have now settled down permanently giving up their migratory nomadic life.

As a result, some of their knowledge systems have already lost, and many others are on the verge of eradication. The traditional method of Bhotiya food fermentation and beverage making was designed in such a way, that it utilized those available crops, which did not make their main food crops. The common fermented drinks of this community are jann and wine. Among the fermented foods is the semi-fermented rice called sez, which is taken as a light snacks by these communities.

SURVEY METHODS

Extensive surveys were made in the Bhotiya dominated high altitude villages of three districts in Uttaranchal such as Pithoragarh, Chamoli and Uttarkashi from 1999 to 2001 to identify and explore the indigenous methods of preparing various fermented beverages and foods.

The information on this indigenous practice was acquired through participatory field research methods such as semi-structured interviews, field inspections, field observations, participation in their social life and events.

PREPARATION OF STARTER CULTURE

The traditional catalyzing agent used in the preparation of fermented food and beverage is called balam in Kumaon and balma in Garhwal region, which is not prepared by all villagers in the society. The alpine grazers called as anwals have specialized knowledge to prepare this starter culture. It is made up of wheat by mixing a number of herbs and spices. First, the raw wheat is washed in water and sun dried, later this is grinded into flour, and then it is roasted over fire and removed before it becomes brown in colour.

The roasted flour is then mixed with spices like long, elachi, kalimirch, leaves of mirchi-ghash, and seeds of pipal. In this mixture, powder of old balam is also added. The addition of old balam powder is a must, without this production of fresh balam is not possible. The mixture so prepared is then thoroughly mixed up with the required quantity of water, and is rolled into a thick paste. This mixture is then pressed between palms to make balam balls of the required size. These balls are then dried in shade and stored for future use for an indefinite period of time.

PREPARATION OF LOCAL BEER

Jann is a traditional soft drink of the Bhotiyas, and contains very low concentration of alcohol. It is commonly prepared out of rice; however, it can also be made out of a good number of substrates of both cereals and fruits. Some of the common cereals from which jaan can be made are rice, wheat, jau, koni, china, oowa, and chuwa. Similarly, amongst the fruits, apple is most desired and is also very delicious.

But jann prepared from koni is considered to be the best in quality. The quality of jann is best judged by its taste, smell and strength. Mostly rice jann is commonly used and is prepared almost in every household in this society, but now its preparation and consumption has declined. In the making of rice jaan, first rice is cooked or boiled for about half an hour or until it becomes soft and edible. The cooked rice is drained off the excess of water and spread on a flat container allowing to be cooled quickly. The cooked rice is then thoroughly mixed with balam powder. The quantity of the balam powder required is proportionate to the quantity of rice to be fermented. This mixture is then kept in an airtight container and is kept in a dark and warm place for fermentation. In cold conditions, the rate of fermentation is slow as compared to warm. But for a good quality jann slow fermentation at low temperature is a required condition. The process of fermentation takes place in the absence of oxygen, and usually after a week of fermentation jann is prepared. However, for a better quality of jann the fermentation period is extended as long as possible but not more than a year. Longer the period of fermentation the less is the undigested remains of rice, and in that case the quantity of jann produce is more.

It has been proved that longer the period of fermentation, there is more and significant reduction in phytic acid content while the availability of in-vitro minerals increases. After the completion of fermentation, the jann so produced is filtered with the help of a sieve. The filtrate is a whitish liquid, which is abandoned or used as animal fodder. Earlier, when Bhotiyas migrated to their winter settlement in lower valleys, before their migration they prepared jaan material and left them for fermentation.

For six months of winter, their entire settlement got submerged under snow, and as result of the internal heat generated due to the external pressure of ice from the top, the jaan fermentation was slow but steady. On their return to the place again in summer the people found their jann ready for drink, and jann produced in this way is considered to be the best in quality. Similarly, the preparation of jann is same from other cereals like koni, wheat, jaw, oowa, chuwa and cheena. Like rice, first the seeds of any of these cereals are boiled in water until they become soft and edible. Then they are mixed with balam powder and the rest of the stages of storing and fermentation, and finally yielding of jann is the same. Only in the case of jaw the seeds are partially grinned before boiling, which enables quick fermentation and optimum yielding. Jann is also prepared from fruits like apple, banana, pumpkin and orange. Apples are first cut into pieces and then are mixed with balam powder for fermentation. The rest of the method is the same, except in case of orange, where either the juice or the complete fruit after peeling is mixed with balam powder and fermented for yielding jann. Banana is used without removing its outer skin.

The preparation of jann from pumpkin is slightly different, where a small cut is made in a large sized pumpkin in such a way that the cut piece is again fitted back to its place. First, the seeds and loose tissues contents of the fruit is removed through the opening, and boiled rice or other substrate mixed with balam powder as usual is poured into the empty space of the fruit. It is then sealed again by placing back the cut piece in its place. The process of fermentation takes place inside as a result of which along with rice the inner soft tissue of the fruit also gets digested, and thus yields jann in due course of time.

PREPARATION OF ALCOHOLIC DRINK

Wine is the distilled liquor containing ethyl alcohol at a much higher concentration than other alcoholic beverages. Rice and jaggery are the common substrate used for preparation of wine. Apart from rice, the cereals like koni, chuwa, oowa and wheat are used in the preparation of wine. However, unlike in the case of jann the taste of the wine does not vary just as to the type of substrate used.

Therefore, choice of substrate does not matter in the preparation of wine. The most commonly available and cost effective materials used in the preparation of wine, is rice and jaggary. Cooked rice on becoming cool is mixed with the powder of balam, the proportion of balam powder required in preparation of wine is much more than what is required in jann preparation. This mixture is then kept in an airtight container for fermentation, and is kept in preferably a warmer place.

To ensure the warmth, either the fermentation container is covered with woolen cloth or else it is kept near the cooking hearth, direct heating is, however, avoided. After about a week of fermentation, when the mixture is in a semi liquid condition, it is distilled in a distillation vessel. The distillate substance is the wine, which is collected in bottles. The undigested residue is called chak, is dirty white in colour, this can be used again for preparation of wine by fortification with jaggary and fresh balam powder. This way chak is recycled or reused in wine preparation. However, this is not used for more than three times, and is given to animals to eat.

DISTILLATION AND COLOURING OF WINE

The traditional distillation method is still practiced in this region, the indigenous set, which is quite simple has three parts parar, jokhal and tal, as called in the local dialect. The parar is a big saucepan like container with flat bottom, and jokhal is a flat wooden device like a dish having an elongated channel with a hole at the centre, and is indigenously prepared by the people. The tal is a simple cooking vessel, but the neck of tal and the bottom of parar is of such a size that they hold the jokhal perfectly.

This whole system is put on fire, on being heated the alcoholic vapour first evapourate and come through the central hole of the jokhal. But on coming in contact with cold bottom of parar the vapour gets condensed into liquid. This liquid is collected in a container, and this distillate is the alcohol or wine. The wine collected in first three to four bottles during the process of distillation contains very high percentage of alcohol, and is always diluted before consumption.

The alcohol content gradually reduces and finally only water evapourates. Traditionally wine is graded into three categories the initial few bottles containing high percentage of alcohol is called paileful; the final few bottles containing very low contents of alcohol is called piskani, and a few bottles in between them containing moderate contents of alcohol is rated good for consumption. For making the wine attractive in appearance, a small quantity of turmeric is hanged right at the mouth of the distillation set through which the distillate is collected. This makes the liquid a light but brilliantly shining yellow in colour.

SEZ (SEMI-FERMENTED FOOD)

The traditional semi-fermented food used by the Bhotiyas is called sez, it is made from rice, and is mostly used as a snacks. Earlier, it was a delicacy and was prepared only during certain festivals. In most cases, sez is extracted while preparation of rice jann. In the case of wine preparation the intermediate stage yielding sez is very unstable. The quantity of balam powder added is the determinant factor for the rate of fermentation.

In wine preparation quantity of balam used is maximum. Thus whenever extraction of sez is required the fermentation process has to be slowed down. To that effect a small quantity of balam powder is mixed with the substrate. Under a slow fermentation it becomes easy to intervene into the process removing the sez easily. Once sez has been removed fresh balam powder is added to hasten the process of fermentation so that jann or wine could be yielded.

PRODUCTION OF JANN, SEZ AND WINE FROM A COMMON CYCLE OF FERMENTATION

All the three different categories of fermented beverage and foods can be prepared from a common fermentation cycle, only when rice is used as substrate. Rice is first cooked or boiled in water for half an hour or until become soft and edible. This is then kept in a flat container to be drained off excess water and also to be cooled down. This boiled rice is mixed with balam powder.

The mixture is kept in an airtight container preferably in a dark and cool place. The container nowadays even plastic vessel is also used. After one or two days of fermentation, the sez is ready for consumption. The required quantity of sez could be removed at this stage. After that the container is again kept airtight for another five to ten days for further fermentation, then jann is produced. Jann is removed by filtration, i.e. by passing the content through a sieve or a piece of cloth. In the remaining mixture, jaggary and fresh balls of balam at a ratio of one ball per kg jaggary is added for the preparation of wine. The jaggary is boiled and cooled, and is mixed with balam powder. This is then added to the mixture and kept for fermentation in a tin container. Earthen ware is not used in wine preparation. The container set for fermentation is made air tight and kept in a warmer condition. Wine is produced within three to four days of fermentation. The emergence of this indigenous knowledge system in this part of high altitudes of the Himalaya was due to the cold climatic conditions of the Bhotiya dominated areas.

The way this society carved a niche in the making and living on the surrounding natural resources for adaptation to the emerging circumstances in the region. However, there is a shift in livings due to the intervention of outside forces, which have been damaging the traditional and self-sustaining systems in the name of development through introducing the outside made products. The indigenous knowledge of making fermented food and beverages developed over a long period of time. However, due to the expansion of road network and market forces, the availability of prepared yeast and modern liquor has changed the quality and quantity of indigenous fermented food and beverages. The age- old indigenous fermentation techniques should be encouraged as it led to the development of nutritious food items, which can cope up the inhospitable climatic conditions of high altitude areas.

ECOLOGY OF FERMENTED FOODS

Fermentation as an Ecological Process

The word ecology conjures images of the outdoors, and discussions of human food tend to focus on things we can see with the naked eye. We would like to highlight the importance of the indoor, microbial ecology of fermented foods, such as beer, cheese, bread, yogurt, and other foods which constitute documnet we describe fermentation as a human ecological process, and suggest that fermentation is a wonderful vehicle for teaching ecological concepts. Food fermentation is practiced by human cultures all over the world. It is a major component of human survival in places where preserved food is a necessity. Production of fermented food does not require knowledge of the biologicallymediated nature of fermentation, because the biota that carry out fermentation are present worldwide.

Fermentation organisms are ambient in the environment, whether humans make use of them or not. The relationships embodied in preserved foods can be treated as microbial ecosystems, sitting on countertops and stored in food cellars around the world. The main components of the fermentation ecosystem include: microbes, organic material to be fermented, a solution in which the fermentation takes place, a vessel with a controlled gate, and various tools which may be used to develop and monitor the fermentation. This is an ecosystem in that it is a complex of living and non-living components that are viewed in terms of their interactions in a specific place.

Beer biochemistry has recently been used to teach food chemistry but the emphasis in fermentation studies is usually on non-living chemical components. As suggested, treat the chemical pathways of microbial metabolism as a black box, in order to shift attention towards the interactions within the microbial environment. Knowledge of microbial metabolism is not necessary for the production of fermented foods, and indeed wasn't even proposed until 150 years ago. Yet evidence of controlled fermentations has been found at the earliest agricultural settlements in China, the Middle East and South America.

Today, all human cultures rely on fermented food products and the microbes that produce them. Fermentation is not only a component of human ecology, but also has an ecology of its own. Over the past 150 years, microbiologists have uncovered this unseen world of ecosystems that have always lived in our food. This document will introduce food fermentation as a human ecological process, with a focus on pickled foods, alcoholic beverages, microbial evolution and domestication.

Fermented Foods

Fermentation is a natural process that unavoidably affects the human food supply worldwide. Wild fermentation bacteria and yeast cover the continents and permeate ecosystems, in the air, soil, water, and guts of animals; they are a natural resource available to people all over the world. Although fermentation is everywhere, it is rarely understood. Fermentation is the microbially mediated conversion of sugars into products such as alcohol and lactic acid. When consumed by humans, fermented foods often introduce microflora that inhabit the human body. Many common foods contain fermentation microorganisms and their by-products. The word "fermentation" will be used simply to refer to the process by which alcohol or lactic acid are produced by living cells in solutions that contain sugars.

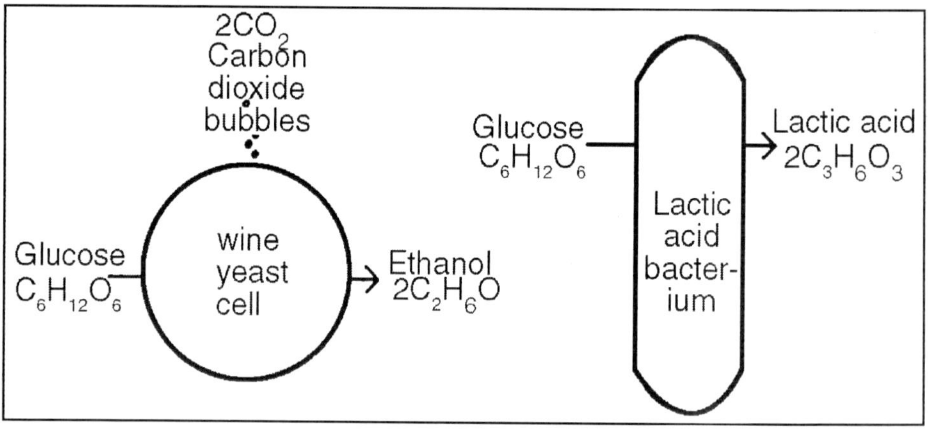

In order to focus attention to inter-special relationships, and relationships to the fermentation substrate, microbial metabolism is treated as a black box in this thesis. Alcoholic fermentation carried on by yeast and lactic acid fermentation carried on by bacteria are central to the fermentation of food and drink. Note: yeast and bacteria cells come in different sizes and shapes. There are two kingdoms of life in fermentation ecosystems: fungi and bacteria. Fermentation fungi include yeasts which produce alcoholic beverages and moulds. Fermentation bacteria are responsible for pickles, cheese, and cured sausages. Generally, yeasts are used to produce ethanol, and bacteria are used to produce lactic acid. There are exceptions: bread yeast is employed to produce carbon dioxide bubbles in leavened dough, and Gluconobacter is a genus of bacteria that can produce acetic acid. Fermented foods are generally produced using plant or animal ingredients in combination with fungi or bacteria which are either sourced from the environment, or carefully kept in cultures maintained by humans. Just as living organisms cover the surface of the earth, fermentation microbes cover the surface of the organisms. Wild yeasts are found living on grapes and bacteria line the human digestive tract. Kimchi, a spicy pickled food that Koreans eat at almost every meal, has scores, perhaps hundreds of species living in it and previously unknown species of bacteria are being discovered in Kimchi microflora. The ecology of fermented foods is still a frontier of discovery.

Ecosystem Succession in Pickled Foods

One can explore basic ecosystem processes in a kitchen or a classroom by making sauerkraut. Making sauerkraut involves a bacterial ecosystem succession in which each population of bacteria create the conditions for the bacteria to thrive.

Making sauerkraut is simple:

- Chop cabbage,
- Layer with salt,
- Weight down the cabbage and salt in a container.

Microbial ecosy stems that live a human households across the globs. In this tablespoons of salt is sufficient to pull the juices out of a gallon of chopped cabbage via osmosis. The salt must not contain iodine or other anti-caking agents. The vegetable juices mix with the salt to create a brine which inhibits the growth of putrefying organisms while creating prime conditions for the growth of Coliform bacteria, which are ubiquitous in the air. Call Coliform the "pioneer species" of the sauerkraut ecosystem. Coliform bacteria produce acids, lower the pH of the kraut, and set the stage for Leuconostoc bacteria to colonize the medium. The Leuconostoc bacteria lower the pH of the sauerkraut further still, thus creating the conditions for Lactobacillus to grow.

Lactobacillus adds the characteristic taste of lactic acid to the food, a smooth note in the otherwise tangy kraut. Lactic acid can create a temporary equilibrium state, which is the ultimate goal of food preservation via fermentation. Refrigeration halts the fermentation process. If left out in room temperature air, the kraut will get more acidic and sour, eventually reaching a point of inedibility.

This phenomenon is similar to the aging of mineral soils, which lose organic matter and become more acidic as the get older. Another way to explore the concept of ecological succession is to make cheese. Dairy fermentations involve the conversion of lactose to lactic acid through several successional phases. Raw milk, after it is collected, contains multiple bacterial populations. Fresh milk has a neutral pH and a warm temperature—perfect conditions for the rapid multiplication of Lactococcus bacteria. Lactococcus immediately begins producing lactic acid, lowering pH, and thus creating favourable conditions for the growth of Lactobacillus bacteria, which convert lactose to lactic acid and lower the pH further still.

By using up nutrients, lowering pH, and producing metabolic wastes, each microbe helps create conditions favourable for its successor. Many cheeses are also "surface ripened" by moulds, yeast, or other bacteria that significantly alter the flavour. Some yeasts may follow Lactobacillus and consume lactic acid. This is the end stage for some live-rind cheeses, whence the fermentation is halted.

The site-specific adaptation of wild microbes can be quite strong: in one study, when cheeses were innoculated with human-selected bacterial strains, the cheeses were actually ripened via a sequence of wild microflora ambient in the environment, who crowded out the introduced bacteria and rendered the innoculum superfluous. Cheese recipes stress the importance of controlled temperature, water content versus salt level, and storage location, which are effectively climate, moisture regime and geography of the dairy fermentation ecosystem. For centuries, cheese-makers have refined their methods of guiding the succession of bacteria and yeast that produce the best cheeses, by creating controlled conditions in which selection pressures determine microbe survival. Although the cheese-makers may have simply thought of themselves as altering temperature, water, and salt they were also altering microbial population growth dynamics, ecosystem species composition, and microbial survival, so that certain flavour compounds were produced in a stable manner. As such, this point of equilibrium was the ecological stopping point in the cheese succession—under proper conditions, a stable cheese can last for weeks, months, or even years, making the nutrition- value of the dairy product a longer—lasting alternative than it would be without the biological transformation.

The same equation roughly applies for all pickled foods and hard sausages: lactic acid fermentation generally involves reducing the amount of water in the food, increasing the amount of salt, and controlling temperature, such that the desired microorganisms lower pH and ultimately produce lactic acid, effectively preserving the food while producing otherwise unavailable flavours and nutritional compounds. Most lactic acid fermentations also produce a salty liquid solution which also may be considered a biologically active fermented food. This is in contrast to alcoholic fermentations in which the final product is usually dead.

Alcoholic Fermentation as a Natural Resource

Alcoholic fermentation ecosystems are dominated by one genus of yeast: Saccharomyces. Beers are produced by fermenting maltose from malted grains. Wines are produced by fermenting sugary fruit juices. Species of Saccharomyces are ambient in the environment, and are present on the skins of fruits such as ripe grapes. Old world grape wines were products of the native yeasts in their regional ecosystems. Modern oenology has shown that there is a succession of fermenting microorganisms, that yeast strain populations differ between batches and years, and wine quality is therefore vineyard and vintage dependent.

The wine yeasts can out-compete the pathogenic onslaught introduced during barefoot stomping without pasteurization, and produce a 12 per cent alcohol wine for the table. Domesticated Saccaromyces combined with different ingredients and environmental conditions, can be manipulated using simple equipment in a pedagogical setting to demonstrate environmental chemistry, population dynamics, nutrient limitation, and competition for finite resources. The components of a finished wine or beer include flavour compounds that also function as non-living chemical components of the fermentation environment.

Controlled alcoholic fermentation involves pasteurizing a sugary solution called a must, and then later adding selected strains of Saccaromyces to the cooled must to convert the sugar to alcohol. The different tastes of wines, ports, meads, beers, and distilled liquors comes from the different relative proportions of alcohol and the other compounds remaining in the final product, as a consequence of must preparation and yeast-strain selection.

Distinguishable flavour compounds include organic acids, esters, carbonyl compounds, sulfur compounds, and residual sugars. This is the environmental chemistry of the must, and there are several books that focus primarily on the chemistry aspects of alcoholic fermentation in relation to yeast activity. Experimental brewing is an application of Liebig's law of minimum. In nature Saccharomyces are limited by the unavailability of sugars. Home-scale alcoholic fermentations are often started by producing a "starter culture" in a plastic bottle consisting of sugar, fruit juice, and yeast. Adding a packet of wine yeast, beer yeast, or even bread yeast should work, because they are all the same species.

The yeast multiplies rapidly and begins releasing carbon dioxide and ethanol within a few hours. The CO2 must be released periodically or else the pressure will build up and burst the bottle. The goal of making a starter culture is to produce a large colony of live Saccharomyces to inoculate a must. The starter culture and the must both go through a climax stage known as high krausen when the maximum quantity of yeast cells is achieved. The goal of making a starter culture is to add it into the must during high krausen.

To demonstrate Liebig's law of minimum, an otherwise difficult to show environmental chemistry concept, alcoholic fermentations may be shown to be limited by the absence of other nutrients. Saccharomyces cannot live on sugar alone. To show, prepare a one gallon must of sugar dissolved in water, and add wine yeast to ferment the sugar. After a short flurry of activity, sugar water fermentations become stagnant or "stuck," as the microbial ecosystem is nutrient—limited. It may be possible to overcome stuck sugar water ferments by adding nutrients: a cup of fruit juice should suffice. One must be careful, however, not to add juice that contains potassium sorbate or excessive sulfites. These compounds are added to prevent commercial fruit juices from fermenting, and they will have the same effect on a must.

Fruits and grains have evolved mechanisms to prevent fermentation from taking place, and yeasts have evolved mechanisms to help them compete for sugars in short supply. For instance, there is a class of yeasts known as "killer yeasts". Killer yeasts are more competitive than other Saccharomyces strains; they use extra-cellular enzymes to kill other yeast strains and then proceed to scavenge the dead yeast for food. Since there is no primary production in the fermentation ecosystem, whatever carbon is added at the beginning is the maximum carbon that will be available for the duration of the fermentation. The yeasts are respiring CO2 out of the system, so it should not be surprising that some strains of yeast have evolved a tendency to predate other yeasts in order to win the competition for finite carbon. With unpasteurized musts, killer yeasts may be added to ensure speedy fermentations, as the killer yeasts also tend to work very quickly. In the absence of primary producers, the fermentation ecosystem is thus an ecosystem of consumers. Nutrient cycling, habitat/niche, and competition for resources may be demonstrated by manipulating the availability of nutrients provided at the outset by the humans who set up the system. Even without the killer yeasts, there is evident cycling of nutrients from dead yeast cells that settle at the bottom of the solution.

There are different fermentation "climates": ale yeasts prefer to ferment at 70°F, whereas lager yeasts do better around 55°F. Rhyzopus oligosporus can't ferment soybeans to tempeh unless it is very warm. The pods of coffee, chocolate, and vanilla beans are fermented outdoors in the sun in tropical parts of the world, and likely provide unique habitat to microbes that fulfil that role. In the absence of oxygen, yeasts ferment grape juice to wine, but in the presence of oxygen, acetic acid bacteria can oxidize the ethanol to acetic acid. These are the micro-environmental conditions of the fermentation food web.

Discussion

The concept of a whole ecosystem is unpopular in some circles and many have abandoned the idea that ecosystems have boundaries. For those who maintain that discrete ecosystems are useful, fermentation projects are an excellent illustration. A fermented food is easier to explain than a large ecosystem such as an archipelago, and it is more immediately useful as well.

Environmental education might do well to add a few fermentation projects to its repertory, even when the intention is to show the lack of autonomy of open biotic communities. San Francisco Sourdough cultures taken to other parts of the world lose their San Francisco flavour qualities after about six months, so a baker producing San Francisco Sourdough bread in New Jersey will have to constantly import new starter cultures to maintain the integrity of a San Francisco Sourdough bread operation. Tasting the fermented foods at different points in time allows for a primary experience of the link between flavour and an evolving biotic community of yeast populations. Where else do humans get to experience the tangible results of a biotic community changing over millions of generations in a short period of time? The repeated fermentation of a single food product in a given place over long periods of time is a process of domestication.

Registered appellations are a product of local yeasts, local soils, and local cave conditions that produce distinct regional wines, even when different regions are using the same grape cultivar. The same may be said for cheeses. For centuries, cheese-makers have domesticated the yeast strains that produce the best cheeses by creating controlled conditions in which human domestic selection pressures determine yeast survival. By altering salt, water, and temperature, cheese-makers were altering microbial environments, affecting microbial survival based on adaptation to the cheese-making processes over centuries. The influence of human choice over fermentation processes reveals different ecosystem responses to these perturbations. Indeed some fermented food cultures are themselves biodiverse, comprised of symbiotically associated bacteria and fungi.

Kefir is a fermented milk product in which lactose has been converted to alcohol and lactic acid. Kefir is produced by kefir "grains," which are tapioca- like colonies of bacteria and yeast. Recent studies have found kefir grains to include populations of Zygosaccharomyces, Candida, Leuconostoc, Lactococcus, Lactobacillus, and Cryptococcus, which grow differentially in successional phases. Adding kefir grains to milk produces a sour yogurt-like beverage within about 48 hours, and if the solution is sealed during fermentation it will develop effervescence. Complete kefir fermentation produces a lactose-free food that lactose-intolerant people can digest. Kefir is being investigated as a leavener for bread, a starter culture for cheeses and a source of kefiran, an insoluble polysaccharide with antibacterial and cicatrizing properties that show potential for use in medicine. Kefir is a stable probiotic food that may be kept for months without spoiling, and the kefir colonies provide a tangible, visible sense of the biodiversity that inhabit this fermented food. Kefir points to a means of solving environmental problems by using diversity instead of eliminating it. The ecology of fermented food can be considered as both a simple model and a domain of complex experimentation.

Fermented foods can be used to construct ecosystem demonstrations that are small-scale and short-term. Fermenting foods can be as easy as following a recipe and the illustration of distinct ecosystem concepts can be achieved by modifying one variable at a time. It is difficult to capture the essence of continental ecosystems, but it is easy to distinguish the boundary of a fermentation container, and to observe the processes taking place within those boundaries, on a microbiological scale.

These processes include, but are not limited to: effect of temperature/climate on species composition, effect of species composition on environmental chemistry, ecological succession and population dynamics such as competition, climax, and equilibrium, the concept of nutrient limitation, selection pressures, domestication, and biodiversity. The deliberate use of fermented foods shows how all life processes are inextricably linked with ecological processes, and that the patterns of culture which last the longest may be those that mimic the dynamics of ecosystems.

□

5

Biotechnological Applications of Enzymes for Food Processing

INTRODUCTION

Food processing enzymes are used as food additives to modify food properties like digestability, texture and shelf life. Major enzymes used in the food industry are for starch liquefaction, saccharification and isomerization reaction. Food Processing enzymes are used in meat processing, dairy industry and in manufacture of pre-digested foods. Enzymes are also used for natural breaking of large sized molecules of carbohydrates, fats and proteins, in fermentation and preparing predigested protein food or preparing amino- acids and specialty foods.

The project discussed in this chapter envisages setting up of a food processing enzyme unit in the state of Gujarat.

MARKET AND GROWTH DRIVERS

The global market for food processing enzymes in 2002 was approximately US $700 million that increased to US $740 million in the year 2004. Food and feed enzymes together had nearly 45 per cent share, followed by industrial enzymes which are used in the detergent industry.

In terms of value, this is contributing approx. US $450 million in the world enzyme market estimated at US $1000 million by the year 2005. However, food processing enzymes find limited applications in India and hence its market also has remained un-tapped till date. Enzymes for food and feed processing industries contribute almost 17 per cent to the Indian market. In recent years, the trend is changing with globalization of food processing industry in India, Food processing enzyme market is fast growing in diverse applications. Biocon Ltd and Novozymes are the two prominent players in the Indian food processing enzymes industry, their sales turnover for 2003-04 and 2004-05 and growth rate is summarized here below:

Table: Sales INR in Millions

Sr. No.	Name of Company	2003-2004	2004-05	Growth (%)
1.	Biocon Ltd.	5020.0	6464.0	29
2.	Novozymes Bangalore	530.0	690.0	30

Growth Drivers

- Population growth, urbanization and rising income levels have increased demand on food items with its spill-over effect seen on the growth of demand of food products and this in turn has spurred the demand of food enzymes in India.
- Technical innovation in enzymatic food processing is a major growth driver for this segment.
- The fast changing food habits, increased use of fast foods, modified foods and instant foods are other drivers for demand of food processing enzymes.
- Health food is a sunrise industry in India and also globally, where food processing enzymes find wider application in manufacturing of these products.

Technology/Process

Fermentation

- Fermentation of a selected microorganism under sterile conditions.
- Production of the desired enzyme by consumption of carbohydrates, proteins, salts, water and energy
- Transfer of the fermented broth to recovery.

Recovery

- Filtration of the fermentation broth.
- Purification of the liquid phase containing the enzyme.
- Concentration of the liquid enzyme to desired enzymatic activity.
- Stabilization and standardization of a liquid product.
- Standardization of a liquid concentrate for granulation.

Granulation

- Formulation and standardization of the enzyme into solid granules to encapsulate the enzyme.
- Providing the right property to the product.
- Preparation of source materials for enzyme extraction of food processing enzymes using physical/ chemical processes.
- Production of food processing enzyme using physical/ chemical/ bio-tech processes.
- Purification process quality control checks packing in air tight bulk packing.

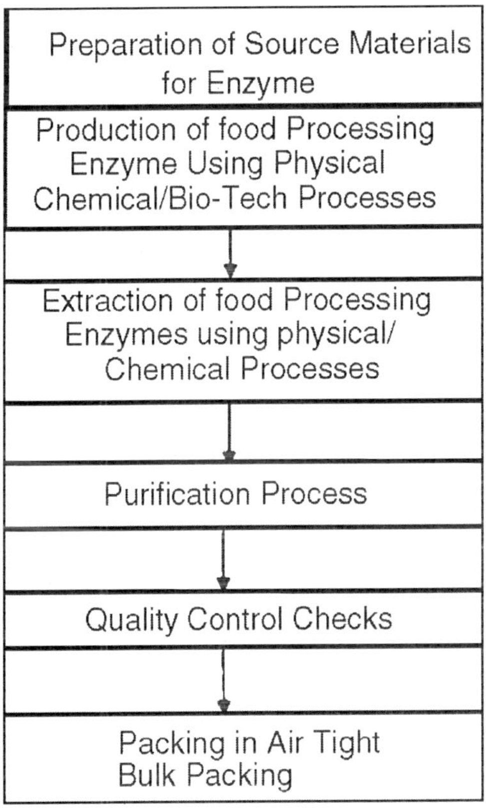

Raw Materials

Food processing enzymes are produced, mostly using all natural materials as source of raw materials. Now, these enzymes are produced in bulk using fermentation techniques-both with solid state and submerge culture in modern process of manufacturing.

In the following Table particulars of various food processing enzymes, their source and applications are summarized:

Table: Food Processing Enzyme—Source and Their Application

Sr. No.	Enzyme	Source	Applications
1.	L-amylase, Bacterial	B.subtillis/ B.licheniformis	Starch conversion
2.	L-amylase, fungal	Aspergillus oryzae	Maltogenic Saccharufucatuib
3.	Amylogluco-sidedase	Aspergillus nigar var,	Starch syringes dextrose, foods
4.	B-Glucanase	B.subtillis/ Peni-cillium emersonil	Brewing and food processing
5.	Neutral protease	B.subtillis	Brewing/ flavouring
6.	Neutral protene	Aspergillus oryzae	Baking
7.	Cellulase	Trochoderma Spp	Cellulose hydrolysis
8.	Invertase	Yeast SPP	Confectionary
9.	Pectinase processing	A.niger	Fruit/wine
10.	Papain	Papaya latex	Meat processing
11.	Rennet	Mucor Spp	Dairy industry
12.	Glucose isome-	Strep Spp	High fructose corn syrup
13.	Lipasa	Mucor arase Spp/ Aspergillus	Dairy Indus/ Fat splitting
14.	Lactase	S.Lactis	Dairy industry
15.	Hemicellulase	A.niger	Baking, fruits, gums
16.	Glucose oxidase	A.niger	Analytical, food processing
17.	Catalase	A.niger	Analytical, food processing

SUGGESTED PLANT CAPACITY AND PROJECT COST

Capacity – 360 Tonnes per annum.

Capital cost is estimated to be INR 50 million.

Table: Estimated Project Cost and Means of Finance

Sr. No.	Cost of project	INR in Millions
1	Land and Land Development	3.60
2	Building and Civil Works.	6.75
3	Plant and Machinery	23.00

4	Misc. Fixed Assets	3.10
5	Preliminary and Pre-operative	4.00
6	Provision for Contingencies	2.70
	Total Fixed Assets	43.55
7	Margin Money for Working Capital	6.45
	Total	50.00
	Means of Finance	
8	Promoters Contribution	16.50
9	Term Loan	33.50
	Total	**50.00**

The proposed project will require approx 6,000 sq. mt. of land with an proposed built up area of 1,500 sq. mt. The unit is proposed to have an installed capacity of 360 TPA. The total fixed cost of the project is estimated at INR 43.55 and INR 6.45 million is the working capital margin which adds up to block capital cost of INR 50.00 million. The unit being proposed to cater to domestic as well as international demand is suggested to have a debt-equity ratio of 2:1. Thus, the estimated term loan amounts to INR 33.50 million and equity at INR 16.50 million.

PLANT AND MACHINERY

The list of main plant and machinery and utility equipments is as mentioned below:

Table: List of Main Plant and Machinery

Sr. No	Particulars	Quantity	Supplier
1.	Preparatory for Enzyme source material including and particle classifier	1 Set	Goldin India equipment Pvt. Ltd., Vadodara Pulverizer, Sifter Riddhi Pharma Machinery Ltd., Mumbai
2.	Fermentor for Enzyme 5000 Letre	2	Alfa-Laval India Ltd., Pune
3.	Glasslined reactors for Enzyme separation Mumbai	2	Gammon India Ltd.,
4.	Steam Distillation Column	2	Dipesh Engineering Works, Mumbai Enzyme Extractor

6	Solvent extraction	1	Desmet Chemfoods equipments India Pvt.Ltd., Mumbai
7.	Enzyme separation	1	Ion Exchange India column Ltd., Mumbai
8.	Basket centrifuges separation	3	Sukhras Machines for final product Pvt. Ltd., Mumbai
9.	Hot air dryer with hot air generator for final product drying	1	Aerotherm India P.Ltd., Ahmedabad
10.	Bag filling and sealing	3	SPA International, Machines Deonar, Mumbai
11.	Oil fired steam gen-eration unit	1	Thermax Ltd., Pune
12.	HT/LT Electrification power	Lot	Kirloskar Electricals and DG set for standby Ltd, Mumbai

UTILITIES

The unit will require utilities in the form of electricity and low pressure steam from non-IBR steam generating mini boiler. The unit will require approx. 220 KVA power and approx. 500 kg steam per hour for the proposed installed capacity of 360 MT/ per annum.

MANPOWER

The proposed project will have manpower requirement of 35 persons which is of two types, technical and non-technical. The proposed food processing enzyme unit will require 4 functional managerial persons, 1 personnel cum administrative manager, 10 technical and 15 non-technical persons, 5 office staff.

SUGGESTED LOCATION

The preferred location for the proposed project is Central and South Gujarat areas close to urban centres, like Ahmedabad, Gandhinagar, Vadodara, Surat and Valsad districts.

PROJECT TIME LINE

The proposed project will have project time line of 5 to 6 months for obtaining various clearances and it will require 10- 12 months for implementation subject to availability of required permission, approvals and resources.

FINANCIAL INDICATORS

Based on the profitability projections worked out for the proposed project, key financial indicators are as summarized below:

Table: Key Financial Indicators

Sr. No	Financial Ratios	1st Year	2nd Year	3rd Year
A	Break-Even Point in% capacity	42.97	38.84	35.47
B	Debt-service Coverage Ratio	1.64	2.26	3.04
C	Average DSCR		2.31	
D	Return on Invest-ment (ROI)	17.66	20.08	22.49
E	IRR		17%	

As perceived from the project cost and means of finance table, the suggested Debt-Equity Ratio for the proposed project is 2:1. The IRR for the proposed unit is approx. 17 per cent projected for a period of 10 years.

CLEARANCE REQUIRED

The proposed unit will have to register itself with Secretariat of Industrial Approvals, Ministry of Industries and Government of India, by filing Industrial Entrepreneur's Memorandum, as it will have plant and machinery investment of more than INR 10 million.

The proposed unit is for manufacturing for food processing enzymes which are critical inputs for the consuming industries. There is fast growing demand of food processing enzymes in the global market and the project envisages export to advanced countries like USA, Canada, UK, Europe and Australia. The unit will require to register their products with Food and Drugs Administration in these countries, apart from registration with Indian and state food administration. The most critical aspect of this product will be its shelf life for export consumers and hence it is critical to meet FDA regulations in consuming countries and Codex standards followed by them. The unit will get EOU registration from RBI, DGFT and with APEDA as registered manufacturer exporter to avail export incentives. Being an exporting unit it will have to follow strict quality standards as accepted in the countries where export is to be made. Indian FDA authorities have laid down standards for food additives including food processing enzymes which will be followed by the proposed unit. It is obligatory to meet provisions under the PFA act for all ingredients and quality aspects for marketing the product in the Indian market.

□

6

Managing Quality and Safety

WHAT IS QUALITY?

The domain of the quality professional has changed. From its humble beginnings in manufacturing, it is now expected, along with other infrastructure professions, such as IT, HR and finance, to contribute at the organisational level. Unlike those other professions, quality expertise can be hard to define, perhaps because there are many views of what business-level quality means. David Straker considers current definitions of 'quality' and offers a new one, considering its ramifications for the quality profession.

At its simplest level, quality answers two questions: 'What is wanted?' and 'How do we do it?' Accordingly, quality's stomping ground has always been the area of processes. From the bread and butter of ISO 9000, to the heady heights of TQM, quality professionals specify, measure, improve and re- engineer processes to ensure that people get what they want.

SO WHERE ARE WE NOW?

There are as many definitions of quality as there are quality consultants, but commonly accepted variations include:

- 'Conformance to requirements' - Crosby
- 'Fitness for use' - Juran
- 'The totality of characteristics of an entity that bear on its ability to satisfy stated and implied need' - ISO 8402:1994
- Quality models for business, including the Deming Prize, the EFQM excellence model and the Baldrige award SO WHAT IS WRONG?

Philip Crosby's definition is easily toppled: if requirements are wrong, then failure is guaranteed. His focus is the domain of QA where, without a specification, quality cannot be measured and thus controlled. You cannot have zero defects if you do not have a standard against which to measure defectiveness.

This reflects the early days, where quality was clearly about product. Quality control, and later QA, was our domain - we didn't care about customers; the research and design department was responsible for designing the job and sales and marketing for selling it. But those halcyon days of definitive specifications and jobs for life are long gone.

Though Juran takes a step further down the value chain, to the use of the product or service, he still presupposes that we can fully understand how the product will be used, which is a great challenge. As Deming himself said, some things are 'unknown and unknowable'.

ISO 8402 recognises this uncertainty with its 'implied need'. It uses the word 'entity' as opposed to the 'product or service' definition of its earlier version, indicating a broadening uncertainty. Nonetheless, it suffers again from a simplistic, single-minded focus - all we need to do is to figure out what is wanted and then deliver it.

The quality models are a step further into broader business. Here, although processes are important, quality is much more about people: customers are there, but so too are stakeholders - employees, partners, suppliers, shareholders and society. Perhaps wisely, the models avoid nailing down a specific definition of quality, leaving us without a definition that encompasses a broader business view.

ISO9000:2000 steps in this direction also, talking about 'customer and other interested parties', but leaves the definition of quality at a rather generalised 'degree to which a set of inherent characteristics fulfils requirements'.

Initial Problems

Let's face it, quality is difficult to define. We want to be precise, to create a quality definition, yet language is limited. Nor does it help that our domain has expanded from the relatively- constrained factory floor into the open realms of a broader business context, and beyond that, to environmental and social domains.

The difficulty of naming quality. In the end, it plumps for a customer focus of quality that ranges throughout the product/service chain: this is still is not enough.

The perception of 'quality' as almost impossible to define, is not confined to our profession; in 'The Timeless Way of Building', architect Christopher Alexander calls it 'the quality without a name'. In the same way that we know a good room when we use one, but cannot define exactly what makes it good, we can name its attributes of quality, but cannot define quality itself. One way to find a good definition of anything is to take a broader view. Alexander does this in his definition of a 'pattern language' for architecture, which reduces the whole of building and town design to 252 simple rule-sets. So can we find a new definition for quality by looking at the bigger picture?

A New Beginning

Now for the audacious part: having knocked the existing definitions of quality and acknowledged that definition is not easy, let's try it nonetheless. In the words of Susan Jeffers, we should 'feel the fear and do it anyway'. The focus of our definition will remain in the general business arena. This is where most of us make our living. What if we follow the early quality mandate and ensure that we meet requirements? Of course, we can go out of business by producing goods that do not sell. So, strike the product/ requirements-only focus.

What if we gave customers everything they wanted? What if they were totally delighted? Sounds good. But what if it cost us so much that we failed to make a profit? Again, we would go out of business. We need customers and products and services to satisfy them, but this is not enough. Why are businesses started? - To meet the needs of the people who start them, of course. So we must also meet the needs of the owners of companies, not all of whom are interested solely in money. Bill Hewlett and Dave Packard started HP to make a difference to society while having fun with the electronic engineering that was their passion. But they were aware that they had to make a profit to pay for their higher goals. Public companies are less egalitarian and have to toe the line that analysts and shareholders demand, which means a return on investment.

Effectiveness and efficiency are words we often use to define quality. Effectiveness is about meeting requirements, usually of customers. Efficiency is doing this at a minimal cost, which meets shareholders' needs. Could we just focus on these? Skip the carpets and cafeterias; pay people the absolute minimum. Perhaps not, as in these times of hyper-competitiveness and scarce talent, your people are your most important asset. Employees have both needs and legs, and if the former are not met, the latter get into action; when you ask too much of your people, those with 'get up and go' are the first to do just that. We can be effective and efficient and still go out of business as our best employees leave and the rest repay our lack of care for them with a lack of care for us.

There are still people who can drive us out of business, from uncooperative suppliers and partners to environmental pressure groups and punitive governments. Where is the common thread? The phrase most commonly heard is 'going out of business'. Deming recognised this when he pointed out that survival is optional.

Testing The Definition

A good definition will withstand all kinds of serious criticism. What about those people who need things? Staying in business means keeping them all reasonably happy, so this works. What about growth? This is an interesting question: why do so many companies seek to grow constantly? If shareholders demand growth, and will take their money elsewhere otherwise, then it is still about staying in business. If our competitors grow, we need to grow to stay in the game.

Growth can be a management trap: If it leads to over-extension or unmanageable diversity, such that the business fails, this is not a quality situation. To quote Ricardo Semler1: 'The biggest myth in the corporate world is that every business needs to keep growing to be successful. That's baloney. The ultimate measure of a business' success is not how big it gets, but how long it survives.'

One of the frustrations we meet in quality is the focus on longer-term company survival; we know that products containing defects will lead to dissatisfied customers. We know that incomplete customer knowledge impairs our ability to correct external problems and repair internal processes. But we come up constantly against managers who are working on short-term problems, such as getting a delivery out today or pacifying an angry customer on the phone. So who is right, given our new definition of quality? The answer is both. Our perspectives may be different and we can both benefit from sharing one another's concerns, but we both want to stay in business, which means focusing on both the short- and long-term.

How do We Stay in Business?

If quality means staying in business, how do we do that? Perhaps there is no single, simple answer, but by exploring the issue, including going back-to- basics, we can take a few steps in the right direction.

WHAT IS BUSINESS?

While we are rushing in where angels fear to tread, perhaps we should scrutinise what we mean by 'business'. Business is not so much barter as value exchange. If business were just about customers and ourselves, it would be easy. We would find what they wanted, make it and sell it to them. But it is not that simple: our problems begin when we find we are at the crossroads of many exchanges of value. There are shareholders, employees, customers, suppliers, partners and governments, all engaged in a complex web of value exchange.

To make things worse, we cannot make all of the people happy all the time. With a limited pool of resources, we try to keep customers happy, while being profitable enough for shareholders, while paying our suppliers, while paying for the new employee rest rooms. Sorry folks, but there is not enough cash to go around. Like any paymaster, as suggested, need to make some tough decisions.

Staying in business then, means playing a dynamic balancing game, optimising value exchange, with an awareness of the very real resource limitations with which we work. This gives us a second level of detail we can use for our quality definition:

What does this Mean for Quality?

Casting a keen quality eye over this revised definition may lead to a certain queasiness. Optimising means making compromises but we have technology: remember Mr Pareto and his law, and Juran's 'vital few'. We are not counting defects but units of value, in terms of value created and of the levels and types of value required to keep each player in the game.

A simple conceptual model is to imagine everyone putting coins into a central pot and then taking them out again at a later time. As long as there is money in the pot, and there are people to play, the game continues. Staying in business means keeping the game going.

A consideration within this game is that some players can easily leave. When they are critical value contributors, they can demand a higher level of value in return. This can lead to low-value customers which many of us tolerate under the 'customer is always right' banner. What we sometimes forget is that if someone is taking too much out of the pot, they can be asked to leave.

If quality is making this game work, then quality professionals need to understand the game. It does not mean abandoning our concern for customers and products: far from it. But it does mean optimising the system so that the whole thing continues to operate. Blind quality is what killed TQM in many companies. Why should I map my processes? - Because it is the right thing to do. Why do I need to empower everyone? - Because it works. The revised view of quality proposed here pushes against such mantras. Thus, one more defining statement is:

If we are to accept this definition, the most important result is that it changes the what we must do as quality professionals. We mustperformanceon the words: understanding, optimising, system, value and exchange. It means understanding how things truly work, both individually and as systems. It means understanding people, what they value and how they effectively trade with others. And it means working out how these imperfect systems can be optimised so our businesses thrive.

An ancient Chinese emperor once asked his wise counsellor's advice for the greatest thing that could happen. The counsellor said: 'Grandfather dies, father dies, son dies.' The emperor was shocked at such a morbid suggestion until he realised that changing this sequence would bring a far greater sadness. The same applies to our companies, which are often much like our children. We can change and advise them in many ways, but the greatest thing we can do is to give them the strength to outlive us.

QUALITY CONTROL

Quality control is a process employed to ensure a certain level of quality in a product or service. It may include whatever actions a business deems necessary to provide for the control and verification of certain characteristics of a product or service. The basic goal of quality control is to ensure that the products, services, or processes provided meet specific requirements and are dependable, satisfactory, and fiscally sound.

Essentially, quality control involves the examination of a product, service, or process for certain minimum levels of quality. The goal of a quality control team is to identify products or services that do not meet a company's specified standards of quality. If a problem is identified, the job of a quality control team or professional may involve stopping production temporarily. Depending on the particular service or product, as well as the type of problem identified, production or implementation may not cease entirely.

Usually, it is not the job of a quality control team or professional to correct quality issues. Typically, other individuals are involved in the process of discovering the cause of quality issues and fixing them. Once such problems are overcome, the product, service, or process continues production or implementation as usual.

Quality control can cover not just products, services, and processes, but also people. Employees are an important part of any company. If a company has employees that don't have adequate skills or training, have trouble understanding directions, or are misinformed, quality may be severely diminished. When quality control is considered in terms of human beings, it concerns correctable issues. However, it should not be confused with human resource issues. Often, quality control is confused with quality assurance. Though the two are very similar, there are some basic differences. Quality control is concerned with the product, while quality assurance is process– oriented.

Even with such a clear-cut difference defined, identifying the differences between the two can be hard. Basically, quality control involves evaluating a product, activity, process, or service. By contrast, quality assurance is designed to make sure processes are sufficient to meet objectives. Simply put, quality assurance ensures a product or service is manufactured, implemented, created, or produced in the right way; while quality control evaluates whether or not the end result is satisfactory.

Importance

Successful businesses inevitably place great emphasis on managing quality control - carefully planned steps taken to ensure that the products and services offered to their customers are consistent and reliable and truly meet their customers' needs.

Multinational corporations have entire departments of highly trained specialists to design and implement their quality assurance programmes. For a custom countertop fabricator, as for other small businesses that make unique, handcrafted products, quality control is also essential.

Such companies cannot rely on a staff of trained experts or the standardization inherent in mass production to take care of quality control. One or a handful of managers must handle it themselves, along with every other management function.

That is part of being a small business person. It is all too often true, though, that fabricators fail to institute their own carefully planned quality control procedures. I would like to suggest a few simple steps that can help a countertop fabricator or any similar small business improve the quality of its products and services.

It is said that when the Japanese business that later became Sony Corporation was founded, the co-founder Mr. Ibuka established the company philosophy by stating that "If it were possible to establish conditions where persons could become united with a firm spirit of teamwork and exercise to their hearts' desire their technological capacity, then such an organization could bring untold pleasure and untold benefits." For decades, Japanese businesses have pioneered management techniques intended to improve quality continuously. American and European companies have spent years catching up.

Modern computer communication gives even the smallest business the means to rapidly access information and advice through the Internet. For those interested in developing or improving a quality control programme.

Forsberg's brief summary of quality management principles follows:

- *Principle 1:*
  - Customer:Focused Organization. Organiz-ations depend on their customers and therefore should understand current and future customer needs, meet customer requirements, and strive to exceed customer expectations.

- *Principle 2:*
  - Leadership: Leaders establish unity of purpose, direction, and the internal environment of an organization. They create that environment in which people can become fully involved in achieving the organization's objectives.
- *Principle 3:*
  - Involvement of People: People at all levels are the essence of an organization and their full involvement enables their abilities to be used for the organization's benefit.
- *Principle 4:*
  - Process Approach: A desired result is achieved more efficiently when related resources and activities are managed as a process.
- *Principle 5:*
  - System Approach to Management: Identifying, understanding, and managing a system of interrelated processes for a given objective contributes to the effectiveness and efficiency of the organization.
- *Principle 6:*
  - Continual Improvement: Continual improvement is a permanent objective of the organization.
- *Principle 7:*
  - Factual Approach to Decision Making: Effective decisions and actions are based on the logical and intuitive analysis of data and information.
- *Principle 8:*
  - Mutually Beneficial Supplier Relationships: Mutually beneficial relationships between the organization and its supplier enhance the ability of both organizations to create value.

Let me suggest a few programmes that countertop fabricators can implement, guided by these principles, to improve quality and customer satisfaction: Call each and every customer a few days after completion of an installation to ask whether the customer is fully satisfied. performancepromptly to resolve customer concerns. Enclose a brief survey form with the final invoice requesting information on the customer's opinions and expectations. Listen with great care to every one of your customer's ideas and suggestions, and thank them for their input.

All management personnel, starting with the owner, must understand and agree that quality management is essential to the success of the business. Once that agreement has been reached, every employee must be involved in the process. All too often, employees are reluctant to report quality problems, feeling that they would be"rocking the boat" or seen as criticizing co-workers to management. Every effort must be made to convince each employee that jobs and prosperity depend on quality products and services, and that teamwork and cooperation are essential in ensuring quality.

Every process required to satisfy a customer needs to be analysed with the goal of improving customer satisfaction. Profitability will inevitably follow. Functions such as sales, extending credit, ordering materials, measuring and templating, shop fabrication, delivery, installation, billing and collection can't be seen as separate, unrelated functions. Problems resulting in customer dissatisfaction or financial losses most often occur when information is being passed from one such process to another. Special care must be taken to ensure that every process connects reliably to the adjacent processes. Most thoughtful analysis should be lavished on any chronic problem areas. For example, if several customers have recently complained about visible seams, then the whole process of assembling seams needs to be analysed in detail, with absolutely nothing taken for granted. An itemized checklist identifying every conceivable factor that could affect seam quality should be developed, with actual observations being made every step along the way. This sort of systematic approach will help develop effective solutions much more quickly and reliably than more haphazard methods.

The attitude that says,"We've always done it that way" is the enemy of continuous quality improvement. Instead, every employee should be encouraged to think,"There is no aspect of how we do our jobs that can't be improved in some way. Together, let's figure out how to do it."

Keep accurate records, and more importantly, analyse that data. Again, in this era of sophisticated $2,000 computers, not even the smallest business has any excuse to avoid analyzing factual information that can be used to improve the quality of its products and services. Job costing is the basic function that is still ignored by many fabricators who bid based on what they think their competitors will bid, rather than on their actual history of costs in completing similar projects. When you can quickly quote an accurate, competitive price on custom work, you are providing an important aspect of quality to your customer - and an assurance that you will remain in business as a profit-making venture able to meet their needs in years to come.

Rely on the training and technical support offered by the manufacturers of your materials and machinery. Read the technical bulletins and manuals, attend and stay awake during the seminars, view the videos, and listen carefully to what their sales representatives have to tell you. Your suppliers are part of the team that enables you to satisfy the needs of your customers.

QUALITY MANAGEMENT

Quality management can be considered to have three main components: quality control, quality assurance and quality improvement. Quality management is focused not only on product quality, but also the means to achieve it. Quality management therefore uses quality assurance and control of processes as well as products to achieve more consistent quality.

Quality Management Evolution

Quality management is a recent phenomenon. Advanced civilizations that supported the arts and crafts allowed clients to choose goods meeting higher quality standards than normal goods. In societies where [[art] responsibilities of a master craftsman was to lead their studio, train and supervise the on, the importance of craftsmen was diminished as mass production and repetitive work practices were instituted. The aim was to produce large numbers of the same goods. The first proponent in the US for this approach was Eli Whitney who proposed parts manufacture for muskets, hence producing the identical components and creating a musket assembly line. The next step forward was promoted by several people including Frederick Winslow Taylor a mechanical engineer who sought to improve industrial efficiency.

He is sometimes called"the father of scientific management." He was one of the intellectual leaders of the Efficiency Movement and part of his approach laid a further foundation for quality management, including aspects like standardization and adopting improved practices. Henry Ford also was important in bringing process and quality management practices into operation in his assembly lines. In Germany, Karl Friedrich Benz, often called the inventor of the motor car, was pursuing similar assembly and production practices, although real mass production was properly initiated in Volkswagen after World War II. From this period onwards, North American companies focused predominantly upon production against lower cost with increased efficiency.

Walter A. Shewhart made a major step in the evolution towards quality management by creating a method for quality control for production, using statistical methods, first proposed in 1924. This became the foundation for his ongoing work on statistical quality control. W. Edwards Deming later applied statistical process control methods in the United States during

World War II, thereby successfully improving quality in the manufacture of munitions and other strategically important products.

Quality leadership from a national perspective has changed over the past five to six decades. After the second world war, Japan decided to make quality improvement a national imperative as part of rebuilding their economy, and sought the help of Shewhart, Deming and Juran, amongst others. W. Edwards Deming championed Shewhart's ideas in Japan from 1950 onwards. He is probably best known for his management philosophy establishing quality, productivity, and competitive position. He has formulated 14 points of attention for managers, which are a high level abstraction of many of his deep insights.

They should be interpreted by learning and understanding the deeper insights and include:

- Break down barriers between departments
- Management should learn their responsibilities, and take on leadership
- Improve constantly
- Institute a programme of education and self-improvement

In the 1950s and 1960s, Japanese goods were synonymous with cheapness and low quality, but over time their quality initiatives began to be successful, with Japan achieving very high levels of quality in products from the 1970s onward. For example, Japanese cars regularly top the J.D. Power customer satisfaction ratings.

In the 1980s Deming was asked by Ford Motor Company to start a quality initiative after they realised that they were falling behind Japanese manufacturers. A number of highly successful quality initiatives have been invented by the Japanese. Many of the methods not only provide techniques but also have associated quality culture. These methods are now adopted by the same western countries that decades earlier derided Japanese methods.

Customers recognize that quality is an important attribute in products and services. Suppliers recognize that quality can be an important differentiator between their own offerings and those of competitors. In the past two decades this quality gap has been greatly reduced between competitive products and services.

This is partly due to the contracting of manufacture to countries like India and China, as well internationalization of trade and competition. These countries amongst many others have raised their own standards of quality in order to meet International standards and customer demands. The ISO 9000 series of standards are probably the best known International standards for quality management.

In recent times some themes have become more significant including quality culture, the importance of knowledge management, and the role of leadership in promoting and achieving high quality. Disciplines like systems thinking are bringing more holistic approaches to quality so that people, process and products are considered together rather than independent factors in quality management.

The influence of quality thinking has spread to non-traditional applications outside of walls of manufacturing, extending into service sectors and into areas such as sales, marketing and customer service.

Quality Improvement

There are many methods for quality improvement. These cover product improvement, process improvement and people based improvement.

In the following list are methods of quality management and techniques that incorporate and drive quality improvement:

- **ISO 9004:2008:** Guidelines for performance improvement.
- **ISO 15504-4: 2005:** Information technology—process assessment: Guidance on use for process improvement and process capability determination.
- QFD: Quality function deployment, also known as the house of quality approach.
- **Kaizen:** Japanese for change for the better; the common English term is continuous improvement.
- Zero Defect Programme: Created by NEC Corporation of Japan, based upon statistical process control and one of the inputs for the inventors of Six Sigma.
- **Six Sigma:** 6σ, Six Sigma combines established methods such as statistical process control, design of experiments and FMEA in an overall framework.
- **PDCA:** Plan, do, check, act cycle for quality control purposes.
- **Quality circle:** A group approach to improvement.
- Taguchi methods: Statistical oriented methods including quality robustness, quality loss function, and target specifications.
- **The Toyota Production System:** Reworked in the west into lean manufacturing.
- **Kansei Engineering:** An approach that focuses on capturing customer emotional feedback about products to drive improvement.
- **TQM:** Total quality management is a management strategy aimed at embedding awareness of quality in all organizational processes.

First promoted in Japan with the Deming prize which was adopted and adapted in USA as the Malcolm Baldrige National Quality Award and in Europe as the European Foundation for Quality Management award.

- **TRIZ:** Meaning "theory of inventive problem solving"
- **BPR:** Business process reengineering, a management approach aiming at 'clean slate' improvements.
- **OQM:** Object Oriented Quality Management, a model for quality management.

Proponents of each approach have sought to improve them as well as apply them for small, medium and large gains. Simple one is Process Approach, which forms the basis of ISO 9001:2008 Quality Management System standard, duly driven from the 'Eight principles of Quality managagement', process approach being one of them.

Thareja writes about the mechanism and benefits: "The process may be limited in words, but not in its applicability. While it fulfills the criteria of all- round gains: in terms of the competencies augmented by the participants; the organisation seeks newer directions to the business success, the individual brand image of both the people and the organisation, in turn, goes up.

The competencies which were hitherto rated as being smaller, are better recognized and now acclaimed to be more potent and fruitful ". The more complex Quality improvement tools are tailored for enterprise types not originally targeted. For example, Six Sigma was designed for manufacturing but has spread to service enterprises. Each of these approaches and methods has met with success but also with failures.

Some of the common differentiators between success and failure include commitment, knowledge and expertise to guide improvement, scope of change/improvement desired and adaption to enterprise cultures. For example, quality circles do not work well in every enterprise and relatively few TQM-participating enterprises have won the national quality awards.

There have been well publicized failures of BPR, as well as Six Sigma. Enterprises therefore need to consider carefully which quality improvement methods to adopt, and certainly should not adopt all those listed here.

It is important not to underestimate the people factors, such as culture, in selecting a quality improvement approach. Any improvement takes time to implement, gain acceptance and stabilize as accepted practice. Improvement must allow pauses between implementing new changes so that the change is stabilized and assessed as a real improvement, before the next improvement is made.

Improvements that change the culture take longer as they have to overcome greater resistance to change. It is easier and often more effective to work within the existing cultural boundaries and make small improvements than to make major transformational changes. Use of Kaizen in Japan was a major reason for the creation of Japanese industrial and economic strength.

On the other hand, transformational change works best when an enterprise faces a crisis and needs to make major changes in order to survive. In Japan, the land of Kaizen, Carlos Ghosn led a transformational change at Nissan Motor Company which was in a financial and operational crisis. Well organized quality improvement programmes take all these factors into account when selecting the quality improvement methods.

Quality Standards

The International Organization for Standardization created the Quality Management System standards in 1987. They were the ISO 9000:1987 series of standards comprising ISO 9001:1987, ISO 9002:1987 and ISO 9003:1987; which were applicable in different types of industries, based on the type of activity or process: designing, production or service delivery.

The standards are reviewed every few years by the International Organization for Standardization. The version in 1994 was called the ISO 9000:1994 series; comprising of the ISO 9001:1994, 9002:1994 and 9003:1994 versions.

The last major revision was in the year 2008 and the series was called ISO 9000:2000 series. The ISO 9002 and 9003 standards were integrated into one single certifiable standard: ISO 9001:2008. After December 2003, organizations holding ISO 9002 or 9003 standards had to complete a transition to the new standard.

ISO released a minor revision, ISO 9001:2008 on 14 October 2008. It contains no new requirements. Many of the changes were to improve consistency in grammar, facilitating translation of the standard into other languages for use by over 950,000 certified organisations in the 175 countries that use the standard.

The ISO 9004:2000 document gives guidelines for performance improvement over and above the basic standard. This standard provides a measurement framework for improved quality management, similar to and based upon the measurement framework for process assessment.

The Quality Management System standards created by ISO are meant to certify the processes and the system of an organization, not the product or service itself. ISO 9000 standards do not certify the quality of the product or service.

In 2005 the International Organization for Standardi-zation released a standard, ISO 22000, meant for the food industry. This standard covers the values and principles of ISO 9000 and the HACCP standards. It gives one single integrated standard for the food industry and is expected to become more popular in the coming years in such industry.

ISO has also released standards for other industries. For example Technical Standard TS 16949 defines requirements in addition to those in ISO 9001:2008 specifically for the automotive industry. ISO has a number of standards that support quality management. One group describes processes and another describes process assessment and improvement ISO 15504. The Software Engineering Institute has its own process assessment and improvement methods, called CMMi and IDEAL respectively.

Quality Terms

- Quality Improvement can be distinguished from Quality Control in that Quality Improvement is the purposeful change of a process to improve the reliability of achieving an outcome.
- Quality Control is the ongoing effort to maintain the integrity of a process to maintain the reliability of achieving an outcome.
- Quality Assurance is the planned or systematic actions necessary to provide enough confidence that a product or service will satisfy the given requirements.

Importance of Quality Management

Quality management is a principle that ensures quality in a company's products and services. There are various types of quality management programmes which include but are not limited to Six Sigma, Theory of Constraints and TQM. Although the approach to solving quality issues vary with the different quality management programmes, the goal remains the same—to create a high quality, high-performing product or service that meets and exceeds the customers' expectations. Quality management is important to companies for a variety of reasons.

Product Quality

Quality management ensures product quality. Some primary aspects of product quality include: performance, reliability and durability. Through the use of a quality management programme, the company can produce a product that performs just as to its stated promises. The will endure normal, everyday use. Use quality management programmes to improve the quality of a product and to design new products. Six Sigma has a specific component called DFSS which is a methodology to build Six Sigma quality into a product or service.

Customer Satisfaction

Quality management ensures customer satisfaction. Conduct customer satisfaction surveys to understand the qualities of the product important to the customer. Also conduct surveys with those who are not the company's customers. This will also provide insight into why these businesses use the services of the competitor. Use customer surveys to target those features of a product or service that need improvement. The quality management programme provides a methodology to use to create the type of product the customer desires.

Increased Revenues

Quality products and services give the company a spotless reputation in the industry. This reputation allows the company to gain new customers and sell additional products and services to existing customers. A quality management programme also removes inefficient processes within the system.

By removing unnecessary processes, employee productivity increases. The employee is spending less time on activities that do not contribute to the product's quality. As a result, the employee is producing more work in less time while the company has not increased the salary. Quality management programmes help recapture lost monies due to inefficiencies.

Reduce Waste

A quality management programme helps companies reduce waste. Companies that house inventory are paying for the storage, management and tracking of the inventory. The costs of having the inventory are built into the price of the product. Implementing a quality management programme reduces the amount of inventory that costs the company money and occupies valuable space. Quality management means that there is a systematic approach to keeping inventories at acceptable levels without incurring waste. Work closely with suppliers to manage inventory using a Just-in-Time philosophy. In short, a JIT inventory system helps the suppliers and manufacturer remain in close communication to become more responsive to the customer.

Teamwork

Quality management systems force company departments to work as a team. Different areas of the company become reliant upon one another to produce a quality product that meets and exceeds the customers' expectations. A quality system incorporates measures that affect sales, finance, operations, customer service and marketing. The balanced scorecard is a one-stop-shop for evaluating how various departments are operating against their performance expectations. Use the balanced scorecard to show how close the company is to the financial, operational, customer service and learning/growth targets.

MANAGING QUALITY

Quality generally refers to a certain degree or level of excellence. The American National Standards Institute and the American Society for Quality Control defined quality as "the totality of features and characteristics of a product or service that bears on its ability to satisfy given needs".

There are two main perspectives of defining quality, one from the customer and the other one from the producer or manufacturer.

- Quality of Design: Quality from the point of view of customer and involves designing quality characteristics into a product.
- Quality of conformance: Quality from the manufacturer's perspective and seeks to ensure that the product is produced according to design. To achieve QOC means improvement in the design of the equipment, materials, training, supervision and control. This quality definition serves as the basis for evaluating quality performance at the shop floor level.

Why is Quality Important?

The world of manufacturing has changed dramatically over the past 20 years. The challenge for firms to become and to remain competitive has never been more pronounced. Bases for competition no longer just focus on cost, but on other key success factors such as quality, flexibility, delivery, service and innovation. Why do firms want to achieve quality? Firms with good quality can command a higher price and will be remembered by customers. But how does quality relate with profitability? What are the costs involved in achieving quality? Because of good quality in terms of product, service and process, companies employing quality management could enjoy market gains as well as cost savings that ultimately lead to better profits for the organization.

What are the Costs of Quality?

But achieving quality has certain costs:

- Costs to control quality: These include the costs to prevent the occurrence of defects and the costs of evaluating the firm's progress towards achieving zero defects. These also consist of the investment made by company on good quality materials, process, technology, and quality inspection.
- Costs of failure to control quality: These refer to the costs incurred if the firm fails to achieve its quality targets and customers get dissatisfied for a poor quality product or service. These include the costs of internal and external failure.

How can Quality be Managed?

Total Quality Management (TQM) is considered an important approach in managing quality. TQM derived its teachings mainly from the following disciplines — Statistics, Organizational Theory, Strategic Management, and Industrial Organization.

The efforts of the company employing TQM are targeted towards meeting cross-functional goals utilizing management techniques, productivity improvement efforts, and various problem solving tools and techniques in disciplined manner.

The ultimate objective of TQM is to achieve customer satisfaction all the time.

Presented below are 12 important considerations if your company is planning to adopt TQM:

- Are you committed to quality?
- Do you plan for quality?
- Is your company customer – oriented?
- Does your company manage supplier quality?
- Are your people involved in quality?
- Do you train your employees on quality?
- Are your workplaces organized and orderly?
- Is quality integrated in your product design?
- Is quality integrated in your processes?
- Does your company measure and monitor quality?
- Does your company benchmark with the best?
- Does your company sustain its quality/productivity efforts?

A SYSTEMATIC APPROACH TO QUALITY MANAGEMENT

To deliver quality to the customer in the face of the complexities identified above, the food and beverage operation must adopt some form of systematic approach. The quality management cycle shown in the Figure has been developed from the basis of the Deming PDCA cycle. This approach was developed to help identify and correct any errors that occur during production or service and to lead to lasting quality improvement.

The foundation of the cycle is one of continual improvement to reduce the gap between customer requirements and the actual performance of the operation. The cycle starts by planning what improvement to make based on a clarification of the problem and the development of hypotheses about the underlying causes. The' do' phase implements a small scale experiment to correct the situation that is then' checked' through measurement. The final step' acts' to implement these quality improvements. The cycle is essentially a learning process and after one cycle is completed another one starts. It is, however, useful to extend this four-step approach to the systematic management of quality throughout an organization, while maintaining the elements of learning and continual improvement.

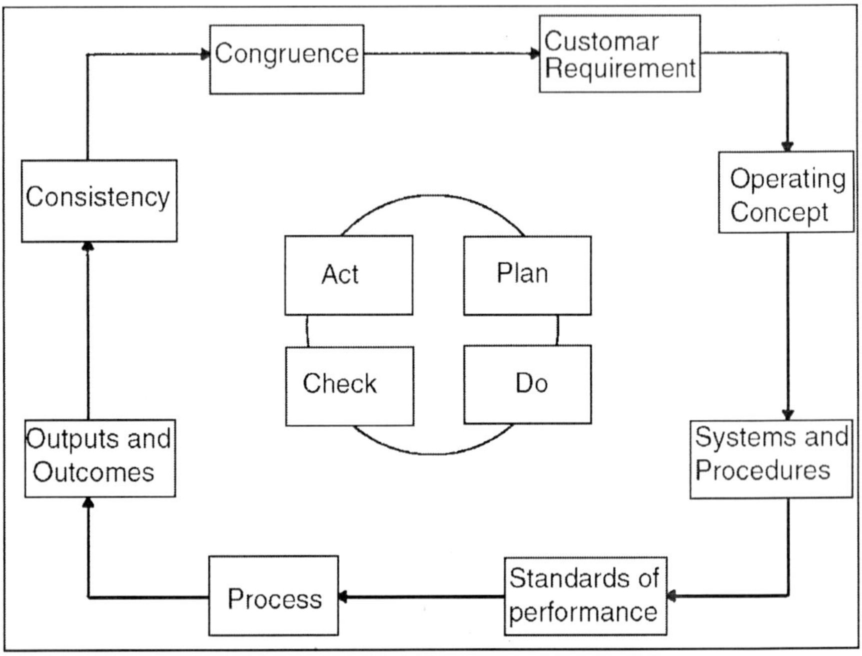

Fig: The Quality Management Cycle.

Planning

The starting point for any quality initiative should be to establish the specific requirements of customers in each of the market segments that the food and beverage operation intends to serve. For example, what does a business traveller expect from a hotel breakfast and in what ways is that different from the weekend leisure visitor?

In reality, it is more likely that there is already a fairly good idea of what the operation will be like. Market research can still help to identify the most important characteristics of the operation so that they can be built into systems and procedures from the beginning. From this customer base, management needs to prepare a detailed operating concept.

This should start from an idea of the corporate mission to develop into a series of core product values and then be translated into a practical service delivery system. They can also be developed into a series of operating standards reflecting the core values that the company feels are important. Heskett et al. have developed a detailed model that describes the integration of the target market segments with the service concept, operating strategy and the design of the service delivery system through positioning, value-cost leveraging and system-strategy integration. This strategic service vision forms the foundations upon which quality can be built throughout the organization. Translating these ideas into a concrete design is a complex challenge that is fundamental to the future success of the operation.

Doing

Once the design of the food and beverage operation has been decided, it is then necessary to fill in the details of the systems, standards and procedures to be adopted. Most businesses will translate these into detailed standards of performance to be found in the standards manual, which will form part of the induction and ongoing training of employees. With all the design and planning done and all systems, standards and procedures in place, the next stage is to activate the operation and ensure it performs on a day-to-day basis.

Checking

Checking that the operation has performed according to the plan can take place at two levels. Firstly, checks can be made that the process has been carried out correctly and then the outputs or outcomes of the operation can be checked. Checking the process can be done either as part of the daily operations or as a periodic inspection. Statistical Process Control is the term used in manufacturing for the collection of process data that can then be monitored against performance norms to identify when processes have or are likely to deviate from established tolerance levels. There are, however, very few examples of the application of SPC to food and beverage operations. A similar approach that the industry uses more widely, especially but not exclusively, in relation to food hygiene, is Hazard Analysis Critical Control Point.

This technique, originally developed in food manufacturing to control hygiene risk, identifies the critical points in the production process and puts into place control measures to monitor performance at these points. As long as these measures stay in control, the quality of the whole process should be assured. Periodic inspection, although not controlling the process as it happens, will check whether all procedures are being followed. The method used here is some form of operational or internal audit, whereby a detailed checklist is developed to cover all aspects of the operation. Some restaurants will have separate checklists for bar/cellar, hygiene, kitchen, restaurant and administration.

Each area can then be further divided into headings. For example, a restaurant quality assurance evaluation may be broken down into cleanliness and hygiene, preparation, presentation/moments of truth, service, timing and guest reaction. Each heading can then have a series of items to be looked for.

For example, under the preparation heading you might check whether all tables are laid up, cruets and sugar containers are filled, promotional material is displayed and ashtrays are available on smoking tables. Each correct item can then be awarded a number of points and totals can be calculated to compare with acceptable levels, previous performance or other restaurants in a chain.

Monitoring the process should ensure that the service delivery system is performing as it should but it will not check the level of customer satisfaction with the service received. Therefore a checking system also needs to be in place to measure the outputs from the system and the outcomes from the customers' point of view. A commonly used method is to use a mystery shopper or quality audit. Mystery shoppers visit the unit as normal customers but prepare a report on their experiences against established criteria. This technique is widely used in fast-food operations, commercial restaurants and international hotels. Other approaches may use some form of customer satisfaction survey.

The SERVQUAL instrument originally developed by Zeithaml et al. has been widely researched and customised specifically for lodging operations and a series of food and beverage applications but is not without its critics.

Acting

The final stage of the cycle is to act on the information collected. Consistency involves acting on any non-conformance to established standards. Quality improvement to move towards zero defects is a continuing process. The introduction of quality improvement teams, quality control circles or corrective action teams may help this move. The focus here is on improving the process. In looking at congruence the focus is on ensuring that the food and beverage concept still matches the customers' requirements. Over time customer expectations will change and there must be some way of highlighting these gaps between expectations and delivery. Once identified these new or changed requirements are passed on to the design team who then start the next round of the cycle.

DEVELOPING APPROACHES TO QUALITY MANAGEMENT

The development of the main approaches to managing quality is shown in the Figure. The diagram shows a movement from early approaches to quality relying on inspection of the finished product through quality control and quality assurance to total quality management.

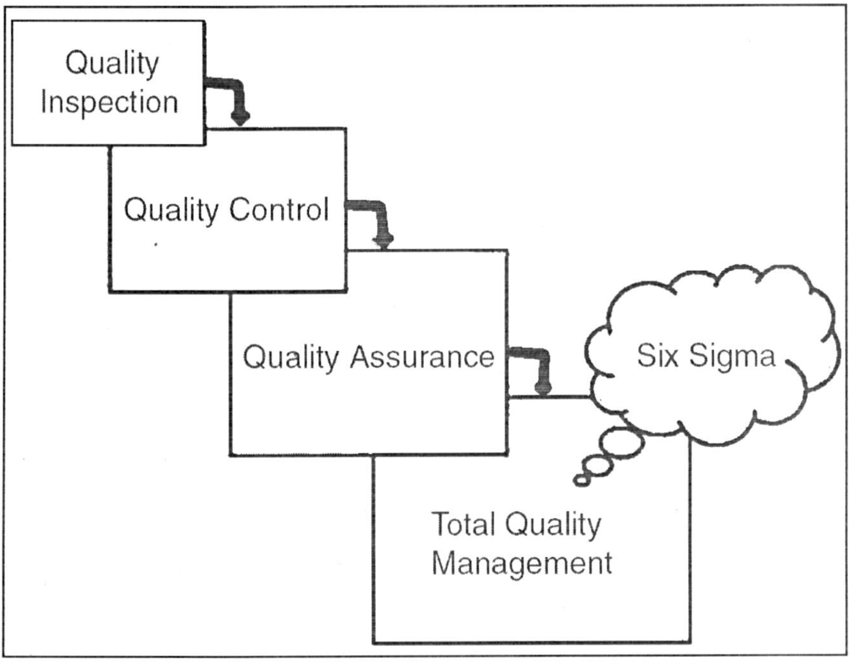

Fig: The Development of Approaches to Quality Management.

Quality Inspection

The earliest and probably the easiest approach to quality is the inspection approach. This simple approach is based on finding defects in a product or service before it reaches the customer by introducing an inspection stage or stages. There needs to be some specification of what the product should be like against which the product can be checked once it has been produced. The checking would probably be carried out by staff employed mainly for that purpose.

If any problems are found, that product will be rejected as non-conforming and will be sent back for re-work – to put the defects right – or for scrap. Manufacturing industry has tended to rely on a separate inspection department to carry out this task, but this is not a model that has been adopted in food and beverage operations. A simple example of inspection is the head chef standing at the hot plate during a banquet passing dishes across to the staff when satisfied with the standard reached. The focus here is firmly on identifying defects. The emphasis is on a lack of quality followed by the rejection of substandard work. The inspection becomes something the staff dread and very negative feelings can be aroused. Quality is a question of checking physical attributes off against a checklist and hoping that nothing has been missed. The emphasis is on putting things right rather than on identifying the cause of the problem and dealing with it at source.

Quality Control

The quality control approach still centres on inspection but recognizes the need for a detailed specification and that quality checks should be made throughout the production process. Using sophisticated inspection methods at appropriate points in the production process, the approach is more likely to find errors and will correct them earlier. The emphasis is still on a find and fi x mentality. Quality control will not improve product or ser vice quality, it will only highlight when it has gone wrong. A non-conforming product or service must be produced before action can be taken to put it right and this leads to inefficiency and waste. The focus has switched for the staff onto finding others to blame for the defects to avoid the ' disciplinary ' action taken against those who make mistakes. The whole focus of quality control is on mistakes.

Quality Assurance

Quality assurance recognizes the inefficiencies of waiting for mistakes to happen and strives to design quality into the process so that things cannot go wrong or if they do they are identified and corrected as they happen. Lasting and continuous improvement in quality can best be achieved through planning and preventing problems from arising at source. Moving the emphasis from inspection to prevention is helped by the introduction of a number of quality assurance tools and techniques such as SPC, blueprinting and quality costing. The approach is also likely to include a comprehensive quality system, perhaps based on the ISO 9000 series. In quality assurance, however, the focus is not just on systems.

Effective quality assurance must involve the development of a new operating philosophy and approach; one that is proactive rather than reactive, that includes involving employees in the process from across normal departmental barriers.

Total Quality Management

The focus on the customer and the scale and nature of internal and external involvement are the main differences between the quality assurance and TQM approaches. In any TQM approach, the driving force is the focus on the satisfaction of customer needs. The whole system must be directed at customer satisfaction and anything that could get in the way of delivering this satisfaction must be removed.

This involves the whole organization, including suppliers, looking for ways to improve continually the products or services delivered. TQM places the emphasis on the people in the organization and their roles, through a broadening of their outlook and skills, through encouragement of creativity, through training and empowerment, in measuring their performance and finding ways to improve it. The emphasis is on a management-led move towards teamwork and participation. Taking this holistic perspective can involve organizations in significant changes in their culture. It may be relatively easy to introduce new systems and procedures, but changing the culture is a much more difficult, but necessary, task.

□

7

Principles of Food and Beverage Control

Food and beverage control may be defined as the guidance and regulation of the costs and revenue of operating the catering activity in a food and beverage establishment. A successful holistic food and beverage control is imperative for any type of food and beverage operation regardless of its size.

The cost of food and beverage can range from 25 per cent to up to 50 per cent depending on the type of operation. In restaurants, food and beverage can be the only source of revenue. In the public sector catering, employee restaurants and similar operations, food and beverages are the main day-to- day expenditure, which is controlled by budgets and possibly a level of subsidy, either on a total company or on a per unit basis.

The amount of control is related to the size of the operation. A large group operation would require a much more precise, detailed, up-to-date information, than a small operation. Additionally a larger operation will be able to support the control with a computerized system when a smaller operation may not be able to afford it. In both instances the type and volume of data required needs to be selectively determined if control is to be meaningful and effective. It is important at this stage to clarify the limitations of a control system.

- A control system can only identify problem areas and trends in the business. The system cannot automatically correct such problem areas.
- A control system will require constant management supervision to ensure that it functions efficiently.
- A control system will need management action to evaluate the information produced and to act upon it.

THE OBJECTIVES OF FOOD AND BEVERAGE CONTROL

The objectives of a food and beverage control system may be summarized as follows:

- Analysis of income and expenditure: The analysis is solely concerned with the income and expenditure related to food and beverage operations. The revenue analysis is usually by each selling outlet, of such aspects as the volume of food and beverage sales, the sales mix, the average spending power of customers at various times of the day, and the number of customers served. The analysis of costs includes departmental food and beverage costs, portion costs and labour costs. The performance of each outlet can then be expressed in terms of the gross profit and the net margin and the net profit.
- Establishment and maintenance of standards: The basis for the operation of any food and beverage outlet is the establishment of a set of standards which would be particular to an operation, for example, a chain of steak house restaurants. Unless standards are set no employee would know in detail the standards to be achieved nor could the employee' s performance be effectively measured by management. An efficient unit would have the set standards laid down in manuals often known as SOPs which should be readily available to all staff for reference. Having set the standards, a difficult problem always for the management of an operation is to maintain these standards. This can be aided by regularly checking on the standards achieved by observation and analysis and by comments made by customers, and when necessary, conducting training courses to re-establish the standards.
- Pricing: An important objective of food and beverage control is to provide a sound basis for menu pricing including quotations for special functions. It is, therefore, important to determine food menu and beverage list prices in the light of accurate food and beverage costs and other main establishment costs; as well as general market considerations, such as the average customer spending power, the prices charged by competitors and the prices that the market will accept.
- Prevention of waste: In order to achieve performance standards for an establishment, targets are set for revenue, cost levels and profit margins. To achieve these levels of performance it is necessary to prevent wastage of materials caused by such things as poor preparation, over-production, failure to use standard recipes, etc.

This can only be done with an efficient method of control, which covers the complete cycle of food and beverage control, from the basic policies of the organization to the management control after the operation has been completed.

- Prevention of fraud: It is necessary for a control system to prevent or at least restrict the possible areas of fraud by customers and staff. Typical areas of fraud by customers are such things as deliberately walking out without paying; unjustifi- ably claiming that the food or drink that they had partly or totally consumed was unpalatable of drinks served; making payments by stolen cheques or credit cards. Typical areas of fraud by staff are overcharging or undercharging for items served and stealing of food, drink or cash.
- Management information: A system of control has an important task to fulfil in providing accurate up-to-date information for the preparation of periodical reports for management. This information should be sufficient so as to provide a complete analysis of performance for each outlet of an establishment for comparison with set standards previously laid down.

Information overload can be a major issue when managing an operation. Often management will be presented with enormous amount of reports and statistical information that they may not know how to use or do not have the time to act upon.

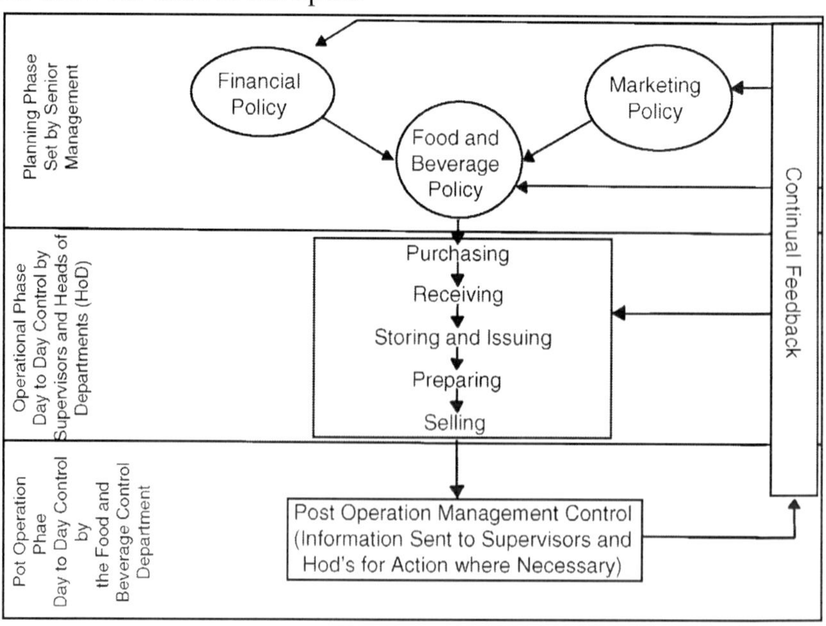

Fig: Holistic Food and Beverage Control System

It is therefore imperative that depending on the size of the operation appropriate control is applied, for example, a small operation may not require daily, weekly and periodic reports whilst a larger operation will probably require them so that management may take both corrective and preventive action quickly.

SPECIAL PROBLEMS OF FOOD AND BEVERAGE CONTROL

Food and beverage control tends to be more difficult than the control of materials in many other industries.

The main reasons for this are:

- **Perishability of the product:** Food, whether raw or cooked, is a perishable commodity and has a limited life. The caterer, therefore, has to ensure that she buys produce in the correct quality and quantity in relation to estimated demand, and that it is correctly stored and processed.
- **Business volume unpredictability:** Sales instability is typical of most catering establishments. There is often a change in the volume of business from day to day, and in many establishments from hour to hour. This causes basic problems with regard to the quantities of commodities to be purchased and prepared as well as to the staffing required.
- **Menu mix unpredictability:** In order to be competitive and satisfy a particular market, caterers must often offer a wide choice of menu items to the customer. Predicting menu item preference on top of customer volume can be a challenge. Effective forecasting as part of the total food and beverage control system is therefore necessary.
- **Food and beverage operation short cycle:** The speed at which catering operations take place, relative to many other industries, allows little time for many control tasks. It is not uncommon that items ordered one day are received, processed and sold the same or next day. It is for this reason that in larger catering establishments cost reporting is done daily or at least weekly. Further problems, particularly with perishable foods, are that with a short life for produce, items cannot be bought very much in advance of their need; and the problem of availability at times of produce relative to the price that can be afforded in relation to the selling price.
- **Departmentalization:** Many food and beverage operations have several production and service departments, offering different products and operating under different policies. It is, therefore,

necessary to be able to produce separate trading results for each of the production and selling activities.

THE FUNDAMENTALS OF CONTROL

Effective control systems and procedures consist of three broad phases: planning, operational and management control after the operation has taken place.

The Planning Phase

It is difficult to run an effective catering operation without having firstly defined the basic policies. Policies are pre-determined guidelines, laid down by the senior management of an organization, which outline such matters as the market or segment of the market that is being aimed at, how it is to be catered for, and the level of profitability/subsidy to be achieved. Policies in general are particular to individual companies and establishments, although example, for hospital catering. A catering operation should have its policies clearly defined before it commences business, and re-defined whenever a major change takes place, for example, when a new theme is chosen for a restaurant to aim for a different market segment. Ideally, in a large organization the policies should be written down and periodically reviewed in relation to the current business and future trends; however, in smaller organizations there is not the communication problem of a large organization and to formally draw up and commit policies to paper is not so vital.

There are three basic policies which need to be considered:

- The financial policy will determine the level of profitability, subsidy or cost limits to be expected from the business as a whole and the contribution to the total profit, subsidy or cost limit that is to be expected from each unit, and then from the departments within them. This involves the setting of targets for the business as a whole as well as each unit and the departments within them. Thus, the financial policy for a large hotel will set profit targets for the hotel, and departmental profit targets for the accommodation and catering as well as other departments. The financial policy for the catering department will set the overall target for the department itself, which will be further divided into targets for the various restaurants, bars and function facilities. The financial policy for an industrial contract catering operation will set the overall target for the operation, the level of subsidy and the level of management fee, as well as the cost limits per unit.
- The marketing policy will identify the broad market the operation is intended to serve and the particular segment of the market

upon which it intends to concentrate. It should also identify the immediate and future consumer requirements on a continuous basis in order to maintain and improve its business performance. It is obvious from the above that the broad market intended to be served by a large city hotel could be broken down into the specific segments of the various types of users of, for example, the coffee shop, the carvery, the cocktail bar, the banqueting rooms, etc. each having specific and different consumer requirements. The interpretation of the marketing policy for a national commercial catering organization into a marketing plan for the next year may include some or all of the following objectives:

- National identity: To achieve a better national identity for all units by corporate design, and by meeting consumer expectations of what a 'popular restaurant' concept should be.
- Customer: The customer profile being the business person, shopper, tourist of either sex, aged twenty-five years or more, commonly using the high street of any major town, requiring food and beverage of good general standard, waitress served, for a typical price of ` n per meal.
- Market share: To achieve, maintain or increase the percentage of 'our' market.
- Turnover: Sales volume to be increased by x per cent on previous year.
- Profitability: Profit to be increased by each unit by y per cent on previous year.
- ASP per customer to be increased by z per cent–to achieve a new ASP of not less than `n.
- Product: The product to be maintained at a consistently high standard.
- Customer satisfaction: The net result must be the satisfaction of every customer.

• The catering policy, which is normally evolved from the financial and marketing policies, will define the main objectives of operating the food and beverage facilities and describe the methods by which such objectives are to be achieved.

It will usually include the following:

- The type of customer, for example high spending business executive, low spending female shopper, short-stay hospital patient, etc.
- The type of menu(s), for example table d' hôte, à la carte, fast food.

- The beverage provision necessary for the operation.
- The food quality standards, for example fresh, frozen, canned, etc. and the grade of produce to be used.
- The method of buying, for example by contract, quotation, cash and carry, etc.
- Type and quality of service, for example cafeteria, counter, waiter, etc.
- Degree of comfort and décor, for example square footage per customer, type and style of décor, of chairs, tables, etc.
- Hours of operation, for example twenty-four hours, seven days a week; 1200–1500 and 1800–2200 hours, Monday–Saturday, etc.

The Operational Phase

Having defined the policies, it is then necessary to outline how they are to be interpreted into the day-to-day control activities of the catering operation. The operational control is in five main stages of the control cycle.

These are:

- **Purchasing:** There are five main points to be considered. evaluations the particular products to be used.
  - **Yield testing:** To identify as a result of tests the yield obtainable from all the major commodities used.
  - **Purchase specifications:** A specification is a concise description in writing of the quality, size, weight, etc. for a particular food or beverage item.
  - Method of buying: By contract, quotation, cash and carry, etc.
  - **Clerical procedures:** It is necessary to determine who originates, sanctions and places orders and what documentation is required for control.
- **Receiving:** There are three main points to be considered:
  - **Quantity inspection:** A person must be nominated to be responsible for physically counting and weighing goods and checking that the quantity and size of items in the delivery matches the purchase order. If there is a shortage in the delivery the purchasing manager or a member of the management must be informed.
  - **Quality inspection:** This is particularly important with perishable foods where inspection may be made by a senior chef. Whenever possible the items should be checked against the appropriate purchase specification.

- **Clerical procedures:** This is a very important aspect as all necessary documentation must follow a set procedure. It includes the acknowledgement of the receipt of acceptable goods and the delivery person' s signature on a 'request for credit' note for returned goods and short deliveries.

- **Storing and issuing:** There are four main points to be considered:
  - Stock records: It is necessary to decide what records are to be kept.
  - **Pricing of items:** The method of pricing of the various types of items must be decided upon so that there is consistency within the operation.
  - **Stocktaking:** The points to be considered here are the level of stock to be held, rate of stock turnover, dealing with discrepancies, identification of slow-moving items, etc.
  - Clerical procedures : There is a need to determine what documentation is necessary, for example requisitions, record cards, bin cards, stocktaking reports, etc.
- Preparing: This is a critical stage in the control cycle, in particular for food. There are three main points to be considered:
  - Volume forecasting: A method of predicting the number of customers using the catering facilities on a specific day, and also of predicting as accurately as possible what items they will eat and drink.
  - Pre-costing: A method of controlling food and beverage costs in advance of the preparation and service stages. It is done by preparing and using standard recipes for all food and beverage items and also by using portion control equipment, for example ladles, scales, optics, standard glassware, etc.
  - Clerical procedures: What documentation is required and the distribution and destination of this information.
- **Selling:** This important stage of operational control needs to take into consideration the following points:
  - A checking system: This is necessary to keep control of the number of covers sold and of the items sold. This may be done through a standard type of waiter' s check system or through a till roll or in the case of hospital patients, by the summary and analysis of completed individual patient menu cards.

- The control of cash: This is vitally important. It is necessary to ensure that all items sold have been paid for and that the money is received or credit has been authorized.
- Clerical procedures: These would be necessary to control items sold and the money received or credit entitled, and would often include a restaurant checking system, meal and sales analysis, cashier' s paying-in book, etc.

The Post Operation Phase

This final phase of food and beverage control is in three main stages:

- **Food and beverage cost reporting:** The cycle of production is very short and the product is perishable. These factors together with the variations in demand for the product necessitate up-to-date reporting at least weekly if not daily.
- **Assessment:** There is a need for someone from the food and beverage management team in the case of a large unit, or the proprietor or manager of a small unit, to analyse the food and beverage reports and to compare them with the budget for the period and against previous actual performance.
- **Correction:** A control system does not cure or prevent problems occurring. When the analysis of the performance of a unit or department identifies that there is a problem, it is up to management to take the necessary steps to correct the problem as quickly as possible.

THE REALITY OF CONTROL

No matter how effective a control system may be there are certain realities that do not allow for any system to be 100 per cent efficient.

The reasons for the deficiency of a system can be:

- The material product is very unlikely to be 100 per cent consistent as to quality or the final yield obtainable from it.
- The employees are unlikely to work to a level of 100 per cent efficiency at all times, in spite of the fact that operational standards may exist.
- The equipment used is also unlikely to work to the level of 100 per cent efficiency at all times, and this could well affect the yield obtainable.
- The customers' choice of dishes can well be different at times to some of the budgeted sales mix, therefore affecting all forecasts.

It is important that the staff should see that control in some form is taking place and that on occasions there is a follow-up and action is taken on irregularities to set standards. Further, the importance and relevance of using percentages as a yardstick necessitates that any percentages used should be directly related to the amount of money involved. A 1 per cent difference to the required budgeted gross profit may not appear very significant at first but when related in financial terms it becomes more significant. For example, in the case of a unit with a turnover of ₹400,000 and with a budgeted gross profit percentage of 65 per cent a 1 per cent difference in the gross profit achievable would represent ₹2,600. Being aware that they are ₹2,600 off budget may be more meaningful to unit managers than just being aware that they are 1 per cent off target. The management of any catering operation has to be fully aware of everything that is taking place within and outside the operation and, to be successful, needs to continually collect, analyse, and evaluate data and take any necessary steps to correct anything which is irregular to the standards set for the operation.

SETTING THE BUDGET AND BREAK-EVEN ANALYSIS

In order to have an effective food and beverage control system a manager needs to have benchmarks where he/she can compare the operations performance.

The Budget

A budget is a plan–expressed usually in financial and/or quantitative terms which reflects the policies of an establishment and determines the business operations for a particular trading period. The trading period is usually of one year, but is often broken down into review periods of either thirteen four-week periods; or alternatively, of thirteen-week quarters, each quarter con sisting of two four-week and one five-week periods. Whichever method is adopted it is necessary that the periods remain the same so as to make it possible to compare results not only with corresponding periods in the same year, but also with the corresponding periods in earlier years. Bank holidays and special events falling into different periods each year should be noted. The term budgetary control refers to a method of control where particular responsibility for various budgeted results is assigned to the managers concerned and a continuous comparison of the actual results and budgeted figures is made. When there are discrepancies between the two, it is necessary to identify the reasons for the variances and to take appropriate action. It is essential that when budgets are set they are clearly seen to be achievable; otherwise they are of little value.

The objectives of budgetary control are threefold:

- To provide a plan of action for a set trading period, to guide and regulate a business in keeping with its stated policies, and to maximize the full use of its resources.

- To set standards of performance for management against which their performance can be measured.
- To set out levels of cost responsibility and encourage cost awareness.

Budgets are prepared by the senior management of an organization in consultation with the various managers and departmental heads so as to ensure a greater level of commitment and an awareness of the aims, objectives, problems and possible weaknesses of the establishment. There are two main types: cap ital budgets; and operating budgets. Capital budgets, as the name implies, are those which are concerned with the assets and liabil ities of an establishment, for example equipment, plant and cash.

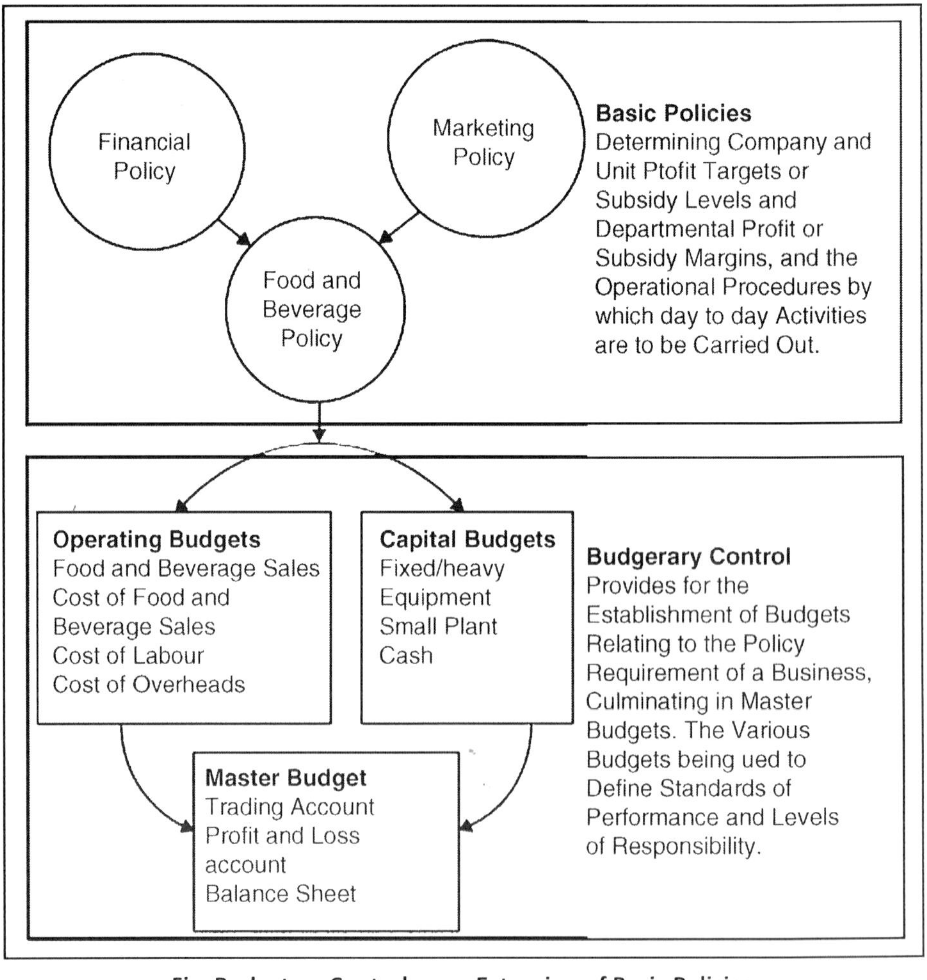

Fig: Budgetary Control as an Extension of Basic Policies

Operating budgets are those concerned with the day-to-day income and expenditure of an establishment and include sales, cost of sales, labour, maintenance, head office expenses, etc. This is the type of budget that food and beverage managers will be mostly concerned with when looking at the food and beverage control system. For simplicity, budgeting may be seen as being in six stages.

The amount of detail and sub division into departmental budgets depends very much on the type and size of the business.

The basic stages are:

- Determination of the net profit required for the business in relation to the capital invested and the risk involved. Alternatively, in the case of non-profit making establishments, the level of subsidy available or required is postulated.
- **Preparation of the sales budget:** This determines the volume of sales necessary to achieve the desired net profit or subsidy and also influences the budgeted costs for food, beverages, labour and some overheads.
- **Preparation of administration and general budgets:** These are for such items as head office expenses, advertising, rates, insurance, etc. Some of these may be regarded as fixed budgets, that is, they are not affected by any change in the volume of business, for example head office expenses, advertising, rates, etc.; while others may be regarded as flexible budgets, that is, they are affected by changes in the volume of business, for example telephones, laundry, etc.
- Preparation of the capital expenditure budget which makes provision for such items of expenditure as new kitchen equipment, restaurant and bar furniture, etc.
- **Preparation of the cash budget:** This is regarded as the most important of the capital budgets and it predetermines the cash inflows, the cash outflows and resulting cash balance at particular points during the period.
- **Preparation of master budgets:** As stated previously master budgets are prepared for the trading account, profit and loss account and the balance sheet.

Costs, Profits and Sales

The cost of operating a catering unit or department is usually analysed under the three headings of the elements of cost.

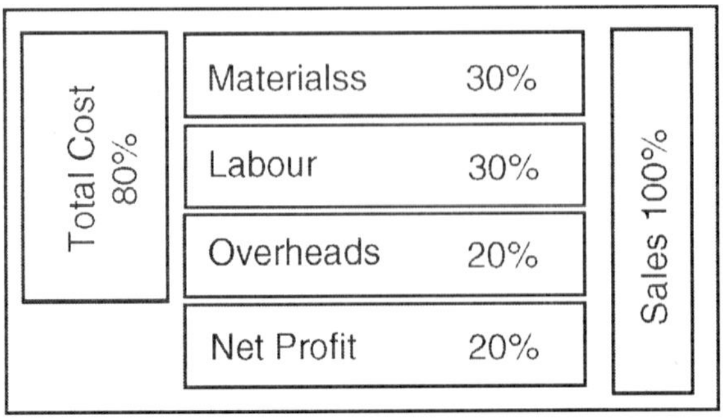

Fig: Typical Example of the Elements of Cost

- **Material costs:** Cost of food and beverage consumed and the cost of additional items such as tobacco. The food cost is then calculated by the formula:

  Opening stock
  \+ cos t of purchases
  – clo sin g stock = Material cos t
  –cos t of staff meals

- **Labour costs:** Wages and salaries paid to all employees, plus any employer contribution to government taxes, bonuses, staff meals, pension fund, etc.
- **Overhead costs:** All costs other than material and labour costs, for example rent, rates, insurance, depreciation, repairs, printing and stationery, china and glassware, and capital equipment.

As most catering operations are subject to changes in the volume of business done, it is normal practice to express the elements of cost and net profit as a percentage of sales. A change in the volume of sales has an effect on the cost structure and on the net profit.

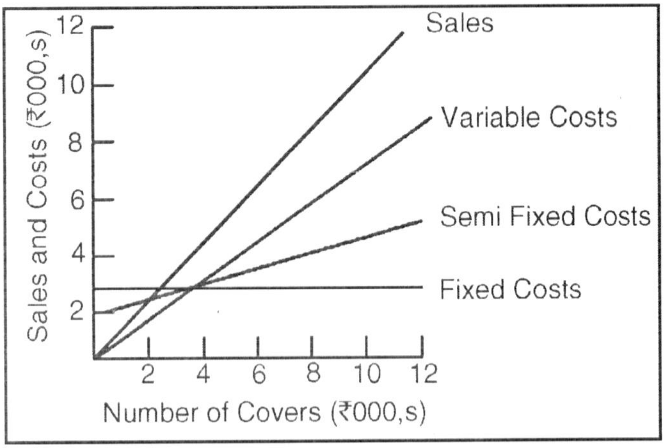

Fig: Fixed, Semi-fixed and Variable Costs

It is necessary to examine costs not only by their nature but also by their behaviour in relation to changes in the volume of sales.

Using this criteria, costs may be identified as being of four kinds:

- **Fixed costs:** These are costs which remain fixed irrespective of the volume of sales, for example rent, rates, insurance, the management element of labour costs.
- **Semi-fixed costs:** These are costs which move in sympathy with, but not in direct proportion to the volume of sales, for example fuel costs, telephone and laundry. Semi-fixed costs contain a fixed and variable cost element, for example, the charge for the telephone service in the India contains a fixed cost for the quarterly charge for the rental of each phone and a variable cost depending on the number of phone calls made.
- **Variable costs:** These are costs which vary in proportion to the volume of sales, for example food and beverage.
- **Total costs:** This is the sum of the fixed costs, semi-fixed costs and variable costs involved.

Three main kinds of profit are normally referred to in food and beverage operations:

- Gross profit = total sales–cost of materials. Note: The term gross profit is often referred to as 'kitchen profit' (food) or 'bar profit' (beverages). Room hire is normally treated as 100 per cent gross profit.
- After-wage profit (or net margin) = total sales–(material + labour costs).
- Net profit = total sales–total costs (material + labour + overhead costs).

All of the normally used as measures of performance against past results and budgeted targets. The statement shows the sales, costs and profit over two consecutive months with the May sales figure showing a 50 per cent increase in business.

It is very common for food and beverage management to be faced with problems concerning the level of food and beverage cost that can be afforded, the prices that need to be set for food and beverages, the level of profit required at departmental and unit level and the number of customers required to cover specifi c costs or to make a certain level of profit.

Typical questions raised are:

- What level of sales is needed to cover the fixed costs of a unit?
- What level of sales is required from a particular unit to achieve `x' s net profit?

- What level of sales is required to increase the net profit of a unit by ₹10,000?
- What will the effect of increasing prices by 5 per cent have on net profit?
- What will be the effect on net profit of increasing the average spend of customers by 50p per meal?
- What increased level of sales must be obtained to cover the spending of ₹1,000 on advertising to promote the restaurant?
- What will be the financial implications of discounting beverages during a proposed promotion?
- What is the relationship between the capital invested in a restaurant and its sales and profit?

Answers to the types of question are normally attempted by using the accepted technique of break-even analysis. Break-even analysis enables the relationship between fixed, semi-fixed and variable costs at specific volumes of business to be conveniently represented on a graph. This enables the breakeven point to be identified and the level of sales necessary to produce a pre-determined level of net profit.

The term break-even point may be defined as that volume of business at which the total costs are equal to the sales and where neither profit nor loss is made. The technique is based on the assumption that: the selling price remains constant irrespective of the volume of business; that certain unit costs remain the same over the sales range of the charted period; that only one product is being made or sold; that the product mix remains constant in cost price and volume and that labour and machine productivity is constant.

Nearly every action or planned decision in a business will affect the costs, prices to be charged, the volume of business and the profit. Profits depend on the balance of the selling prices, the mix of products, the costs and the volume of business.

The break-even technique discloses the interplay of all these factors in a way which aids food and beverage management in selecting the best course of action now and in the future. Pricing is a multi-dimensional problem, which depends not only on the cost structure of a business and its specific profit objectives but also on the level of activity of the competition and the current business economic climate.

Essentials of a Control System

With the advancements in points of sale technology, food and beverage control has become even easier to establish even to small operations. There are a number of companies that now offer software that will offer solutions to any restaurant.

The main components of such a software system may include:

- **Menu planning:** Historical data will enable to forecast menu item popularity and profitability making it easier for the manager to plan future menus.
- **Production control:** Menus can be used to determine precise sales and production quantities, ensuring great control over kitchen production and usage of goods, reducing wastage of perishable goods.
- **Stock management:** The system may maintain stock levels in any number of individual store locations, tracking the issues and consumption of raw materials, as well as wastage and weekly or monthly stock checks.
- **Purchase ordering:** The system can base on minimum stock levels and/or forecast demand from production planning and match delivery notes and invoices. Some systems will even place an automatic order once stock levels are detected to be under minimum required.
- **Menu analysis:** Individual customer menu choices can be automatically recorded and analysed.
- Financial management reporting.

These components are often fully integrated into the electronic point-of-sale system, so that all data inputting is automatically done. It is important that when examining an existing control system or preparing to install a system into a new operation that the following points should be taken in consideration.

- Any control system should be comprehensive and cover all the outlets of an establishment and all stages of the food control cycle.
- The cost of maintaining the system should be in relation to the saving to be made, the level of sophistication of the control system usually increasing with the increase in the volume of sales and the complexity of the menu.
- The control system should be easy to operate and to be understood by all levels of staff.
- The control system should be seen by staff to be working. That is, that the management act in a positive way to adverse trading results and follow up on future results to check if the corrective action taken is effective.
- To be effective the information produced must be accurate and up- to-date.

BASIC CONCEPTS

Before we consider methods of food and beverage control we need to have an understanding of the four basic concepts in food and beverage production control. These are planning, standard yields, standard recipes and standard portion sizes. When PYRS are practised in a food and beverage operation they should aid management in controlling costs, setting standards and achieving customer satisfaction. The production of beverages needs to be tightly controlled as the contribution to profits from beverages is usually higher than that from food.

Production Planning

Production planning, or volume forecasting as it is also known, is the forecasting of the volume of sales for an establishment, for a specified time period, for example a day, a week or a month.

The aims and objectives of production planning are as follows:

- To facilitate food and beverage cost control for the establishment.
- To facilitate the purchasing of items, particularly perishable ones, and ensure appropriate stock levels are maintained.
- To reduce the problem of food that is left over and how it is to be re-used, beverage wastage or customer dissatisfaction when insufficient foods and beverages are available.
- To gear production to demand by forecasting the number of meals and drinks to be served for a given meal period.
- To enable a comparison to be made between actual and potential volume of sales, and for corrective action to be taken if necessary.

An initial forecast is made either at a set period in advance, for example a month, or when the major food orders are placed. This initial forecast estimates the total number of meals to be sold by the establishment and the estimated total of each menu item. In the case of a large hotel with a variety of catering outlets, a more detailed forecast would be made for each individual outlet. Factors that need to be taken into account at this stage are the season, and hence the weather forecast for that time of year; past popularity of menu items; major events occurring in the area–fêtes, shows, etc. that are likely to attract a larger than average number to the establishment' s normal catchment area, any sales campaigns currently being promoted by the operation, etc. The initial estimate is later adjusted, usually one or two days prior to the day of production, so that a more accurate forecast may be made. On the basis of this updated information, any changes that may need to be made with regard to staff scheduling, food purchases and requisitions, etc. should be made as soon as possible. There are a number of aids or management tools that may be employed by an establishment to assist the forecasting and planning of production.

Standard Yields

The standard yield of a particular food product is the usable part of that product after initial preparation, or the edible part of the product after preparation and cooking; for example, the standard yield for a whole fillet of beef is the number of fillet steaks that will be available for cooking and final sale to the customer after the fillet is trimmed and any unwanted meat removed. Any usable trimmed meat should be taken into account with the standard yield. In large establishments buying in large quantities of food per week, standard yields may be available for almost all the commodities– meat, fish, vegetables, etc. In smaller establishments standard yields may only be determined for the more expensive cuts of meat or fish such as whole fillets, lobsters, salmon, etc.

The development of standard yields by an establishment has a number of advantages:

- Standard yields determine the most appropriate and advantageous size/weight to buy a particular commodity in.
- They assist in determining the raw material require-ments for the production levels anticipated from the production forecasts, and therefore act as an aid in the purchasing of the establishment' s foodstuffs.
- They act as a 'double check' for the purchasing department. Should an unsatisfactory delivery of meat, for example, be made to an establishment and is unnoticed at the receiving bay, this delivery is subject to a second 'checking' procedure in the kitchen where the meat should yield a standard number of portions.
- They act as a safeguard against pilferage or wastage occurring in the kitchen as the actual and potential yields can be compared and this acts as a measurement of the efficiency of the production department.
- Finally, they are an aid to accurate food costing for particular dishes offered on an establishment' s menu, as the cost factor can be established.

For beverages the standard yields of beverage products may, with few exceptions, be accurately calculated, because for the majority of beverages there is little wastage and all the contents of, for example, a bottle of spirits may be used. For the purpose of beverage control all beverages bought in to an establishment should have standard yields calculated, on which the pricing of each drink may be based, and to control wastage and pilferage. If, for example, a 75 cl bottle of wine is bought in, allowing 15 cl of wine to a glass, five good measures should be obtained.

Standard Recipes

A standard recipe is a written schedule for producing a particular menu item, specifying the name and quantity of the item to be produced, the constituent ingredients necessary for its production and the method of preparation. This is the basic information contained in a standard recipe although it may also include such information as the costing of the dish, its nutritional value, etc. Detailed recipe cards are usually kept in the food and beverage control department for cost and price updating, only the basic information needing to be included on those cards that are displayed in the production area–often together with a photograph of the end product. Recipe management software has replaced the manual system.

Along with the standard recipes the nutritional information of each item is readily available as well as the recipe costings. Linked to an EPOS total food costs at the end of the day can be automatically calculated and easily reported to managers. The use of standard recipes by an establishment has a number of advantages.

- Accurate food and beverage costings can be determined for particular dishes/drinks and from this the cost per portion may be calculated. It is necessary to have the food cost of a dish for the purpose of pricing it for sale to the customer, in order to make the required gross profit. For some items it is not possible to make a gross profit, of, for example 65 per cent, whereas for other items the gross profit made may be higher; by having this type of information, the food and beverage department is able to balance the menu prices so that overall the necessary gross profit is obtained from the menu.
- In certain institutional establishments, such as hospitals, it is important to know the precise nutritional value of the dishes being given to certain patients. By itemizing the ingredients for a particular dish the nutritional value of it is easily calculated.
- They are an aid to purchasing and internal requisitioning. By taking into account the following day' s production forecast requirements the head chef is able to use the standard recipes to calculate the quantities of foodstuffs he/she will require the following day. In some catering establishments the head storeman may have a copy of the standard recipes and when the next day' s forecast requirements are sent, the head storeman is responsible for calculating the quantity of foodstuffs that need to be sent to the kitchen.
- Standard recipes are particularly useful in the preparation of items in the kitchens, both as a reminder to present staff of the

preparation procedure, and also as an aid to the training of new employees. More importantly the use of standard recipes in the production area ensures that the customer will always receive a standardized product.

- Standard recipes are an aid to menu planning. New additions to the menu, for example, may be accurately costed and balanced with the other items on the menu, not only in terms of price, but also in appearance, flavour, colour, etc.
- They may be used as a basis for compiling standard portion sizes which, if used in conjunction with standard recipes and standard yields, will together form the basis of a very effective production control system.

Standard recipes should also be compiled for the majority of beverage products offered for sale by the establishment. Like standard yields, standard recipes may be very accurately produced as all the contents of a drink may be itemized on the standard recipe. Obviously only a certain number of standard recipes may be produced for an establishment, and this is where the sales histories discussed earlier may be particularly useful–they do at least ensure that the recipes for the most popular drinks have been standardized.

With such a variety of components with which to make different drinks, it would not be practical to write standard recipes for every possible combination; so the bar staff should be provided with a book or books chosen by management on how to prepare those varieties of drinks that may be rather unusual or rare. Computer terminals and visual display units may be used in bars where the mixing and service details of various drinks can be displayed to order giving a speedier visual recipe than using a book. Bar staff should also be provided with the correct equipment for measuring and mixing drinks. Standard bar equipment would include such items as a fruit knife and board, sticks for cherries and olives, ice bowls, fruit squeezers, a cocktail shaker and stirrer, etc.

Standard Portion Sizes

A standard portion is the quantity of a particular food item that will be served to the customer; the quantity may be measured in terms of ounces or a numerical quantity. The portion sizes of the food items are determined by management in conjunction with the heads of both the kitchen and restaurant departments. Standard portion sizes in the operation may be established in several ways.

- By buying in pre-portioned food items, for example 8 oz rump steaks, pre-wrapped packs of butter and condiments, etc.

- By buying in food items in bulk and portioning them in the production kitchen before service, for example, pre-plating salads to be served in a display cabinet in a cafeteria line.
- By portioning food items as they are being served to the customer, for example, food in hot bain-maries in a cafeteria line being plated and served when the customer requests the food item.

In establishments operating more than one level of service, there may be varying portion sizes for the same food items, for the different catering outlets. For example, in a hotel the coffee shop offering a table d' hôte menu may serve a 6 oz rump steak, while the silver service restaurant offering an à la carte menu would serve an 8 oz steak. Standard portion sizes, like standard recipes, are an aid to food costing, as once the standard portion size has been established the gross profit may be calculated for that dish.

Any fluctuations in the sizes of the portions, for example serving larger portions, will therefore be reflected in the restaurant' s gross profit, particularly so if this is occurring with a number of menu items. Details of the standard portion sizes should be made readily available to all necessary employees. The food and beverage costing department should regularly review the portion size of a particular food item with reference to its current price, as it may be necessary either to reduce the standard portion size if the cost of a particular food item has increased substantially; increase the selling price; or possibly, remove the dish from the menu for a period until the cost price is acceptable.

In the kitchen and restaurant, the standard portion sizes of a dish are often combined with the standard recipes, and together they may be displayed on a wall chart to which all employees may refer.

As with standard recipes, standard portion sizes for beverages should be easier to control than those for food products. With some beverages, for example a bottled baby orange juice, all the contents of the bottle will be emptied into the customer' s glass. Other beverages such as spirits need to be measured before being poured into the customer' s glass, the use of optics being an accurate method. Another aid to control the portion size is to use standard glassware for specific drinks. In the India, for example, alcohol measurements are specified by law and managers can be heavily fined or even lose a licence if they are found not to comply with specifications.

METHODS OF FOOD CONTROL

Depending on the size of the operation food control methods may be automated or manual. We see examples of a recipe management software which can then produce automatic reports of daily/weekly/monthly food costs. Inventory or stock control is an imperative management tool to ensure that food costs are controlled and losses minimized.

The basic tools that enable the correct functioning of the inventory control cycle are:

- **Purchase order:** Completed by the Chef and are normally forms that are in triplicate with one copy for the supplier one for the accounting and one remains with the chef.
- **Delivery note:** Issued by the supplier and delivered together with the goods to the operation.
- **Invoice:** Issued by the supplier and normally send directly to the accounts department.
- **Requisition:** A note issued by the production unit to the storeroom requesting the issuance of goods.

These are FIFO and LIFO. FIFO stands for First in First out meaning the goods that were received first should be sold to customers. Because of the high levels of perishability of goods, FIFO is the method most commonly used in food and beverage operations. The LIFO method stands for Last in First out and in fine dining restaurants where the freshest ingredients are expected to be used this method is normally utilized. Depending on which method is used closing inventory may be valued differently using the oldest or the latest prices of the stock to value the whole stock. However with computerized systems, it is very easy to use actual cost of each item therefore allowing managers to be far more accurate than ever in the costings of their inventory.

Weekly/Monthly Food Cost Report

The following is an example for the calculation of the monthly food costs for an operation where detailed information is not thought to be necessary, or for a small or owner-managed unit where the control is an everyday part of the manager' s activity, in order for the operation to be successful. The weekly/ monthly food cost report is almost a reconciliation report on an activity that is tightly controlled daily by management.

The advantages of this method are:

- It is simple and quick to produce.
- It can give and indication of the general performance of the unit.

The disadvantages though are:

- This information is only produced after seven or twenty-eight days of operation.
- It provides no intermediate information so that any undesirable trends may be corrected earlier.

- It does not provide the daily or to-date information on purchases, requisitions and sales for a unit with an average of ₹2,700 a day turnover.

A Daily Food Cost Report

This food cost method is suitable for a small to medium-sized operation, or one where a not too sophisticated method is required, or where the costs involved in relation to the savings to be made do not justify a more involved method.

The advantages of producing this basic food report are:

- It is simple and easy to follow.
- It gives a reasonably detailed account of the general performance of the business on a day-to-day basis.
- It records the daily stock level, daily purchases, daily food requisitioned and daily food sales and enables the daily food cost percentage to be calculated. This information is used for preparing to-date totals.
- The to-date food cost percentage smooths out the uneven daily food cost percentages and highlights the corrective action to be taken, if necessary, early in the month. The uneven daily food cost percentage is often is often caused when food is requisitioned on one day to be processed and sold on subsequent days.

The disadvantages of this basic food report are:

- Although simple and easy to prepare, the report relies heavily on the accuracy of the basic information to be collected, for example the total of daily purchases, daily requisitions, etc.
- It is not totally accurate as it ignores such things as the cost of the staff meals; food transferred to bars, for example potato crisps, nuts, salted biscuits, trays of canapes, etc. which are given away free in the bars to customers and items such as lemons, limes, etc. which are included in certain drinks; and beverages transferred to kitchens, for example wine, spirits, beer, etc. for use in the cooking of specific dishes.

A Detailed Daily Food Cost Report

This food cost report is a development of the previous report and refines the accuracy of the report by taking into account the cost of beverages transferred into the kitchen, the cost of food transferred out of the kitchens to the bars, and the cost of employees' meals.

- It is more accurate than the two previous food reports illustrated that it includes additions to the cost of food for beverages transferred to the kitchen and deductions for the cost of food transferred from the kitchen to the bars and for the cost of all employees' meal. It also separates purchases into those that go straight to the storerooms and those that go direct to the kitchen and are charged immediately to the kitchen. The result of these additions and subtractions is that the true cost of the food sold to customers is more accurate than previously.

- The accuracy of the to-date food cost percentage is refined to take into account all daily transactions and these figures should be fully relied upon to be the basis against which corrective action may be taken.

The disadvantages of this type of report are that it is more detailed than the previous reports and it relies very much on the accuracy of the collected information, for example, the collection of all the requisition notes and the accurate extensions of the pricing of items; the collection of the goods received sheet and the checking of it against delivery notes, credit notes, invoices, etc.

Calculation of the Potential Food Cost

The potential food cost is the cost of the food under perfect and ideal conditions. The potential food cost of an operation is the principal and most effective method of evaluating the actual food cost. Any variance higher than 1 per cent between the potential and actual costs should be investigated. The potential food cost may be calculated in a variety of ways, but because of time it is usually costed per menu for each selling outlet twice a year or more frequently if the menu changes. This means that the potential figures will differ between breakfast, lunch and dinner menus and between selling outlets, where the prices of items may vary. The calculations are in three main steps.

- For each individual menu item multiply the number of portions actually sold during a 'sample' week as determined by the restaurant sales analysis, by the potential food cost per portion, to obtain the total potential cost of food sold for that week.
- Multiply the same portions actually sold by the menu selling prices, and arrive at the potential total sales. the potential food cost percentage.

To be able to do the calculations it would be necessary to have the following information to hand:

- A detailed sales analysis of all items sold in the various outlets, together with their selling prices.

- Standard recipe cards of all the menu items costed out.
- Summary of potential food cost, obtained from the standard recipe cards.
- Average market price for the main ingredients taken from invoices, food marketing reports or food cost indices reports.

It is not unusual for there to be a difference between the actual and the potential food cost figures. Usually the actual cost of the food sold is higher than the potential for such reasons as food being a perishable commodity, the difficulty of being exact when forecasting food production requirements and that a small amount of waste is almost unavoidable. Any large differences in the figures will reflect a lack of adherence to established standards, or pilfering or sheer carelessness resulting in an excessive amount of waste. As stated earlier, any variance in excess of 1 per cent should be investigated.

METHODS OF BEVERAGE CONTROL

There are many different methods in use today to control costs, the various methods depending on the size of the operation, the volume of business, owner or managed operation, etc. and the level of sophistication of control required. Each of the different methods in use could be classified under one of the following six basic types of beverage control systems.

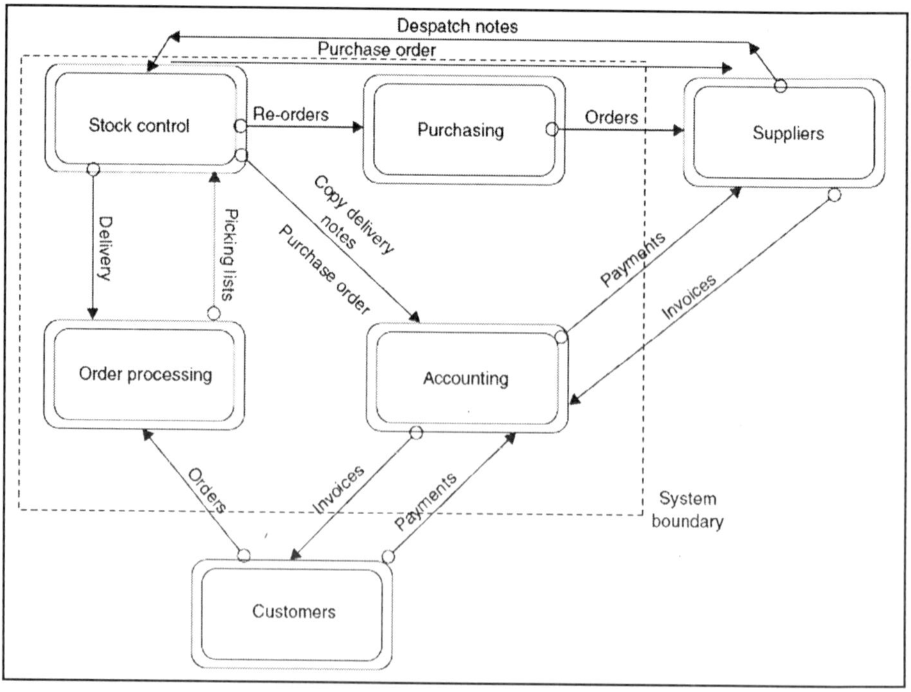

Fig: Inventory Control Cycle

Whatever method is adopted, it would be of little value unless the previous steps of control had been efficiently implemented and enforced, that is, the control of purchasing, receiving, storing and issuing; production planning; the establishment of standard yields, standard recipes, standard portion sizes and inventory. The inventory control cycle is of course applicable to beverage inventory as well, with FIFO been the most used method whilst LIFO may find application in situations where some stock may be kept back for later use. For example, some wine may be kept in the cellar and not sold so that it may age a little more.

Bar Cost System

This system is similar to that for the basic food cost report and the detailed food cost report. It may be produced for each bar separately or for all of the beverage operations.

Par Stock or Bottle Control System

This is a simple yet effective method of beverage control and is particularly useful for the smaller type operation where there are few full-time control staff. The following points should be noticed.

- The level of par stock is established for each bar, that is, to establish for each beverage the number of bottles required for a busy day plus a small safety factor. This number is determined to be the stock level to be held in the bar at the beginning of the service each day. To simplify the system only full bottles are counted, partial bottles are not counted.
- The number and type of empty bottles are noted each day, this being the amount and type to be requisitioned for the day.
- The potential sales are based on the quantities issued at selling price and are compared to actual revenue received.
- Adjustments to be made to the initial selling price if many mixed drinks are sold. This may only be necessary if the difference between the potential and actual sales figures gives cause for investigation.

The particular advantages of this system are its simplicity and ease of operation. The system assumes that over a short period the level of partial bottles remains relatively constant so that it becomes unnecessary to count each bottle' s contents to determine the total sales. Theoretically, the sales value of today' s issues should equal yesterday' s revenue. This would be unlikely, however, but over a short period the sales value of issues to date should equal the revenue to date figures.

Potential Sales Value System

This system is designed to control beverage sales and therefore beverage the bottle and the selling price for each drink. The sales value of each drink is called the potential sales value. The system requires as a basis for its operation, established standards for a bottle code number system, drink recipes, drink sizes, glassware and par stocks. Whenever the bottle size, drink size or recipe change a new calculation must be made and recorded, as this can affect the price of a drink and should require the price to be reviewed.

The various calculations which have to be made to establish the potential sales values are concerned with:

- **Full bottles of spirits:** The potential sales value of a full bottle of spirits, etc. which at times may be sold over a bar is equal to the selling price established by management. As little handling is involved in selling a full bottle, its price will usually be lower than when sold by the individual glass.
- **Spirits, etc. sold by the glass:** The sales value for a bottle of spirits, wine, etc. which is to be sold by the glass is calculated as in the following example. Potential sales value for a bottle of whisky: Size of bottle 70 cl Size of a straight drink 2.5 cl Selling price per drink ₹ 4.50 Number of drinks per bottle 28 (as determined by management) 28 (number of drinks) _ ₹4.50 (selling price per drink)
  - `126.00 (potential sales value)
- **Soft drink and mineral water sales:** The potential sales value of soft drinks, etc. depends on the pricing policy of the establishments; it could, for example, be:
  - A fixed price when sold on its own or when with another drink, for example, gin and tonic water.
  - At a lower price when served as part of a mixed drink, for example, a straight 2.5 cl drink of whisky may cost ₹4.50; a split bottle of dry ginger may cost ₹0.99; as a mixed drink whisky and dry ginger may be priced at ₹4.99 and not ₹5.49 as would be the case in fixed pricing.
  - The cost of soft drinks is included in the price when selling spirits.
  - It should be noted that if a lower or inclusive pricing system is adopted, adjustments must be made when preparing the control sheets so that an accurate potential sales figure is calculated.

- Cocktails, etc: If all drinks served to customers were sold as straight drinks or full bottles, it would be simple to calculate the potential sales value. When drinks are sold as cocktails containing two or more high selling price items it often requires an adjustment to be made when preparing the control sheet.

When the sales of mixed drinks on analysis are found to be low, there would be little need to go into great detail to calculate the allowances for the various mixed drinks. It is only when the actual money taken in the bars differs from the potential sales value by say more than 2 per cent that detailed analysis of sales and allowances needs to be done.

The Millimeter System

This method is recognized as the most accurate method of determining the amount of beverage sold. It is used at times when investigating the cause of an unacceptable difference recorded between the actual and potential results in a beverage report.

It is, however, a complicated and difficult system to operate for large units with a full range of beverage services unless aided by a mini computer.

The system requires:

- An accurate and detailed analysis of all sales by type and brand of drink sold, for each selling outlet.
- The calculation of the actual consumption of each type and brand of drink based on the daily physical stocktake, giving opening and closing stock levels of bars, plus any issues, and minus any transfers out to other bars. All drinks sold are converted back to the number of millilitres of each type and brand of drink sold using the standard beverage recipes. The total consumption of each kind of drink per sales bill has then to be compared with the actual consumption determined from the physical inventory and any adjustments.

The main disadvantages of this control system are:

- The time required to analyse sales and to take stock levels daily.
- The time required to calculate the daily consumption for each selling outlet.
- Additional difficulties if a large number of mixed drinks are sold and if drinks of different sizes are sold in each selling outlet.

Banqueting and Function Bar System

Should the banquet department have its own storage and bar areas it can operate and be controlled in the same way as any other bar. If, however, a bar has to be set up for each separate banquet or function, it will be necessary for an authorized person to requisition for each event from the main cellar and then immediately at the close of the event to return all unsold beverages.

Bottles issued would be the quantity issued from the cellar for that function. Bottles returned are the bottles and part bottles unused and returned to the cellar. The number of bottles issued minus bottles returned should be equal to the number of bottles and part bottles used. The actual cost is the purchase price paid per bottle, or half or split. The potential sales per bottle drinks per bottle.

Automated Beverage Dispensing System

The use of automated beverage dispensing systems is becoming more and more of a norm. As the cost of technology drops these systems can be afforded by medium-sized operations and when linked to an EPOS system inventory control reports can be compared to sales reports and discrepancies of actual stock can be identified much easier. The bottles of beverage are inverted and connected with small bore pipes within a locked storeroom, to each selling outlet. Large operations that may often use casual staff will normally invest into such technology.

The advantages of this method are numerous, but include the following:

- The drink size is pre-set and the drink automatically measured.
- The yield is consistently higher than when using other methods as the bottles drain completely into the dispenser.
- Each drink can be metered by the selling outlet. This helps with inventory control and the calculation of estimated bar revenue.
- It prevents bar staff from handling bottles. Every drink that they need for a customer is obtained by just pressing the correct drink button on the dispenser.
- Many beverage dispense machines are connected to microcomputers so that they can measure the drinks, dispense, display the prices, print the guest' s bill, as well as maintain the inventory and analyse drink sales.

There are some disadvantages in using beverage dispensing machines, such as:

- Unsuitability for certain types of beverage operations, for example, a cocktail bar in a luxury type hotel where the clientele expect personal service with the mixing of their drinks.

- The cost of installing dispensing machines is high, although the higher level of control should help to repay the initial costs relatively quickly.
- In general, they are only suitable for use in bars with a very high volume of sales and where the customer is not so concerned with traditional bar service.

The management techniques used in beverage production planning are therefore very similar in concept and method to the techniques used for food production planning; if anything even tighter standards may be laid down for beverage production for the reasons already discussed.

A similar recipe file for beverages may also be produced–either manually or by use of a computer and again the use of a computer for beverage planning should be seriously considered for the long-term cost savings and tighter control it can offer the establishment.

EPOS REPORTING

Electronic data storage has both been a blessing and a curse at the same time. The availability of so much information can often overload managers to the point that they end up not using any of the information after all. Here we briefly look at typical reports that a manager can extract from an EPOS system. It is important to understand that a manager can obtain such reports for any specific period be it daily, weekly, monthly or annually or it can even be a report between two dates. In that way reports can be customised for the periods that are important to control for that specific operation.

Menu Item Preference

From a control point of view this report is extremely important. It allows the user to identify potential menu items that are not doing very well and possibly eliminate them from the menu, or identify the items that sell extremely well and ensure that enough ingredients are ordered to ensure no customers are left unsatisfied due to a menu item that was not available.

Menu Item Profitability

This report extracts information from the stock control module of the system and gives accurate profitability per menu item. This together with the menu item preference report can be easily converted into a menu engineering report. The example shows the potential of the EPOS reporting provided the restaurant management wishes to input food costs into the system. In small operations that change their menu weekly and sometimes daily the management decision to not input all the data can often be made.

Sales by Meal Period

Identifying how well the restaurant is doing for each meal period is extremely important as it allows the manager to identify the hours of the day that he may need less or more staff, as well as focusing any marketing and promotions to that particular day.

Sales by Server

Sales by server help identify members of staff that may need further training to enable them to up sale items or reward members of staff that are doing exceptionally well.

Category Report

Often food and beverage items are placed in a specific category, for example appetizers, seafood, whiskies or beer. This enables the manager to see at a glance as to how well a particular category of food or beverage might be performing in terms of popularity and profitability.

Table Waiting Times

Another interesting report is a report that illustrates the time passed between stages of the meal experience. This is not very accurate as the system will only start measuring from the time the order has been put through the system but it can keep records of how long the meal has lasted and time lapsed between courses. Extremely useful tool in helping the manager to ensure quality of the meal experience in terms of service efficiency.

FOOD AND BEVERAGE CONTROL CHECKLISTS

Recent advances in technology have helped with food and beverage control but often one cannot understand the basics of the control system or what they should be looking for when trying to identify errors in the system. Although it would be impos sible for us to address every corrective action that should be taken when standards are not being met we can produce a control checklist that can be used as a tool to identify the weak areas of a control system.

Although the checklists are not exhaustive for every type of operation, it provides a good starting point and can be adapted to fit the type of operation the reader may have in mind.

The major reasons for food cost variances from the established standard for a unit include the following:

- Inaccurate arithmetic to paperwork: This also includes the paperwork of suppliers.

- Inefficient stocktaking.
- Poor revenue control: Lack of systematic procedures and practices.
- Poor menu: Unrelated to market conditions and requirements, lack of sales analysis and up-dating of menu.
- Poor purchasing, resulting in higher food costs, overstocking and wastage.
- Poor receiving, inferior goods being accepted, short weight of goods being signed for.
- Poor storing, poor rotation of stock resulting in wastage, poor security.
- Failure to establish and/or maintain standards for volume forecasting, standard recipes, standard yields and standard portion sizes.
- Failure to account accurately for all staff and management meals.
- Food control not being seen by staff to work, resulting in staff failing to maintain desired standards.

Beverage control is not so difficult or involved as food control. What at times is a problem is the dishonest employee and this is usually difficult to detect.

The typical problems are bar staff who:

- Bring in their own bottles of spirits, etc. sell the contents to customers and then pocket the money. This results in a busy bar with disappointing cash takings.
- **Drink at work:** Bar staff who help themselves to the odd drink soon get into the habit of it unless it is quickly detected. This results in lower than should be cash takings or customers hav ing short measure drinks which 'compensate' for the bar staff free drinks.
- Fail to 'ring-up' each drink sold and pocket the money taken from the client. This results again in lower cash taken.
- Provide free drinks for friends, again, resulting in lower bar takings.
- **Dilute drinks:** When a group of customers order their third or more 'round of drinks', they are less likely to identify weak drinks, the difference being pocketed by the bar staff.
- **Under-charge the customer:** The customer, being an accomplice of the bar staff, orders a drink, pays for it and is then given change in excess of what it should be. This results in bar takings being lower than they should be.

- **Short-change customers:** SThis is the all too common problem of bar staff giving customers less change than they should do and pocketing the difference for themselves.

If the spirits are on optics, or beers, spirits and minerals automatically dispensed to controlled measures, any discrepancy will almost certainly mean an error in cash handling made deliberately or by carelessness.

The types of problems are usually only discovered when good beverage control procedures are in operation, the identification of the dishonest employee being made as a result of such steps as changing bar staff duties and shifts, taking daily bar inventories, changing till drawers during a busy shift and checking the cash with the till reading, and by observation of the bar by an unknown member of the management or security staff.

The only highlights the necessity for the personnel department to carefully interview and take up several references before employing any new bar staff.

Checklist for the Smaller Operation

A quick checklist for the smaller operation for food cost variances from the established standard would include the following:

- Check the arithmetic of all major figures.
- Re-check stock figures and total, and in particular look for unusual figures in relation to the norm. The percentage of the total consumption of each category of commodities should be constant for any given menu over a period. Once a standard has been established, variations from it will indicate a problem, for example, if the meat consumption percentage was up it could well indicate pilferage, fraud, wastage or an increase in price and management attention should be focused towards this.
- Re-check sales figures and check against meals served.
- Check for unusual variances in sales. This could be caused by a major change in the weather, a national holiday, etc.
- Check for unusual changes in the sales mix.
- Check for unusual changes in price of major and costly food items.
- Check stores, refrigerators and waste bins for evidence of over purchasing, over preparation and unnecessary wastage.
- Check on meals taken by staff.

REVENUE CONTROL

To control the revenue of a unit, particular attention must be paid to the major factors which can have an influence on the profitability. Therefore it is essential to control the main factors which can affect the revenue of a business, such as the menu–beverage list, the total volume of food and beverage sales, the sales mix, the average spend of customers in each selling outlet at different times of the day, the number of covers served and the gross profit margins. It is important to note, particularly in commercial oper ations that somewhere in the total control system there is a need for the accountability of what has been served to the customer and the payment for what has been issued from the kitchen or the bar.

The payment for food and beverage may be made in many forms such as cash, foreign currency, credit cards, cheques, travellers' cheques, luncheon type vouchers and signed bills. All staff handling cash should be adequately trained in the respective company' s methods. It is a common practice for a cashier's or waiter's handbook/manual to be produced so that an established procedure may be followed with the specific aim of ensuring that cash security is efficiently carried out at all times.

A typical handbook/manual would contain information on the standard procedure to be followed for such things as:

- **Opening procedure:** Instructions here would include procedures about checking the float, having a float of specific denominations, checking the till roll, recording waiters' bill pad numbers, etc.
- **Working procedure:** Instructions on how to accept payment and the procedure to follow.
- **Closing procedure:** Instructions on any documentation and recordings to be completed, cashing up, recording of credit cards, cheques, etc.
- **Procedure for accepting foreign currency:** What currency is to be accepted, how to obtain the current exchange rates, how this is to be recorded, etc.
- **Procedure for accepting credit cards:** Which credit cards are to be accepted, how they are to be checked, method of processing credit cards for payment, recording of credit vouchers, etc.
- **Procedures for accepting vouchers such as luncheon vouchers:** Which vouchers are acceptable, how this is to be recorded.
- **Procedure for accepting cheques:** How cheques are to be made out, customers to produce a valid cheque guarantee card, checking that signatures correspond, etc.

- **Procedure for accepting travellers' cheques:** What travellers' cheques are acceptable, what currencies are acceptable, witnessing and checking signatures, how this is to be recorded.
- **Procedure for a complimentary or signed bill:** Check against current list of authorized persons and their signature, how this is to be recorded.

PROFIT SENSITIVITY ANALYSIS AND MENU ENGINEERING

Maintaining and improving an adequate level of profit are essential for all businesses today to survive–particularly with the increasing level of competition tempting customers not only to change from their usual type of restaurant, but also from the many other types of leisure businesses all chasing the same customers' restricted amount of disposable income. Among the problems often facing the food and beverage manager is how can the profitability be maintained or increased. Should the prices for some or all items be increased and by how much, and/or food and beverage items costs be reduced, and/or labour costs reduced, and/or the number of customers increased, etc. Two accepted methods of profit improvement are PSA and menu engineering.

Profit Sensitivity Analysis

PSA is concerned with identifying the 'critical' or 'key factors' of a business and establishing how they rank in influencing its net profit. The emphasis of PSA is on net profit and the examination of those areas that responded positively to change. In order to undertake PSA the 'profit multipliers' of the business must firstly be calculated.

The method is:

- Identify the 'key factors', financial and operational of the business. Key factors may be number of covers, food and beverage costs, labour costs, revenue, price per cover, etc.
- Assume a change in one 'key factor' at a time of say 10 per cent, whilst holding all others constant.
- Calculate the resulting change in net profit.
- Calculate the PM:

$$PM = \frac{\text{Percentage of change in net profit}}{\text{Percentage of change in key'factors'}}$$

- List the PMs in order of size.
- Analyse the results.

Menu Engineering

Menu engineering is a marketing orientated approach to the evaluation of a menu with regard to its present and future content, design and pricing. Its origins are based on the famous Boston Consulting Group portfolio technique, a matrix specifically designed to analyse individual business performance in a company with a range of different business interests. The concept of menu engineering requires food and beverage managers to orient themselves to the contribution that menu items make to the total profitability of a menu. It highlights the good and the poor performers in a menu, and provides vital information for making the next menu more interesting and appealing to the customers, and hopefully more profitable.

Menu engineering is a step-by-step procedure that focuses on the three main elements:

- **Customer demand:** The number of customers served.
- **Menu mix:** An analysis of customer preference for each menu item.
- **Contribution margin:** An analysis of the contribution margin for each menu item.

The pre-requisites for using this technique are:

- The standardization of all recipes, so that the food costs can be accurate.
- The accurate sales analysis of each menu item, daily and by meal period.
- The use of a personal computer, so that simple spreadsheets, with standard calculations, may be done accurately and with speed.

Using the simple matrix, menu items can be plotted, representing their performance with regard to volume and cash contribution. The four squares of the matrix commonly have names indicating the performance of items in a particular square.

- **Stars:** Menu items high in menu mix (popularity) and also high in contribution margin.
- **Plowhorses:** Menu items high in menu mix (popularity) but low in contribution margin.
- **Puzzles:** Menu items low in menu mix (popularity) and high in contribution margin.
- **Dogs:** Menu items low in menu mix (popularity) and low in contribution margin.

The analysis of the data to undertake menu engineering can be done using a standard computer spreadsheet package. This takes the form of a large grid compromising of rows and columns where labels, formulae and values can be entered. When in operation, the formulae and values can be changed if required, giving instantaneous re-calculations of the figures, and hard copies printed and retained for easy reference. Whilst spreadsheets can be compiled by hand, the time taken would be lengthy and the opportunity to frequently undertake 'what if' exercises less likely. It should be noted here that the success in being able to move menu items 'up' the matrix to the status of a 'star' could

SYSTEMS OF REVENUE CONTROL

There are two basic approaches to recording and controlling food and beverage sales.

- **A manual system:** Which is commonly used in small and in exclusive type catering units.
- **An automated system:** Which is commonly used in units with several outlets, in units with a very high volume of business and in up-to- date companies with many units.

Manual System

As technology is becoming increasingly affordable even for the very small businesses we become more relied on technology without having an understanding of the basics of a system. Furthermore even the best EPOS will at some point malfunction or a printer may be out of order, and then the business will need to have a back up plan and know how to use a manual system. Here we examine two basics of a manual system the sales check and the role of the cashier which in a computerized system it becomes defunct as every server can have his/her own float as the adding and printing of the bill is automatically done.

Sales Checks

One of the simplest steps to take when attempting to establish sales control procedures is to require that each item ordered and its selling price are recorded on a waiter' s sales check.

Using some form of a check system serves the following functions:

- To remind the waiting staff of the order they have taken.
- To give a record of sales so that portion sales and sales mixes and sales histories can be compiled.
- To assist the cashier and facilitate easy checking of prices charged.
- To show the customer a detailed list of charges made.

An additional aid is to use numbered checks and control these tightly, recording all cancelled and missing checks.

It is more common to find duplicate or triplicate check being used as an aid to control for the following reasons:

- They provide the kitchen, buffet or bar with a written record of what has been ordered and issued.
- They authorize the kitchen, buffet or bar to issue the food and/or beverage.
- They provide the opportunity to compare the top copy of the check with the duplicate to ensure that all that has been issued has been charged and paid for.

The Cashier's Role

In addition to following precisely the unit' s procedure for the handling of all revenue transactions within the restaurant or bars, it is normal practice for the cashier working a manual system to be required to complete the following:

- To issue check pads to the waiting staff prior to a meal period, to record the numbers of the checks issued in each pad, and obtain the waiting staff' s signature for them; and on the completion of the meal period to receive from the waiting staff their respective unused check pads, record the numbers, and sign for the receipt of those returned. This information to be recorded on the check number issue control sheet.
- To check the pricing, extensions and subtotals of all checks and to add any government tax charges and to enter the total amount due.
- To receive and check money, credit or, when applicable, an approved signature in payment for the total amount due for each check.
- To complete the missing checklist for each meal period. This is an aid to the cashier in controlling what checks are used. The respective check numbers on the list are crossed out when payment is made. When a missing check is identified, investigation to be carried out to find the reason for this, and if no satisfactory explanation is forthcoming, to inform a member of management on duty. Missing checks to be marked on the missing checklist.
- To complete the restaurant sales control sheet for each meal period. This form requires that all revenue received is recorded under specific headings such as cash, cheques, credit card transactions, etc. From this control sheet basic data–such as the number of covers served or the average spend per customer on food and beverages–is quickly obtained.

- To complete the necessary paying in of all cash, etc. in accordance with the unit' s established practice. This could be direct to a bank whether a small independent unit, or a unit of a large company, or to the head cashier' s office if a large unit with many outlets.

Problems of the Manual System

In brief, the basic problems of controlling any food and beverage operation are:

- The time span between purchasing, receiving, storing, processing, selling the product, and obtaining the cash or credit for the product, is sometimes only a few hours.
- The number of items held in stock at any time is high.
- A large number of finished items are produced from a combination of the large number of items held in stock.
- The number of transactions taking place on an hourly basis in some operations can be very high.
- To be able to control the operation efficiently, management ideally requires control in formation of many types to be available quickly and to be presented in a meaningful way.

The full manual control of a food and beverage operation would be costly, time consuming and data produced would frequently be far too late for meaningful management action to take place. Certain aspects of control such as regularly up-dating the costings of standard recipes, calculating gross profit potentials, and providing detailed sales analysis would seldom be done because of the time and labour involved. A manual system providing a restricted amount of basic data is still widely used in small- and medium-sized units although they are likely to be replaced in the near future by machine or electronic systems.

The day-to-day operational problems of a manual system are many and include such common problems as:

- Poor handwriting by waiting staff resulting in:
- Incorrect order given to the kitchen or dispense bar.
- Wrong food being offered to the customer.
- Incorrect prices being charged to the customer.
- Poorly presented bill for the customer, etc.
- Human error can produce such mistakes as:
  - Incorrect prices charged to items on a bill
  - Incorrect additions to a customer' s bill
  - Incorrect service charge made
  - Incorrect government tax charge made.

- The communication between departments such as the restaurant, dispense bar, kitchen and cashiers has to be done physically by the waiting staff going to the various departments. This is not only time consuming but inefficient.
- Manual systems do not provide any quick management information data, any data produced at best being normally twentyfour to twenty-eight hours old, as well as being costly to produce.
- Manual systems have to be restricted to the bare essentials because of up-to-date information.

COMPUTERIZED SYSTEMS

EPOS technology and windows based software specifically designed for the food and beverage operation seem to have replaced every other type of machine based system. Although it is tempting to simply talk about EPOS systems only, it is important we also look at some of the older technology that still may be used in some countries and is still used in very small operations around the world.

Pre-Checking Systems

Pre-check machines are somewhat similar in appearance to a standard cash register and are designed to operate only when a sales check is inserted into the printing table to the side of the machine. The machine is operated in the following way.

- A waiter has his/her own machine key.
- A check is inserted into the printing table and the particular keys, depending on the order taken, are pressed giving an item and price record as well as recording the table number, the number of covers and the waiter' s reference number.
- A duplicate is printed and issued by the machine which is then issued as the duplicate check to obtain food and/or beverages.
- For each transaction a reference number is given on the sales check and the duplicate.
- All data is recorded on a continuous audit tape that can be removed only by authorized persons at the end of the day when the machine is cleared and total sales taken and compared to actual cash received.

The advantages of the system are:

- The sales check is made out and a record of it made on the audit tape before the specific items can be obtained from the kitchen or bar.

- Analysis of total sales per waiter is made on the audit tape at the end of each shift.
- No cashier is required as each waiter acts as his/her own cashier, each keeping the cash collected from customers until the end of the shift and then paying it in.
- As each waiter has his/her own security key to operate the machine, there is restricted access to the machines and no other way by which pre-checks can be provided and used in exchange for items from the kitchen or bar.

Pre-Set Pre-Checking System

This is an up-date on the basic pre-check machine. The keyboard is much larger than the previous machines, and has descriptive keys corresponding to all items on the menu which are pre-set to the current price of each item. A waiter pressing the key for, say one cheeseburger would not only have the item printed out but also the price.

A control panel, kept under lock and key, would enable management to change the price of any item, if required, very quickly. It is also possible to have a running count kept of each item recorded and at the end of a meal period by depressing each key in turn to get a print out giving a basic analysis of sales made.

Electronic Cash Registers

These are very high speed machines which were developed mainly for operations such as supermarkets and were further adapted for use in high volume catering operations. They are robust machines that apart from printing the customer bill they can also provide basic reports such as sales by type of product, payment method, etc.

The advancement in EPOS technology and the low costs are making Electronic cash registers a thing of the past, although in small operations that do not require heavy inventory control and detailed reporting an ECR is still the choice due to its much lower cost.

Epos Control Systems

At a basic level a point-of-sale control system is no more than a modern ECR with the additional feature of one or several printers at such locations as the kitchen or dispense bar. Some systems replace the ECR with a 'server terminal', which may be placed at several locations within a restaurant, and is a modification of an ECR in that the cash features are eliminated making the terminal relatively small and inconspicuous.

The objectives for having printers are:

- To provide an instant and separate clear and printed order to the kitchen or bar, of what is required and by and for whom.

- To speed up the process of giving the order to the kitchen or bar.
- To aid control, in that items can only be ordered when they have been entered into the ECR or terminal by an identifiable member of the waiting staff and printed.
- To reduce the time taken by the waiter in walking to the kitchen or bar to place an order and, as frequently happens, to check if an order is ready for collection.
- To afford more time, if required, for customer contact.

Printers are it times replaced by VDU screens. Server terminals are part of a computer-based point-of-sale system. These special terminals are linked to other server terminals in the restaurants and bars within one system and, if required to, also interface with other systems so that, for example, the transfer of restaurant and bar charges may be made via the front office computer system.

The advantage of a computerized point-of-sale system is that it is capable of processing data as activities occur, which makes it possible to obtain up-to- the-minute reports for management who can be better informed and able to take immediate and accurate corrective action if necessary.

This type of point-of-sale control system has been taken one step further with the introduction of hand-held terminals or mobile points of sale. These hand-held devises can use radio frequencies or infrared or bluetooth technology to communicate from the guest' s table direct to the kitchen and bar preparation areas. MPOS offer a number of advantages: food and beverage orders are delivered faster and more efficiently to preparation sites; waiters in turn can attend more tables; with a two-way communication service staff can be notified if an item is out of stock; all food and beverage items ordered are immediately charged to the guest' s bill, which is accurate and easy to read; finally, operations can reassess their labour utilization and efficiency, certain members of the service staff, for example, can take the simple orders, while others can spend more time with customers to increase food and beverage sales.

Touch screen technology utilized by the systems enable the server to use EPOS and MPOS technology with minimal training as the systems often resemble a Microsoft windows type interface.

FORECASTING

For food and beverage control to be successful one of the important management tools is successful forecasting. In smaller restaurants managers may often have an intuitive idea about how many customers to expect on any given day. In larger operations however a more scientific approach is required.

Lack of storage space and perishability of the produce are only two of the reasons why effective forecasting is imperative for the success of a food and beverage operation. The main considerations of forecasting is not only how many people will turn up at any given period but also what menu items are they likely to consume and at what time of the day.

Getting it right all the time is an impossible task however with the correct techniques it is possible to have an educated informative guess that is based on research and not assumptions. Forecasting does not only affect purchasing of food and beverages but it also affect all other areas of the business such as the pricing, production, number of employees to hire, to name a few.

In order to be successful in forecasting accurately some of the type of information would need is:

- Sales history
- Turn down history
- Cancellations and no shows trends
- Competitor data
- Market trends at local, national and international levels
- The weather forecast
- Information about special events and new attractions.

Even a change in the weather can affect menu item sales, on a cold day, for example, chances are that customers would prefer a hot soup rather than a cold salad as a starter. There is a number of forecasting software that is available to food and beverage managers and these use some of the methods briefly described here:

- **Multiple regression analysis:** Used when two or more independent factors are involved–widely used for intermediate term forecasting. Used to assess which factors to include and which to exclude. Can be used to develop alternate models with different factors.
- **Non-linear regression:** Does not assume a linear relationship between variables–frequently used when time is the independent variable.
- **Trend analysis:** Uses linear and non-linear regression with time as the explanatory variable–used where pattern overtime.
- **Moving average analysis:** Simple moving averages–forecasts future values based on a weighted average of past values–easy to update.

- **Weighted moving averages:** Very powerful and economical. They are widely used where repeated forecasts required–uses methods like sum-of-the-digits and trend adjustment methods.
- **Adaptive filtering:** A type of moving average which includes a method of learning from past errors–can respond to changes in the relative importance of trend, seasonal, and random factors.
- **Exponential smoothing:** A moving average form of time series forecasting–efficient to use with seasonal patterns–easy to adjust for past errors–easy to prepare follow-on forecasts–ideal for situations where many forecasts must be prepared–several different forms are used depending on presence of trend or cyclical variations.

OPERATING RATIOS

Food cost in relation to food sales, beverage cost in relation to beverage sales, etc. there are many more that are used and found to be of value. The following is a brief explanation of those that are frequently used.

Total Food And Beverage Sales

The total food and beverage sales should be recorded, checked and analysis of these figures is usually done daily for large establishments and for those that are not operating a manual control system. The analysis would show separately the food sales and the beverage sales per outlet and per meal period.

The importance of this yardstick cannot be emphasized enough other than to remind the reader that it is cash and cash only that can be banked and not percentages or any ratio or factor figures.

Departmental Profit

Departmental profit is calculated by deducting the departmental expenses from the departmental sales, the expenses being the sum of the cost of food and beverages sold, the cost of labour and the cost of overheads charged against the department, and the profit being usually expressed as a percentage of the departmental sales, for example:

Departmental profit (₹1,200) = $\times \frac{100}{1} = 15\%$

Food and Beverage sales (₹1,200)

The departmental profit should be measured against the budget figures for that period.

Ratio of Food/Beverage Sales to Total Sales

It is worthwhile for food and beverage sales to be separated from each other and to express each of them as a percentage of the total sales. This would be a measure of performance against the established standard budgeted percentage as well as indicating general trends in the business.

Average Spending Power

This measures the relationship between food sales and beverage sales to the number of customers served. If food sales are ₹750 and the number of customers served is seventy, the average spend by each customers is ₹10.72.

The ASP for beverages is usually related to the number of items recorded on the till roll, rather than to the number of customers, and the total beverage sales. Thus if ₹600 is the recorded beverage sales and an analysis of the till roll showed that 200 drinks had been sold, the average spend per drink would be ₹3.00.

What is different here is that a customer may order several drinks during an evening and therefore the average amount spent on a drink is more important than the ASP per customer. To calculate the ASP for bottled wine sales in a restaurant or at a banquet though could be a useful exercise.

Sales Mix

This measures the relationship between the various components of the total sales of a unit, for example:

Sales mix	%	Sales mix	%
Coffee shop sales		**Restaurant sales**	
Food	20	Food	25
Beverages	5	Beverages	10
Banqueting sales		**Banqueting sales**	
Food	20	Beverages	5
Beverages	10		100

In addition, a sales mix may be calculated for the food and beverage menus for each outlet under group headings such as appetizers, main course items, sweet course, coffees, etc.; and spirits, cocktails, beers and lagers, etc.

This would not only highlight the most and least popular items, but would at times help to explain a disappointing gross profit percentage that occurred in spite of a good volume of business; the reason often being that each item is usually costed at different gross profit percentages and if the customers are choosing those items with a low gross profit this would result in the overall gross profit figure being less than budgeted for.

Payroll Costs

Payroll costs are usually expressed as a percentage of sales and are normally higher, the higher the level of service offered. It is vital that they are tightly controlled as they contribute a high percentage of the total costs of running an operation. Payroll costs can be controlled by establishing a head count of employees per department, or establishing the total number of employee hours allowed per department in relation to a known average volume of business. In addition, all overtime must be strictly controlled and should only be permitted when absolutely necessary.

Index of Productivity

This is calculated by the formula:

$$\frac{\text{Sales}}{\text{Payroll (including any staff benefit cost s)}}$$

The index of productivity can be calculated separately for food sales, beverage sales or for total food and beverage sales. The use of the term 'payroll costs' in the formula includes not only the appropriate payroll costs, but also any other employee benefits such as employers' pension contributions, medical insurance, etc.

The index of productivity would vary depending on the type of operation, for example, a fast-food restaurant with a takeaway service would have a high index of productivity, as the payroll costs would be lower than a luxury restaurant employing highly skilled and expensive staff with a high ratio of staff to customers, which may have a relatively low index of productivity.

As payroll costs can be controlled and should be related to the forecasted volume of business, a standard index of productivity can be established to measure how accurately the two elements are related.

Stock Turnover

This is calculated by the formula:

$$\text{Rate of stock turnover} \; \frac{\text{Cost of food orbeverages consumed}}{\text{Average stock value (food or beverage) at cost}}$$

The rate of stock turnover gives the number of times that the average level of stock has turned over in a given period. Too high a turnover would indicate very low levels of stocks being held and a large number of small value purchases being made. This is costly and time consuming for whoever does the purchasing as well as costly for the purchases as no price advantage can be taken of the standard quantity offers made by suppliers. Too low a turnover would indicate unnecessary capital tied up in an operation and therefore additionally a larger control and security problem.

Sales Per Seat Available

This shows the sales value that can be earned by each seat in a restaurant, coffee shop, etc. As in the part about rate of seat turnover, the seat is the selling point and is required to contribute a certain value to turnover and profits.

Rate of Seat Turnover

This shows the number of times that each seat in a restaurant, coffee shop, etc. is used by customers during a specific period. Thus, if in a 120-seater coffee shop 400 customers were served in a three-hour lunch period, the rate of seat turnover would be 400 divided by 120, that is, 3.33. As the coffee shop staff can only sell food to customers while they are seated at a table, the importance of the rate of seat turnover is highlighted.

Sales Per Waiter/Waitress

Each waiter/waitress will have a known number of covers for which he/she is responsible. This would vary depending on the style of food and beverage service offered. As salespeople for the restaurant or coffee shop, their takings should be of a predetermined target level so as to contribute to a satisfactory level of turnover and profit.

Sales Per Square Meter

This is self-explanatory in that the space of all selling outlets needs to be used to its best advantage so as to achieve a desired turnover and profit. This can be calculated on a square foot/meter basis. As the square footage per customer varies with the type of food and beverage service offered, so must the costs to the customer so that an establishment is earning the desired turnover and profit per square foot of selling space.

□

8

Menu Planning

INTRODUCTION

The menu is the primary selling tool of any establishment that offers food and beverage for sale. For the customer it identifies the items that are available, shows prices and any other charges and together with other external features may characterize the style of food service offered. From the establishments perspective the menu should meet the objectives of the marketing policy, the catering policy and the financial policy. The marketing policy should guide the catering policy so that the products on offer and the style of operation best meet the needs of the target market. The catering policy is concerned with the size and style of menu to be offered together with an appropriate style of service and this will impact on space requirements, level and type of equipment purchased, and the level of skill and number of staff required. The financial policy aims to achieve revenue and profitability to budget through pricing, cost control and volume.

TYPE OF MENUS

Although there are many types of eating establishments offering many types of meal experiences, there are basically only two types of food menus: the table d' hôte; and the à la carte. From these two types of menus there are in practice many adaptations of each.

Table D' Hôte

Table d' hôte means food from the hosts' table and may be identified by:

- Being a restricted menu.
- Offering a small number of courses, usually three or four.
- A limited choice within each course.

- A fixed selling price.
- All the dishes being ready at a set time.

MAGNOLIA

SUNDAY ROAST MENU

STARTERS

Cream of Broccoli and Shropshire blue stilton soup
Served with crusty bread
Chicken liver, brandy and basil terrine
Served with red onion chutney,
salad and toasted crusty bread
Mushrooms
Cooked in a creamy garlic sauce
English Asparagus
Sautéed with butter and crispy cured ham
Scottish smoked salmon
Served with lemon

MAINS

Roasted Sirloin of Scottish Beef
and Yorkshire pudding
Whole Poussin Roasted
Roasted Pork leg
With crackling and fresh apple sauce
Whole Sea Bass
Stuffed with herbs, garlic and lemon
All of the above are served
With seasonal vegetables and potatoes

DESSERTS

Baked Apple with sultana's
and a light caramel sauce
Lemon tart with berries
and a berry Coulis
Chocolate and orange liquor cake
With cream and caramelised orange
Selection of Cheeses
Shropshire blue Stilton, Soignon Goats cheese, Somerset Brie, Mature cheddar

TWO COURSE ₹13.95 THREE COURSE ₹16.95

*12.5% discretionary charge will be added to your bill

Fig: Example of a table'hôte menu

This type of menu usually contains the popular type dishes and is easier to control, the set price being fixed for whatever the customer chooses, or being set depending on the main dish chosen and occasionally may offer and additional item at a supplementary price. It is common practice in many restaurants for a table d' hôte menu to be offered to a customer together with an à la carte menu.

Table d' hôte menus can be offered for breakfast, lunch and dinners. Their many adaptations are used for:

- **Banquets:** A banquet menu is a fixed menu at a set price offering usually no choice whatsoever to the customers, unless the client informs the caterer in advance that certain guests require, say, a vegetarian or kosher type meal, and is available to all guests at a predetermined time.
- **Buffets:** Buffet type meals vary considerably depending on the occasion, and the price paid, from the simple finger buffet, where all items prepared are proportioned to a small size so that the customer may consume it without the use of any cutlery, to the exotic fork buffets where hot and cold food is available and where many large dishes will be carved and portioned for the individual guest. Buffets are frequently prepared for such occasions as wedding receptions, press receptions, presentations and conferences. Buffets can be classified as a form of table d' hôte menu as they offer a restricted menu, a limited choice of only what is on the buffet; a predetermined set price and all the dishes are available at a set time.
- **Coffee houses:** A coffee house menu is a more recent form of table d' hôte menu that is commonly used today in hotels and restaurants. This type of menu is characterized by:
  - Being a set menu offered often for twelve to eighteen hours of the day.
  - Being reasonably priced, with often each dish or part of the menu individually priced.
  - Offering a range and choice of items that are suitable for snacks, light meals, lunch or dinner.
  - Offering a limited range of foods that are either already cooked, are of the convenience type food category and require little preparation time, or are simple and quick to cook, for example omelet' s, hamburgers, etc.

  - A simplified form of service being offered, for example plate service, counter service, etc.–In some establishments the coffee shop menu may be replaced for two to three hours with a special breakfast menu offering a restricted choice when there is a need to serve a very large number of people in the shortest pos sible time.
- **Cyclical menus:** These are a series of table d' hôte menus, for example for three weeks, which are repeated again and again for a set period of, for example, four months. These are often used in hospitals and industrial catering as an aid to establishing a pattern of customer demand for a menu item and as a result assist in purchasing, preparation of items and staffing requirements.

À La Carte

À la carte means a free choice from the card or menu and is identified by:

- Being usually a larger menu than a table d' hôte menu and offering a greater choice.
- Listing under the course headings all of the dishes that may
- be prepared by the establishment.
- All dishes being prepared to order.
- Each dish being separately priced.
- Usually being more expensive than a table d' hôte menu.
- Often containing the exotic and high cost seasonal foods.

Part of an à la carte menu may contain a plat du jour or 'speciality of the house' part. This consists usually of one or two main dishes, separately priced, which are already prepared and change daily. À la carte menus are, because of their size and the unknown demand of each item, more difficult to control than the typical table d' hôte menus.

- `11.00 Tagliolinmi (hand made) of fennel and salami
- `12.00Caramella (little sweets) of sustainable prawns, rocket and chilli
- `11.50Tomato and mozzarella risotto, basil pangratatta Main Courses:
- `16.00Duck confit (from Gascony), tomato and potato 'al forno'
- `15.00Char grilled fish of the day, cardamom and horseradish
- `13.00Aubergine, spinach and goats cheese, grilled red chilli sauce
- `15.00Twice cooked pork belly, soy, ginger and spring onion
- `16.00Pan fried organic salmon fillet, cherry tomatoes and mint

A MENU FOR JULY

Fresh bread & butter ~ ₹1.50
Green & black olives ~ ₹2.50
Strawberry Bellini ~ ₹6.00

SOUPS	
₹6.50	Pea, zucchini and their flowers
	Beetroot, cardamom & sour cream
STARTERS	
₹9.50	Prosciutto di san Danielle with summer artichokes
₹9.00	Smoked mackerel, baby leeks, spinach & pickled ginger
₹8.50	New potato, French bean, radish & green olive salad
₹9.50	Mozzarella di bufala, black figs & purple basil
₹8.50	Deep fried vegetables, anchovies & sage, chopped red chilli
Rice and Pastas	
₹11.00	Tagliolinmi (hand made) of fennel & salami
₹12.00	Caramella (little sweets) of sustainable prawns, rocket & chilli
₹11.50	Tomato & mozzarella risotto, basil pangratatta
Main Courses	
₹16.00	Duck confit (from Gascony), tomato & potato 'al forno'
₹15.00	Char grilled fish of the day, cardamom & horseradish
₹13.00	Aubergine, spinach & goats cheese, grilled red chilli sauce
₹15.00	Twice cooked pork belly, soy, ginger & spring onion
₹16.00	Pan fried organic salmon fillet, cherry tomatoes & mint

There will be a discretionary 12.5% service related charge added to your bill!
Acorn House asks you politely to retrain from smoking, for every ones sake!

Fig: Etract of an à la carte Restaurant

There will be a discretionary 12.5 per cent service related charge added to your bill! Acorn House asks you politely to retrain from smoking, for every ones sake!

A special promotion menu is a form of à la carte menu which is at times offered to the guest in addition to the à la carte menu. This type of menu is concerned with the selling of a particular part of a menu to increase the interest for the customer, to increase the average spending by the customer and in turn to increase the turnover and profit for the caterer.

Promotions may be made by specially printing attractive menus for such items as:

- Shellfish, when an increased variety of shellfish and special dishes would be made available.
- Soft fruits, when various types of berry fruits such as strawberries, raspberries, loganberries, etc. would be featured in special dishes.
- The game season, when pheasant, grouse, etc. would be featured in pâtés, soups and special main course dishes.

- Dishes cooked or prepared at the table, for example crêpes Suzette, steak Diane, etc.
- Dishes that utilize seasonal produce many of which are included in the items above.

MENU OFFERING

Much has changed in the presentation and service style of the food and beverage offering. Traditionally high-level service consisted of trolley service where food was either cooked or carved at the table and vegetables were silver served or alternatively silver service where each component of the meal was served individually from silver flats or dishes. Table or family service followed this where the main item was plated and vegetables and accompaniments were placed in dishes on the table for guests to help themselves.

At the lower end of restaurant service was plated service where the whole meal was pre-plated and finally self-service where the customer selected and collected their meal from a service counter. Menu development followed these service styles so that the more expensive trolley or silver service styles reflected in more expensive menu items, printing and general restaurant ambience. Changes in food presentation style initiated by nouvelle cuisine and continued through the development of celebrity chefs now finds plated service regarded as the normal choice in many of the worlds top luxury restaurants.

The chef literally creates the dish on the plate complete with vegetables, sauces and accompaniments creating a presentation or picture of the dish. Menus need to reflect this change in presentation style and the change in status of plated meals. In particular menu descriptions need to be both informative and accurate because all items are already on the plate and customers may have also developed a wider range of and greater use of adjectives similar in many ways to that used to describe works of art, and for the chef restaurateur this is the image that they want to portray as part of the establishment' s and their own identity.

Content of Food Menus

The content of food menus varies with the type of menu, the segment of the market it is aimed at, the occasion, the food cost available, the country or region, etc. Table d' hôte menus are often of three to four courses only. A hotel room service breakfast menu will offer three or four courses from both a traditional breakfast and a continental style breakfast together with a number of ancillary items such as newspapers, magazines or early morning beverages and will also offer a range of breakfast delivery times depending on the establishment.

A' la carte menus often differ for lunch and/or dinner periods, although it is not uncommon for the same à la carte menu to be offered throughout the day. In the India, for example, traditionally the heavier type items, for example thick vegetable-based soups, farinaceous dishes, meat puddings, meat stews, steamed fruit and sponge puddings, would normally be found on a lunch menu; whereas the lighter and often more delicately flavoured dishes would be found on a dinner menu, for example speciality consommés, poached fish with delicate flavours and often complicated garnishes, hot and cold sweet and savoury soufflés, etc. However, many of these traditional dishes now feature on menus at any part of the day as part of a marketing campaign in what marketers would refer to as retro dishes or dishes that where popular in the past, went out of fashion only to re-emerge once again on our menus. This applies particularly to dishes that intuitionalists suggest are bad for us, for example steamed suet puddings for which, nostalgia is a strong buying force. For a traditional full à la carte menu, the courses or parts of the menu would be divided up into a possible 14 parts.

It is from this full outline of the sequence of parts that a table d' hôte menu or a special luncheon or dinner menu could be constructed. The combination of the various parts of the menu depends very much on the occasion, the prices to be charged and the wishes of the customer. There is an established order of sequence of parts of the menu, which by tradition are followed. This accepted sequence enables the caterer to compile the separate courses on table d' hôte and à la carte menus and to suggest to clients suitable special and/or function menus of varying lengths.

It is very seldom the practice for all of the possible courses of a menu to be served, but as a general rule it is possible to state that when a large number of courses are served that the portion sizes are relatively small. The classical European menu structure identified by M. J. Leto and W. K. H. Bode consists of 16 courses excluding coffee. They are in order of service cold starter, soups, hot starters, egg and farinaceous, fish, small hot meat dishes, large meat joint, small cold meat course, sorbet, roast with salad, vegetable course, potato course, warm sweet course, cold sweet course, cheese course and fresh fruit.

Menu Planning

As stated earlier the menu is the key marketing and selling tool available to the restaurateur and as such meticulous attention to detail is the key to making this work successfully and is a positive step towards a profitable food and beverage enterprise. The menu communicates a wide range of information to the customer both in terms of the words used to describe dishes, referred to as 'copy' and more subliminally through colour, layout, quality of material used, and style and needs to be reflected conceptually throughout the whole restaurant.

New menu concepts can rejuvenate a restaurant:

- In his new restaurant at the Compleat Angler hotel in Marlow, Dean Timpson explains that he can focus much more on the food offering. After more than seven years as executive chef at Marlow's Compleat Angler hotel, Dean Timpson was offered the opportunity of opening a restaurant with his name above the door at the 64-bedroom property.
- Almost `1m was spent on creating fine-dining restaurant Dean Timpson at the Compleat Angler and the hotel's other eaterie, the brasserie-style Bowaters, by dividing the former Riverside restaurant in two.
- Timpson explains that cooking for a far smaller number of covers than before and being able to focus exclusively on the restaurant– which is open for lunch Wednesday to Sunday and for dinner Tuesday to Saturday–is allowing him to significantly raise the level of cooking. He has also sourced new suppliers for the restaurant, so is working with the very best ingredients. At lunch, as well as the à la carte, Timpson offers a threecourse market menu for ₹24.50, with three options per course. Crayfish and smoked salmon tortellini with red chard is among the current starters on this menu, with fillet of turbot with pea and truffle risotto among the mains, and passion fruit mousse with mango jelly and coconut ice-cream a dessert option.
- In the evening, alongside the à la carte, a six-course tasting menu is offered and is selling strongly, with about 25 per cent of diners choosing it. Meanwhile, the à la carte features five dishes at each course, with dishes selling evenly across the menu, says Timpson. Duck eggs from a local farm are put to good use in a starter of scallops with English pea purée and a confit of pork belly is a similarly seasonal alternative to start.
- At main course Timpson is particularly proud of the loin of rabbit and langoustine with prune purée and cabbage. 'It's a dish I've been working on for six years, and I've now got it exactly as I want it,' he says. 'It's a lovely balance between earthy, savoury and sweet flavours'.

What's on the menu:

- Duo of foie gras with pineapple purée and caramelized pineapple, ₹14
- Quail ballotine wrapped in Parma ham with rhubarb purée and pickled walnuts, ₹13

- Cornish red mullet with saffron mayonnaise and a tomato dressing, ₹12.50
- Roast suckling pig with pak choi and Granny Smith apple sauce, ₹26
- Cornish monkfish wrapped in Parma ham with marinated tomatoes and asparagus, ₹23
- Fillet of sea bass with orange dressing, baby spinach, clam and razor clam lasagne, ₹27.50
- Dark chocolate soufflé with mint ice cream, ₹7.50
- Strawberry parfait wrapped in chocolate with honeycomb caramel, ₹8
- Chilled apricot soup and apricot mousse served with champagne, ₹7.50

The menu, together with other physical attributes of a property contributes to creating a level of expectation from the customer. Meeting this customer expectation or in fact exceeding this expectation should be the primary objective of the restaurateur in the quest for a successful and profitable business.

Because the menu plays such a pivotal role in operational style, pricing structure and overall concept design it is important at the planning stage that the location is right for the planned menu type, that the market exists within this catchments area and that it works with regard to the local competition.

In an affluent residential area a small restaurant may be successful with high priced, high quality items and a low volume of customers whereas in a less affluent area, perhaps with a high student population on restricted budgets a small restaurant may have more success with a takeaway menu. These two examples are rather polarized and often boundaries are not quite so clearly defined but it serves to demonstrate the need to consider these aspects before embarking on a restaurant style or menu plan).

Themes

The design of a menu concerns more than the typography, colour, graphics, and shape or production material, important as these areas might be. Today' s consumers are well aware of a modern computers ability to produce high quality print and graphics. With a little sophisticated software and a good quality colour printer production of high quality colourfully designed menus with large amounts of graphics is relatively simple and inexpensive. A catering business, therefore, relies more heavily for its overall design appeal on what and how it describes the menu items. The use of language often causes difficulty particularly mixing different languages, for example English and French. By adding

French the restaurateur may seek to add classical named dishes but by mixing the language the dish is described in pseudo-English or French and often becomes an unrecognizable hybrid. If part of the restaurants theme is to represent another country then the menu may be written in the corresponding language but it is essential that an accurate description of each dish be given properly translated into English. In this way special themes or events can be reflected in the menu design and content.

Menu Presentation

Comparatively lower production costs and modern materials should ensure that menus are always kept clean and presentable. Damaged, soiled menus or those that have prices overprinted or in some cases where new prices have been stuck over existing prices are not acceptable and customers will regard the establishment as being of a low standard. Menus should be easy to read, clear and precise and enable a customer to calculate approximately how much they are likely to spend and show clearly if any additional charges are to be made, for example service charge.

Menu items should have accurate descriptions where required, reflect the expectations of customers in terms of the style of restaurant the menu portrays and the service style they should expect. The menu should reflect the restaurant offering in line with current market trends and customer expectation. 'Menus should be designed to market the restaurant, entice diners to eat.

The average customer spends only two minutes reading the menu. The term " reading " may be an overtly optimistic expression of what is no more than a quick scan. In only two minutes your menu must communicate the full range of food and beverages offered and sell the guest on what to purchase to both satisfy them and your financial objectives'.

Layout of the Menu

The larger the menu the more time consuming it is for customers to make their selection of food or wine. However, if it is too short customers may not be entirely satisfied by what is offered. Caterers need to adjust the length of their menu to the particular needs of their customers; bearing in mind that the longer a menu becomes the more management control will be necessary.

What often is particularly confusing and embarrassing–unless the customer is very knowledgeable–is the length of wine lists offered in many restaurants. Unless wine lists of this type are extremely well laid out and contain additional help to customers to aid their selection, they will do very little to help the potential sales of a restaurant. The layout of a menu should take into consideration how a customer normally reads a menu.

This skilled use of the important areas on a menu must be utilized to enable an establishment to achieve its budgetary targets.

Size and Form

The size and shape of a menu can add to and complement the uniqueness of the facility. A food or beverage menu must be easy for the customer to handle and in no way confusing to read. The various forms that the menu can take are unlimited, from a menu chalked up on a blackboard, to a large illuminated display board with photographs, conventional menu cards, tent cards, placemats, menus printed in the shape of a fan or even hand printed onto silk handkerchiefs as mementoes for the guests at a banquet.

There are cost implications, particularly where the services of a professional printing company are involved and therefore consideration for the length of time that a menu might be used or the level of soiling that might be expected should be included as part of the decision-making process.

MENU PRICING

Menu pricing needs to fulfil two needs, for the caterer the need to make adequate profits and for the customer the need to satisfy getting value for money. In both cases the requirement for accuracy is paramount. Customers today are more sophisticated in their dining habits, more people eat out, many are well travelled and nearly all have gained perceptions of quality and value for money from watching celebrity chefs and other food programmes on television.

A restaurateur' s policy on pricing should take a holistic view of the business and include expected return on investment, market demand, competition, where price should be measured against quality, industry standards for style of operation, location, particularly where this may impact on business overheads including staff costs, rents and council charges.

Because much of the time spent on analysis of profitability and pricing, often referred to as menu engineering, it is easy for restaurant owners to lose sight of the fact that they are actually talking about pounds, dollars, euros, etc. and that percentages do not always reveal the true story.

Pricing Models

There are a number of well-established pricing models commonly used some of which are better suited to commercial undertakings whilst others are more frequently used in 'not for profit organizations'. In this respect benchmarking against others in the sector may provide a good 'feel' for a suitable pricing model.

Cost Plus Pricing

Cost plus pricing takes the ingredient or food cost element of a menu item and simply adds a predetermined multiplier or markup. Most commonly used where a simple pricing model will provide the desired return and there are few additional costs. Typically, this could be something like a house wine where little further expense will be incurred and the restaurateur simply multiplies the buying price by say three, so cost price is ₹4 selling price becomes `12 plus or including any sales tax.

This simple pricing approach may aid decision making when for example on the telephone to a supplier or perhaps in a market. By simply applying a set multiplier they can get a good estimate of selling price. Alternatively by adding a fixed markup of say 150 per cent the wine becomes ₹10. This simplistic pricing method also allows the chef or buyer to make quick purchase.

Competition Pricing

Competition pricing as the name suggests copies the prices of competitors. As a short-term strategy this may achieve increased business but it can easily spiral out of control into a price war. What are unknown are the competitors cost structure and margins maybe severely compromised.

Rate of Return Pricing

The basis for this method is an attempt to establish a break-even matrix based on predicted costs and sales. So, for example, if a restaurant investment is ₹300,000 and the required return on this is 20 per cent then the restaurant seeks profits of ₹60,000 per year. By modelling the costs, sales price and volume the emerging data will indicate what levels this needs to be in order to achieve the desired return. It would then be necessary to take it a stage further and carry out a feasibility study to see if the model fits the operational style of the restaurant. This model is unlikely to give definitive menu prices although they may be indicative and therefore help in the initial restaurant setup decision.

Elasticity Pricing

This pricing method considers the market and its sensitivity to price change. If the restaurant operates in a market where price is a determinant of demand a lower price may increase volume sufficiently to give better profitability. The market may also allow supply to be a determinant of price thereby allowing price increase without undue effect on volume. Fast-food operations, particularly branded burger restaurants in urban areas have been demand led and very price sensitive, particularly when market share becomes an important aspect, however when these same restaurants are located on motorway service stations they become supply led and prices can increase.

Backward Pricing

Backward pricing considers what the customer or market will bear in terms of price. Often used in manufacturing, for example confectionary or canned drinks less common in restaurants but useful when trying to establish or develop a new product. Requires fairly accurate ingredient and processing costs to be established and relies heavily on volume forecasts.

Prime Cost

Prime cost and its variant actual cost endeavour to provide more accurate cost models. Prime cost attempts to calculate labour cost in addition to food cost and actual cost attempts to include overheads. Both of these may be modelled via data from electronic point of sale systems over time and may also be benchmarked against industry standards for the sector. For example, it maybe established that Pizzeria' s have an average food cost of 20 per cent, an average labour cost of 30 per cent, average overhead costs of 30 per cent and require a return on investment of 20 per cent. In this model if pizza ingredients cost ₹1 the operator has ₹1.50 towards labour, ₹1.50 towards overheads and ₹2 towards return on his investment that equates to a selling price of ₹5 plus sales tax where applicable.

Whilst this model is more sophisticated and has the propensity to be more accurate modelling against industry standards or using data from the operations EPOS system can be misleading. In the first cost matching across all categories may not be possible and in the second EPOS data by its nature is historic and previous sales may not be attainable in the subsequent trading period, a drop in volume will load each remaining sale with additional levels of cost.

Departmental Profit Margins

The approach to menu pricing must follow from the outline of the basic policies and from the determined departmental profit targets. Each department will have a significant role in the total organization and its individual profit targets will normally be unrelated. For example, in a hotel the profit required from the à la carte restaurant may well be far lower than that of its coffee shop. The existence of the à la carte restaurant may be mainly of an image status for the hotel as against being a major profit contributor. What is necessary is for the total sum of the individual departments' contributions to equal the desired contribution to the revenue for the whole establishment.

Differential Profit Margins

It is unusual to apply a uniform rate of gross profit to all of the items found on a food menu or beverage list, although this simplistic method of costing can at times still be found in the non-commercial sector of the industry. In the non-commercial sector of the industry one of the advantages is that where a uniform rate of gross profit is applied, reference to the takings can quickly show the costs at 40 per cent gross profit irrespective of the sales mix and an immediate comparison can be made to the actual usage of materials. The reasons for not applying a uniform rate of gross profit in the commercial sector, that is, it ignores such things as capital investment; it emphasizes the cost too much; it ignores competition; etc. Further, it could distort the range of prices and values of items on a menu in that a low food/beverage cost item would end up being priced at a very low price, while a high food/beverage cost item would be exorbitantly priced.

In addition, it does not allow any flexible approach to the selling of items. Differential profit margins take into account the sales mix of items from a food menu or beverage list and hopefully provide the competitive balance of prices so that in total it is attractive to the customer and achieves the desired gross profit and revenue for the department.

Special Pricing Considerations

Sales Tax: Depending on the government in power, it is likely that some form of sales tax may be enforced during its period of office. It is important to the customer to know whether prices displayed or quoted are inclusive of this sales tax or not. Additionally, the caterer needs to realise that any money collected on behalf of the government has at some time to be paid to that government and that it should not be included when calculating revenue or average spend figures, etc.

Service Charge: This is an additional charge, made to customers, at a fixed percentage of the total cost of the food and beverage served. The fixed percentage is determined by management, printed on the menu/beverage list, with the objective of removing from the customer the problem of determining what size of tip to give when in a particular establishment. As this charge is to be distributed to the staff at a later date, usually on a points system, it should be treated similarly to a sales tax and not included in the calculation of revenue for food and beverages or in the calculations of average spend figures.

Cover Charge: This is an additional charge to a meal in restaurants to cover such costs as the bread roll and butter and items included but not priced on a menu. Care should be exercised as to whether to implement this or not as it is most likely to cause aggravation to some clients when it is applied.

Minimum Charge: Restaurants to discourage some potential clients from using the premises and to discourage clients from taking up a seat and only purchasing a very low priced item often enforce this.

Menu Pricing Application

The exact method of pricing used by an establishment will depend on such matters as which sector of the industry the establishment is in; the level of profit/subsidy required; its basic policies; etc. It is important though to remember that the price in itself can be a valuable selling tool and a great aid in achieving the desired volume of sales. Whilst menu pricing is not quite a science there are a number of ways that the restaurateur can remove some of the guesswork by adopting one or more of the pricing models previously discussed.

Table d' hôte Menus

This type of menu is characterized by being a restricted menu, offering a small range of courses with a limited choice within each course and at a fixed selling price. The price may be just one price for any three courses chosen, or may vary in price depending on the main course chosen.

The method of pricing chosen should take into account the departmental profit required and the differential profit margins of the menu. Based on the forecasted sales take-up by guests, the average should be taken to fix the price. The average may well be the true figure, rounded off, when the objective is to attract as many customers as possible to choose from the menu; or alternatively, it may be an average plus figure when it is being offered with an à la carte menu and it is not desired to encourage too many guests away from the à la carte menu by making the price differentiation too attractive.

À la Carte Menus

This type of menu is characterized by being a larger menu than a table d' hôte menu offering a greater choice of courses and dishes within each course, and each item being individually priced. The method of pricing here is again to take into account the departmental profit required and the differential profit margins for each course and then to price each item separately using standard recipes. In addition, note should be taken of the potential sales mix within each course so as to achieve the desired profit margin.

Banqueting Menus

This is a specific type of table d' hôte menu offering normally no choice to the customers. The specific difference in pricing this menu is that apart from the food and often the liquor, all the additional items are normally priced and charged separately. Examples of such items are flowers for each table, a band, meals and refreshments for the band, services of a toast master, hire of a microphone, printing of a special menu for the function. Many companies are now trying to customise this restricted choice, for example Marriott have created a package for business functions that combine menu choices with technology requirements banqueting style operations.

The pricing of a banquet menu for a client is commonly found to have a flexible element to it, in that it is not uncommon for a banqueting manager to offer additions to a menu at no additional cost to the client in order to obtain the business during a slack trading period or for a particular gap in a week. For example, the banqueting manager may offer as a free addition to the standard printed menu such things as a soup course, a sorbet, petits fours, etc. Further, the charge for the hire of the function room may be reduced or removed altogether.

Pricing of Beverages

The method used to price beverages is similar to that for pricing foods. As in the case of foods, first, the departmental profit target and gross profit percentage should be set, followed by differential profit margins based on the sales mix achievable. The sales mix breakdown depends on the type of operation and how detailed the breakdown of sales is required. The gross profit percentage of house brand beverages is usually higher than on other brand beverages as it is normally made available by the supplier at a special discounted rate. Pricing may be more accurately calculated for beverages as little, if any, processing of the drinks takes place; drinks being purchased by the bottle or by a specific stated measure from a bottle of known standard size. The mixing of drinks is, like food, usually prepared using a standard recipe particular to an establishment.

Subsidized Operations

There are many operations within the non-commercial sector of the industry that are subsidized in some form or other. Subsidies may take the form of completely free premises, capital equipment, services, and labour or the catering department may be required to pay a percentage of these costs with the balance being the subsidy. Pricing in this situation may, for example, require the sales revenue to cover the food costs only; or food costs plus specific named expenses; or food costs plus a named percentage as a contribution to all overheads.

Pricing in this situation is frequently done on a cost plus basis, depending on the level of subsidy. When more than the food/beverage cost has to be recovered, it is important that prices are competitive enough to encourage a high enough volume of sales. Recipe costing and menu testing software, for example StarChef. NET or fourthhospitality are readily available allowing the restaurateur to compare performance of various menu items using different recipes for price comparison. Menu engineering examined by authors Kasavana and Smith, and Keiser et al. consider the menu in terms of cost, margins and volume analysed to identify menu items under four performance types, namely, plowhorses, stars, dogs and puzzles. Plowhorses are highly popular menu items with average to low contribution margins, stars are highly popular menu items with high contribution margins, dogs have low popularity and low contribution margins and puzzles have low popularity but high contribution margins. As we can see this analysis focuses on the contribution margin, that is the difference between the cost of ingredients and the selling price for each menu item.

This is a relatively straightforward approach with information readily at hand but it ignores both overhead and labour costs that are more difficult to attach to individual menu items. Attaching a level of work output or productivity is time consuming, may vary over time or by staff member. Overhead may be averaged across each menu item but this may be grossly inaccurate. Ignoring either of these has the potential to be very misleading as the following example suggests. Let us examine the 'Stars' a high volume and high contribution menu item like Pizza.

The ingredient costs for a cheese and tomato pizza are very low in comparison to selling price yielding on average a gross margin in excess of 85 per cent. However, making pizza is a time-consuming process and cooking pizza is energy intense because a high oven temperature needs to be maintained throughout the service period.

In many cases pizza is also finished as the order is received into the kitchen so in addition to the preparation time it is labour intensive at the time of sale requiring the restaurateur to plan labour levels accordingly. Pricing remains a relatively flexible task, depending on the ease and cost of menu printing and should be considered with a view to appealing to the target market and restaurant sector in which it is situated. Pricing to low may make to item attractive but will not generate the desired return, pricing to high may put customers off.

Adding Value

In pricing a menu it is necessary to consider the relationship between menu items so that the pricing structure appears balanced and acceptable in today' s marketplace. A general observation suggests that starters and desserts are priced at similar levels and main dishes on an upward sliding scale starting just higher than the most expensive starter or dessert.

From the customers perspective however, the ingredient value often has everything to do with the perception of value of the price being charged.

It is this dilemma that makes pricing a difficult and complex process because much of modern pricing is based on perceptions of added value, supply and demand, trends and fashion, perceptions of quality and market forces and it is the caterers responsibility, skill, training and value adding techniques that allows high profits to be made on low ingredient costs. As an example, let us consider one food item that has been around for at least the last fifty years, the fish cake. Fish cakes were one of the staple food items used in welfare catering, cheap and easy to produce, ideal for using up fish and potato leftovers and easy to buy in ready-made.

Using fresh ingredients it typically costs less than one-pound per portion to produce and using leftovers the cost is literally pence. In a staff restaurant they may sell for three to four pounds per portion, in a typical high street restaurant, with the addition of a few salad leaves, a little flavoured mayonnaise and an imaginative menu description they will sell for ten or eleven pounds per portion and in both restaurant examples, through appropriate marketing it allows the caterer to capitalize the value added and the customer to consider the item value for money.

In this way items on the menu with relatively low food costs and therefore high contribution margins are beneficial to profitability. Reputation also allows the restaurateur to add value to the dining experience so for example, a restaurant that can claim to have three Michelin stars may offer an exclusive menu that commands a substantial price.

MENU KNOWLEDGE

When we consider that a menu is the primary sales tool for any restaurant operation it follows that product/menu item knowledge is important. Aside from issues concerning allergies, special diets or preferred tastes discerning customers will expect waiting or sales staff to have a thorough understanding of all dishes both in terms of ingredients and preparation and cooking. Good menu knowledge is an essential aid in the sales pro cess, it provides an opportunity to discuss and where appropriate to up-sell more expensive or more profitable dishes. It also gives the customer assurance that the establishment is managed professionally.

Sales Mix

Although generally food costs only account for 20–30 per cent of menu item cost averaged across the menu there are often considerable variations. It may be seen from the example above that different food or beverage items may carry significantly different levels of profit contribution.

Other examples include the cost of making a soup as compared with an offering of smoked salmon or the cost of producing a steak and Guinness pie as opposed to an offering of grilled steak and although these dishes in themselves invite pricing differentiation overall the menu needs to have a complimentary pricing structure so that the differentiation appears well structured and meets all the other pricing criteria for customer acceptability. Sophisticated sales data analysis through the use of EPOS systems allows the caterer to examine changes in profitability as changes to the mix of sales go through the system.

Analysis of the sales report will identify sales trends and the effects that these have on profit margins, service requirements and kitchen production. By making adjustments to menu content the caterer is able to manipulate sales mix that can influence revenue, service and production demands. The level of sophistication for menu planning that EPOS systems provide and the reports.

Nutrition

The 21st century has seen much public concern over the nutritional content of food. The provision of food and beverage in certain categories of establishment has required caterers to pay particular attention to nutrition and traditionally these have included schools, hospitals, prisons, the armed forces and any establishment regarded as having a 'captive market'.

More recently public awareness has made nutrition or rather the lack of the correct nutrition a greater concern across the whole strata of society.

Obesity at all ages, poor eating habits within the school meal service leading to poor eating habits later in life, levels of nutrition in hospitals and care homes as changes in demographics lead to a more elderly population the part that food plays in behavioural studies both for school children and prisoners.

Whilst food remains fashionable and trendy in other sectors of society, lifestyle, image and high-level publicity for more healthy food means that caterers in all sectors need to take account of nutrition as part of their regular review of menu planning and design.

Menus and the Law

There are a number of legal issues connected with the preparation of both food and beverage menus. Menus need to be accurate but they also need to be honest in their descriptions of what is on offer. The law requires that all descriptions applied to meals or their accompaniments must be accurate, whether given in writing or by illustration, on menus, blackboards, windows or any other means, including verbal descriptions by staff.

Food labelling law states clearly that failure to inform customers honestly or to give misleading information is an alleged criminal offence.

The legal framework and enforcement of compliance in these areas is part of the responsibility of the local council Trading Standards department. The local council also has responsibility for issues concerning public health via the environmental health department and liquor licensing.

Food Description Problems

Using the term 'chicken fillet' or 'chicken breast' on a menu implies that you are providing a whole unprocessed product. If you then use a product where packaging is labelled 'reformed' or 'chopped and shaped' then it is not an unprocessed product and therefore the menu description should reflect this.

An example of an item that commonly causes problems in this respect is the dish Chicken Kiev described as a chicken breast stuffed with garlic butter coated with egg and breadcrumbs and deep fried, it is a product that is commonly 'bought in' rather than made on the premises and a close examination of the label will reveal that it is often a reformed reshaped product.

Furthermore to use the term 'home-made' when the product has in fact been bought in or 'home cooked' when the product is merely an assembly of convenience products put together and cooked is also an offence so, for example, opening a can of stewed steak and kidney into a dish then adding a frozen pastry lid and baking it in the oven would not constitute a home cooked steak and kidney pie.

Some products are required to contain minimum quantities of ingredient before they can be sold, for example burgers have to contain a minimum or 80 per cent meat before being sold as a burger.

Descriptions of cooking methods also come under scrutiny; roasted joints of meat that have been steamed and flash roasted should not be described as roasted meat. The roasting process is a clearly defined process and is not the same as the process available in highly technical ovens that use very low temperature steam over a long cooking process. This process considerably reduces weight loss because the product does not lose much moisture and is subsequently coloured via a short period of high temperature.

Whilst this process has obvious advantages for the caterer the end product bears little resemblance to a properly roasted joint. Other common terms used in error are cheese when it is a cheese substitute, smoked when really the product is smoke flavoured and butter when margarine is used. There are a further range of descriptions about which the caterer needs to be completely certain, which are factually correct before using them, for example stating that food is fresh or low calorie, that it is suitable for vegetarians, vegans or coeliacs, that it is a proprietary brand product for example Hellmann' s mayonnaise when it is for example a decanted Tesco own brand product, that a product has come from a certain region for example Scotch beef when it is not from that region or where to your knowledge ingredients used have undergone an irradiation process and this is not declared.

In making statements concerning the weight of a menu item, for example steak, it is important to state that the weight quoted is when raw, a 160 g fillet steak will weigh up to 40 per cent less if cooked to well done. An example of a food specification and these can be written for most menu items which will enable more accurate menu descriptions to be followed.

BEVERAGE MENUS/LISTS

The criteria used to prepare a wine menu, or drinks list, are the same as those used when preparing a food menu. Wine menus and drinks lists fall under the requirements of licensing regulations some of which are described and these can change from time to time and those operating licensed premises need to be aware of these changes. The use of the wine menu, or drinks list, as a selling tool cannot be emphasized enough. Customers eating in a restaurant do not have to, and will not feel embarrassed if they do not purchase a drink. It is the caterer' s ability to interest and gain the confidence of customers that is likely to lead them to purchase a drink.

Most beverages require fewer staff to process them and the profits from them is therefore higher than those from food and so it goes without saying that this is an area that requires time and attention from the caterer to obtain the full benefit. Beverage lists should be specifically prepared for the particular unit in which they are being sold, because the requirements vary greatly. A restaurant themed to a country or region might offer both food and beverages from that area' s wines and beers.

To use a generalpurpose wine menu may not be suitable but such is the power of 'brands' it might be prudent to include a few as these are likely to aid sales. What is also important with beverages is that there should be a follow-through with the correct serving temperature being adhered to and the correct traditional glassware used, particularly when available to make the brand. The sales of wines and cocktails in hotels and restaurants are generally lower than they should be for such reasons as poor selling, overpricing and the snobbery that goes with wines and cocktails which tend to put customers ill at ease.

Types of Beverage Menus/Lists

The various types of beverage menus are numerous, but for simplicity they may be grouped as being of six kinds: full wine menus, restricted wine menus, banquet/function menus, bar menus, room service beverage menus and special promotion beverage menus.

Full Wine Menu or Lists

This kind of menu would be used in an up-market hotel or restaurant where the customers' average spend would be high and where the time available to consume their meal would be likely to be in excess of one and a half hours. Like all menus, a full wine menu is difficult to design. Certain wines must be on the menu if a restaurant is of a particular standing; it is the question of the selection of wines within the various types based on the manager' s experience and the analysis of customer sales that make it difficult to keep a correct balance and restrict the choice to reasonable limits. Because of the size and cost it is often the practice to have the menu contained within a quality cover and to be of a loose-leaf form so that the individual pages may be updated when required and replaced.

It is also the practice for many restaurants to give a brief description of the major types of wine as well as provide a map to show the origin of the wine. The price range for this type of menu is high because of the quality of the products.

The layout would usually be in the following order:

- House wines
- Champagnes and other sparkling wines
- Red wines
- White wines
- Port, sherry, liqueurs
- Cognac, armagnac, gin, vodka, vermouth, whisky
- Beers, lagers
- Mineral waters, fruit juices.

Restricted Wine Menus or Lists

This kind of menu would be used in a middle type market operation where the demand for a full wine menu is very limited. It is also likely to be used when a highly skilled wine waiter is not required and where the waiting staff serves all food and beverages. The planning of a restricted wine menu is difficult and can best be done by an analysis of previous wine sales. It is usual that this type of menu would feature a few well-known branded wines with which the majority of customers can identify. The price range for this type of menu would be lower than that of a full wine menu and would need to bear some relationship to the food menu prices. Another feature on a restricted menu is likely to be the sale of wine by the carafe and by the glass.

Banquet/Function Menus

This type of menu is of the restricted type in that it will offer fewer wines than a full menu. The contents of the menu will depend very much on the type of banqueting being done, but in general it is usual to offer a selection of wines with a varying price range so that it will suit a wide range of customers and their tastes.

Again, banqueting wine menus will usually list some well-known branded wines. A point which must not be forgotten with branded wines is that customers frequently will know the prices charged for them in the local supermarket or wine store and therefore the caterer must be very careful as to the markup on these wines so as not to create customer annoyance.

Bar Menus and Lists

This type of menu is basically of two types–the large display of beverages and their prices which is often located at the back of or to the side of a bar and is often a legal requirement in many countries; or small printed menu/lists which are available on the bar and on the tables in the bar area. The large display of menus and prices would be in a general type of bar where the everyday types of drinks are served; the small printed menus/lists being found in lounge and cocktail bars. The cocktail bar menu/list usually contains cocktails; mixed drinks; sherries and ports; liqueurs and brandies; wine; and minerals and cordials. The layout for a cocktail bar menu/list need not follow any set order, the emphasis for the layout being on merchandising specific items.

Room Service Beverage Menu

The size and type of a room service menu will depend on the room service offered. For a luxury type unit the menu will be quite extensive, being a combination of items from the full wine list and from the bar list. In a middle type market unit the menu is likely to be quite small, being a combination of items mainly from the bar list plus a few wines only from the restricted unit wine menu/list.

Because of the high labour costs for room service staff, a practice today in many hotels is to provide a small refrigerator in each bedroom stocked with a limited quantity of basic drinks. There are many types of beverage units available specifically for use in bedrooms, some of which include a computer- based control system, which automatically records the removal of any item from the unit and records it as a charge to the customer.

Special Promotion Beverage Menus

This type of menu may take many forms from a free pre-function reception to promote a particular beverage, to the promotion of after-lunch and afterdinner liqueurs by the use of attractive tent cards, or to the promotion of the cocktails of the month. Fortunately the suppliers willingly give assistance with beverage promotional menus by providing free advertising and promotional material and by offering the particular beverage free or at a special purchase price.

Licensing

The new Licensing Act 2003 came into force on 24th November 2005, the key aims of which are to allow more flexible opening hours, provide a single premises licence to supply alcohol, regulated entertainment and refreshment late at night and provide a new system of personal licences relating to the supply of alcohol.

A full explanation of the 2003 act can be found on the India government web site. The local authority rather than the magistrates' court issues premises licences and personal licences. For most restaurateurs applying for a licence will be done through a solicitor or specialist agency and will require the applicant to have as a minimum qualification the National Certificate for Licensees or the National Certificate in Licensed Retailing.

Description on Beverage Menus

Much of the regulation that covers food menus also applies to beverage menus or wine lists but there are additional regulations concerning portion sizes. Beer and cider can only be sold in 1/3 pint or 1/2 pint or multiples of 1/2 pints unless sold in cans or bottles. Any glass used to sell draught products must be crown stamped unless dispense is by pump measure. Spirits must be sold in measures of 25 ml or multiples thereof.

A notice must be displayed in the bar area informing customers of the measures served. Wine sold by the glass can only be dispensed in measures of 125 ml, 175 ml or multiples thereof and any glass used to sell wine by the glass must be crown stamped. Unstamped glasses may be used where wine is sold either by the carafe or the bottle.

It is interesting to note the mix of both imperial and metric measure that is enshrined in licensing regulations. As with branded food items one branded spirit, beer or soft drink cannot be substituted by decanting into another branded container so Sainsbury' s Cola cannot be sold as Pepsi Cola and Sainsbury' s vodka cannot be sold as Stolichnaya.

It is an offence to adulterate beer or spirits with water or other substances to make it go further.

The General Rules for the Serving of Wines

The practice of serving a different kind of wine with each food course is seldom observed today other than for the very formal occasion or for a special gastronomic event. The choice of wine by a customer is highly individual and the once traditional rules of what wines should only be served with a particular food are not always observed today.

Some aspects of the practice that have stood the test of time and are accepted and commonly practiced today are:

- The progression of wines in a menu would be that light and delicate wines are served before fuller bodied wines, that simple wines are served before the higher quality wines and that young wines are served before the older wines.
- When several wines are to be served with a menu the order of serving is normally accepted as being first a dry white wine followed by a red wine and finishing with a sweet white wine.

- Wines from several countries may be served with a meal providing that there is an affinity between the different wines and that they are accepted partners with the food.
- Champagne may be served throughout a meal with dry champagne being served with all courses other than with the sweet course when semi-sweet champagne would be better suited.
- Rosé wines may also be served throughout a menu although it would be unusual for a formal or special gastronomic occasion.
- Dry white wines are normally served with fish, shellfish and white meats such as poultry, pork and veal.
- Red wines are normally served with red meats, for example beef, and with game, for example all game birds, venison and hare.
- Sweet white wines are normally served with the sweet course.
- Port is accepted as being ideal for serving with cheese and dessert.

□

Index

□□□